Returning to the Source
The Way to the Experience of God

by
Wilson Van Dusen

Real People Press

Copyright © 1996
Real People Press
Box F
Moab, Utah 84532
(801) 259-7578
(801) 259-4042 (Fax)

Cover photo by Steve Andreas.

ISBN: 0-911226-36-2 clothbound $19.00
        0-911226-37-0 paperback $13.50

Library of Congress Cataloging-in-Publication Data:

Van Dusen, Wilson.
    Returning to the source : the way to the experience of God /by
Wilson Van Dusen.
        p.   cm.
    Includes bibliographical references and index.
    ISBN 0-911226-36-2. — ISBN 0-911226-37-0 (pbk.)
    1. Experience (Religion) 2. Mysticism. I. Title.
BL53.V26   1997
291.4'2—dc20   96-44858
                                                              CIP

Other useful books from Real People Press:

Core Transformation: Reaching the Wellspring Within, by Connirae
Andreas and Tamara Andreas. 1993. Cloth $21.50, Paper $13.50.

*Heart of the Mind: Engaging Your Inner Power to Change with Neuro-
Linguistic Programming,* by Connirae Andreas and Steve Andreas. 261
pp. 1989. Cloth $19.00, Paper $13.50.

Is There Life Before Death? An anthology compiled by Steve Andreas, 208
pp. cloth $19.95.

The name *Real People Press* indicates our purpose: to publish ideas and
ways that a person can use independently or with others to become more
real—to further their own growth as a human being and to develop relationships and communication with others.

1 2   3   4   5   6   Printing   99   98   97   96

Dedicated to the One who woke me up,
while others slept, showing me how to present
these matters.

So, then, since the Lord God the Creator is love itself and wisdom itself, and the universe was created by Him, being in consequence a work, so to speak, issuing from Him, it must be that in each and every created thing there is some goodness and truth from Him. For whatever is accomplished by and issues from anyone, derives from him a character similar to his.

Reason can also see that this is so from the order which each and every thing in the universe was created in, in which one thing exists for the sake of another, and in which one thing therefore depends on another, like the links in a chain. For all things exist for the sake of the human race, that from it may come the angelic heaven by which creation returns to the Creator, its source. From this comes the conjunction of the created universe with its Creator, and by that conjunction its everlasting preservation.

—Emanuel Swedenborg, *Conjugial Love*, 1768

The Book Cover

This world is a theater of representations of the spiritual. In many traditions God is seen as the Sun of heaven which emits a warm, inviting, loving glow. All other things seem dark in comparison. Between us here and the sun of heaven are the rocks and waves of the ocean of our experience. The light of the sun shines across the waves and comes right to each of us, wherever we are, showing us the way home. Follow your light to return to the Source.

Table of Contents

Foreword

Jean Giono's wonderful story "The Man Who Planted Trees" begins with this statement:

> For a human character to reveal truly exceptional qualities, one must have the good fortune to be able to observe its performance over many years. If this performance is devoid of all egoism, if its guiding motive is unparalleled generosity, if it is absolutely certain that there is no thought of recompense and that, in addition, it has left its visible mark upon the earth, then there can be no mistake.*

I feel fortunate to have known the author of this book for over thirty years. It is quite extraordinary to be in his presence, because he has no "agenda," no criticism, judgment or wanting you to be different in any way. Instead there is an immense respect and curiosity, and an interest in why God has brought this person into his life, and what is to be experienced and learned through this meeting.

I have always been interested in the larger questions of ultimate meaning, and have sought out a wide variety of psychological/spiritual teachers over the last half-century. Although I have learned much from many, all too often the teachers I found did not live what they taught: the judgmental teacher of openness and acceptance, the grim teacher of joy, the promiscuous teacher of abstinence, the

*Chelsea Green Publishing Co., White River Junction, VT, 1985, p.7.

vi

vegetarian who snuck away from the ashram for a pepperoni pizza, and on and on.

Often these teachers not only had feet of clay, but brains of butter—sloppy thinking or dishonest argumentation or evasion, and they often had great difficulty dealing with the practical tasks of day-to-day living.

In contrast, the author of this book fully lives what he teaches, his thinking is honest and straightforward, and he is immensely capable in the practical world. All of this makes me much more interested in what he has to say about spiritual realms. He has had a sea career and holds a US license as Second Mate, Oceans unlimited, and under the Panamanian flag, Master, Oceans Unlimited. He taught for many years and now voluntarily teaches Coast Guard officers eleven courses. He also wrote the course and trains candidates for a knighthood. He holds a PhD in clinical psychology and worked for many years with the most serious cases of mental illness.

But his life is not all serious. He is a precision target shooter who reloads his own bullets. In his back yard he has a wild bird sanctuary complete with a bird hospital. He zips around town on a motorcycle. One day a week he can be found putting away books in the county library children's room "like a giant in the Kingdom of Lilliput." Many of his friends don't know he has written seven books and knows something of the experience of God.

He is now retired in a small town. His wife is a fiber artist and they enjoy all the arts together. In his late years he has begun to set down the side of his life few even knew existed.

Because he had profound mystic experiences as a small child, long before learning about religion and doctrine, his approach to it is fresh, experiential, and undoctrinaire, leaving all the mystification out of mysticism. For him, a mystic is simply someone who sees and feels the larger whole, one who makes wonder, awe, and beauty into the central focus of his life. By treasuring and cultivating these experiences, they come to blossom more fully and more frequently, opening the small ego to more universal experience.

In many ways this is a practical book, providing both ways of thinking and ways of doing that can lead us toward the experience of enlightenment. But it is also a meditative book, to be read leisurely, a small portion at a time, and repeatedly, allowing meanings to emerge more fully and sink more deeply into our experience.

Like a meaningful prayer or a treasured memory, what is presented here is a gentle reminder of what many of us have forgotten, to be returned to as a sanctuary from the hectic and distracting pace of day-to-day living.

Each time I have edited a section of this book, I have felt nourished, quieted, lightened, cleansed, and refreshed. Whenever I have put these ideas into practice, my life has become easier and more interesting and enjoyable in a quiet and fundamental way.

Whether or not what is presented here is true, in any ultimate sense, or in a life beyond this short journey we are all on, I have found it to be true in my life, now in the present moment. That is truth enough for me.

—Steve Andreas

1
Introduction

Oh, utterly simple
And ever present.
Do you think you can hide
In so many forms?
Not as long as I
and all my kin
Carry you
In our heart.

Oh, how to describe
The utterly simple?
Where to find
The ever present?
While suffused
By an ocean of love
Even silence
Is most eloquent.*

 This book revolves around a simple observation. Some people find their way into the joys of mystical or transcendent experiences—the direct experience of God. The elements in human experience that can lead into this direct experience of God are relatively common, and are easily available to the agnostic and atheist as well

*All poetry without a reference citation is by the author.

as the believer. I hope to describe the mystical experience until you begin to understand so many aspects of it that you will be able to recognize it and discover it in your own experience. The experience of God is not rare and difficult to obtain. It is our understanding of it that needs great improvement.

I am a lifelong and natural mystic. I have known the direct experience of God countless times. What is it like to be a mystic in this world? In part, it is sad. Mystics can go through a long period in which they have experiences of God, but they remain unsure. Once after I gave a talk in a church an old woman waited until the crowd of people who came up to me afterward cleared. I saw that she was not long for this world. Acting very circumspectly, she recited a short dream in which a golden sun came to her, and asked if it was God. I first thought of my standard reply, "We need to get into the dream, and to see what is in it." But then I was struck by the total emotional impact of the larger situation. This old woman is dying, and it matters very much to her if she met God even once in this life. I said, "Yes, it was God," and we both broke into tears. But how sad. She had the marks of a very spiritual person, whose life was embedded in God. And yet she asks desperately if once she met Him. To me she represents most of mankind. She is already well on her way, but she does not recognize the signs.

Once I went to see a gifted abbot, the head of a Byzantine monastery. He said most of his monks and nuns have the direct experience of God, but he is careful not to tell them that it is. This quite startled me. He did not validate the monk's experiences for fear they were not mature enough yet. They might get prideful if the abbot said, "That is of God." There is a vast realm of people who have met God, and suspect it, but remain unsure. Fine mystics write to me, and I am always careful to validate their experience. It cheers them up and gives them confidence in their way. If they have come out on that universal plain where all mystics meet, I then greet them as a fellow mystic even though they have elements in their experience that are different from mine.

As a mystic, the experience of God is always present, very familiar, very simple and direct. So it is distressing to me that others don't also have this familiarity. A friend of mine was overwhelmed by a five-second profound and genuine vision. In the midst of a gathering of Catholics, with her drink in her hand, she suddenly lost all awareness of this world, and found herself in the presence of the Sacred

Heart of Jesus. Then she was back in the gathering. No one noticed the difference. Though she was a lifelong Catholic she did not know such direct and powerful an experience was really possible. She later became angry at the church for not indicating this possibility. She has worked for decades to return to it. She described it as ecstasy, and simply did not believe me when I said I have known ecstasy countless times.

Some people want some thunderbolt out of heaven to knock them down. In my experience such thunderbolts occur, but are rare. Most mystical experience is very direct and simple, like the soft glance of a lover that says it all. U.S. television reflects a culture that craves the big sensation—great explosions and car smash-ups, and death. If you translate this attitude into the mystical realm we would expect God to do it big, and put on a grand show for us. I once approached God in somewhat this attitude, wanting a Big Sign. By direct knowing, without words, I was led to reflect on the scope of the known universe in all its complexity and immensity, and was asked, "Is this not enough sign?" I felt taken aback. If one is not satisfied with the entire created universe as a sign, then nothing much else will do either!

One thing that will surprise some readers is that I concentrate on the smallest signs. They can't get too small to notice. The finest way into the direct experience of God is to learn to recognize the little signs you already have, here and now, in the commonplace. God is in all the little, ever-present signs we are missing. All have known this kind of experience, countless times, and yet it is rarely recognized for what it is.

With all the volumes that have been written about God, one would think that there would be clear descriptions of the experience. I have read a good deal of the accounts of saints and mystics, East and West. Very often they totally omit the specific details of their inner experiences. Saints particularly tend to come out with rather standard doctrine. They conceal their direct experience partly out of modesty. It sounds immodest to say, "I have known God; God came to me and said . . ." To some it may even sound insane. The writings of saints typically leave out descriptions of what actually happened to them. I have often thought how much I would like to interview a saint, so that I could learn what his or her experience was really like! Instead they give us what they feel we should know. They teach how to reach God, and basically these directions describe their path, not what they reached at the end of it. Saints recount the doctrine of their particular faith—as though to say, "Though this is standard stuff, it is what I have found to be true." One of the marks of a mystic is that they tend to reaffirm their tradition. They stand in the tradition, but give it a deeper meaning. Some Christians need to be reminded that Christ was an Orthodox Jew who lived the Jewish tradition. He gave Judaism so much more meaning that it broke away as Christianity. There are many paths, but all have the same heart.

If we want to look at mysticism as a human process, the literature is scant. William James (1),* Evelyn Underhill (2), and others have described the essential aspects of the experience. Several have tried to elaborate stages. But in my own experience the stages seem blurred, or all going on at once. I distrust any sort of categorizing. Are there eight or twelve kinds of mystics? I don't know. I have only personally met twenty or so. Besides, God hasn't told me and I didn't want to bother God with such a trivial question. Each mystic I have known has been a unique person but all reflect the same heart, despite the stylistic differences in how they present themselves. The Sufi's effusive love poetry seems very different than the matter-of-factness of St. Theresa of Avila. I understand and appreciate both, and I also recognize their different style and culture. To me a lot of Psalms, the Book of John, and the Gospel of Thomas are highly mystical, but others would surely derive hard doctrine from the same sources. I greatly admire Mahayana Buddhism, but even this, while representing some of the world's greatest mystical tradition, is lacking. It is mostly about how to reach the state. Only by implication do some Buddhist authors describe the experience itself. So if one wants the direct experience of God, the world's literature is relatively slim. For many nuances I will have to draw on my own experience. Mystics come from many different faiths, with different cultures and styles, but they all point towards the same center. One must know the center to see the broad agreement they represent.

To me there is a sharp difference between mystics and scholars on mysticism. Mystics seem like family and friends; they are so easy to recognize. We are soon in broad dialogue with so many understandings. But scholars of mysticism are usually quite different. They seem unmystical to me, pedantic and heavy, poised to dispute

*All references are numbered, and appear in the Reference Section.

rather than to understand. Medieval scholars debated how many angels could stand on the head of a pin. To a mystic it is a silly question. Angels are spiritual. A pin is natural. All the angels in the universe fit very nicely on the head of a pin. Every abstruse question one can raise about mysticism is answered in the simplicity of the experience itself.

There are experiences so close to mysticism that we will have to look at them. One major one is the whole area of aesthetic experience. For me, all beauty leads to the mystical. But many people who enjoy beauty deeply wouldn't think of linking it to mystical experience, and still less to religion. I suspect that those who would separate aesthetics and the mystical are putting a restrictive meaning on the mystical. Many have negative reactions to anything that smacks of religion, and I don't blame them; they got religious indigestion at some early age and never wished to suffer that again. I see anything beautiful as a plain example of the eternal; the direct experience of God and the beautiful are the same thing, though I am aware many would say otherwise.

My aim is to explore all aspects of the direct experience of God. Anchored in the realm of human experience, we will look at many aspects of experience which point beyond themselves to something more. This is a broad realm, like a Japanese garden, and we can pause to notice a pond with a leaf floating in it, the sounds of running water, a graceful bush, a bridge, and the various things that make up the garden. In part the mystical experience is "all there is at once," which is why many mystics gave up describing it—from which comes the ancient idea that the mystical is dark or hidden. I don't find it hidden at all. It is in plain sight. But like appreciating the Zen garden, we need to linger to experience each aspect of it in order to come to an appreciation of the whole.

We will begin with a first look at the mystical to orient you to the realm. Then I will deal with different aspects of the mystical, beginning with mystery and awe. In describing each aspect I will be attempting to point out the *little shift* in viewpoint that leads into the experience of God. I stress *little shift* for none of these shifts are difficult or abstruse. It is as though we are walking around a gem and I am attempting to describe each facet. Of course the gem is all the facets combined, but taking them one at a time we break the "all at once" into simpler components for the sake of understanding. People differ, so a given person may be reached better by one facet than another. Each facet is, in effect, a way into the mystical experience, and practiced mystics use several of these facets.

There is another aspect of the mystical experience that is inescapable. It is not possible to come into the direct experience of God without also learning about yourself, because the God you would find is in yourself. The way to it is through yourself, and this way is paved with obstacles and self-discoveries. Very often the effort to know God requires some improvement of your understanding and outlook before this is possible. Self-discovery is a facet though, not the whole. It is as though we want to approach something, and find we have to get some rubbish out of the way first— our rubbish, no one else's.

The mystic experience can vary from a momentous instant that colors the life, to a life more and more adapted to such experiences. I am in the tradition of all the mystics—Emanuel Swedenborg, Meister Eckhart, Plotinus, St. Seraphim of Sarov, the anonymous author of *The Cloud of the Unknowing*, Rabindranath Tagore, the countless Sufi and Buddhist mystics, and so many others. They feel like near-relatives and friends of mine. We speak the same language. I easily understand and walk with them, even though we are separated by centuries of time.

Though I have explored various religious doctrines, I simply do not grasp the mystical in doctrinal terms. There are liberal and very conservative followers of the mystic Emanuel Swedenborg. I joined both groups because I identified with Swedenborg but not with one side against the other. I see all religions as correct and useful in different ways. Religions to me are like a marvelous garden. I cannot say I like only the oak tree. The pine and the redwood have their own form and beauty. I enjoy also grass, flowers, bushes, and all things that grow. How can I be both Buddhist and Christian? It is easy. Both are true. In fact both express much the same truth. As a mystic I enter religion where it identifies with the universal. This is a level beyond religious doctrinal differences, which to me look like foolish misunderstandings within the family.

In the midst of much news of ethnic and religious wars and killings I went into the garden where my wife had thoughtfully planted various colored flowers. I asked the flowers why they don't get into killing each other? Surely the reds should conquer the yellows, to be supreme. And there is a deep purple tulip. In silence their differences said, "Is there not a joy and wonder in our differences? See how our differences enrich the whole." It is man's doing to try to raise all plants alike, as on a farm, where people have to laboriously pluck out weedy differences.

By examining religious experience as a process, as a human experience, I simply cut across all religious boundaries. I am working at the foundation of all religions. My examples are primarily from Christian sources only because this literature is handier to me—not because of a preference for one or another. I am naturally ecumenical, one who enjoys all the plants in the garden. I was dismayed to find that some use the term ecumenical to imply an understanding between Christian groups, but all others are excluded! I once had a vision in which I was a Jewish prophet of old, alone in a cave, in great agony dealing with The One God. I cried out the name of God. In our tradition (as a Jew) the name of God was too sacred to mouth. But I discovered it could be said in desperation when it involuntarily erupts through the person. It is experiences like this that have made me of the Universal Church—the one that is everywhere, in all cultures, through all time.

The mystic experience is the highest joy that humans can experience. In order to explore its human basis and source, my approach is phenomenological, the careful and direct description of human experience. My formal training in clinical psychology introduced me to a dreadful number of schools of thought, each with their own leaders. When I discovered Europeans describing human experience as directly and carefully as they could, with total disregard for schools and theories, it was though I had finally come out on a verdant pasture with real grass and trees and sky. I was charmed when a fine description of sickness made me feel sick, and a description of obsession made me feel obsessive. I worked for years in a mental hospital and was honored when I finally got into the world of hallucinating schizophrenics. My pure phenomenological finds of hallucinating psychotics were so startling that my professional colleagues, who dealt for years with the same patients, simply did not believe me. Once I lectured to a mixed audience of patients and staff. I recounted what the average patient's experience of hallucinations was like. My professional colleagues were unimpressed, but patients came up with tears in their eyes and thanked me for understanding their experience, even though I had not met them before. As a person trying to understand and describe hallucinations, the compliments of these patients was like a Nobel Prize. I could not ask for anything higher than to have the people who lived these experiences thanking me. I later wrote of these things (3).

The more we experience the universal basis of religion the less significant are the doctrinal differences. Debate arises where experience is fragmented and in conflict. When one's experience is of the unified whole, of the universal, then debate falls silent. In order to illuminate this shift from struggle to the peace of unity I will have to remind you at times of the struggle of being in the ordinary world, and the need for darkness as well as light. In deepest darkness we can see even the slightest traces of light.

Though I have found value in all religions, most religion seems so badly handled. I attended services for a year in a major faith, but I simply found it too boring and too shallow to persist in it. Most religious works bore me to tears. Much of it seems like some political propaganda. I can see the pitch coming. I was recently asked to review a book supposedly based on Emanuel Swedenborg, a great mystic and a friend of mine. The whole theology of the book I was to review can be summed up by an old joke. A mother sends her son off to church and anxiously awaits her son's evaluation when he gets home. She was, of course, hoping religion would "take." She asked, "What was the sermon about?" The son answered laconically, "About sin." This was not enough for his mother so she anxiously asked, "Yes, but what did he say about sin?" And the son summed it up thus, "He was agin' it." That is what most religious works seem like to me. They are agin' something, mostly against enjoying yourself. In contrast I will be talking about religious experiences which are the essence of joy—a transcendent joy one cannot create but can find.

It has gradually dawned on me that the joy I will be addressing here is seldom recognized as a hallmark of mystical experience. A mystic "sees God" or has some "cosmic insight," but few say how pleasant it is. I once described in a magazine for the Eastern Orthodox a way of using one icon for a long-term meditative experience (4). I was roundly criticized in the next issue by an Orthodox nun who saw in my article the work of the devil. Her proof of my being in league with the devil was that I was enjoying myself! In reply to the nun I tried to be gentle. I said there are two basic paths in religion. Hers was the ascetic way, a way of denial and suffering. Mine is that of harmony with God and transcendent joy. I don't put down her way; I have had too little denial and suffering even to understand the ascetic way. I have known major mystics who found their way through asceticism, but it seems a long and painful way, approaching even death. I don't understand or appreciate it. It simply is not my way. To me it seems so easy to enjoy heaven that I just feel pity for those whose only way is the long way through suffering. It always seems like collecting green stamps in heaven—so many stamps per hour of suffering. I was pleased when a holy monk of my acquaintance said the ascetic way can easily become a self-centered sport. He fasts a day a week but this is for his sake, not for "green stamps" or a heavenly contest.

Skeptics often see a dark correlation between one's God and oneself. It is as though our Gods are really fashioned by us, and reflect us, and may not have any other reality. I agree! This suspicious correlation between our God and ourselves is not to be denied. Certainly the stingy man has a God who honors frugality, and he can back it up with Biblical quotes. Crooks see everyone as crooks. A few saints are soaked in so much good that they see good in all others.

Far from shying from the suspicious link between us and God, I would explore it and play with it. There is such a deep connection between our nature and our God that it behooves us to examine it. So in one of my meditations I practice being God and doing it better. One of the things you run into here is the interconnectedness of all things (a good Buddhist doctrine) so sometimes I hesitate to change even a "jot or tittle" of it. For beginning monks in Tibetan Buddhism there are exercises in which one recreates the whole universe. Perhaps God *depends* on me becoming a better God, in which case I better work at it. Perhaps the whole of existence is designed as a lesson for us, just for our edification, that we wake up to the God of all. Just as Plato said that people ought to "die daily," I also suspect they should be God for a time. I am sure most of you, as God, would seek to end war. "Blessed are the peace makers for they will know peace." When I hear from Africa that the Tutsis are killing the Hutus and vice versa I say to God, "Come on now. This is such a crude joke." A friend of God can be honest and forthright with Him.

I can ask you of your God and get some picture of your internal life. One way to do this is to simply ask a person what they would do if they were God. To those who insist on great rational understanding of religion to get into heaven I create a scene. I make them God standing at the Gate. Here come a long line of the totally mentally retarded, many pushed in wheelchairs. Some cannot hold up their head, or walk, or talk. Many have been spoon-fed their entire lives because putting food into their own mouth was too complicated. Now clearly they hardly know much. I ask my God-friend do you admit them? Most see the fallacy. They thought of all people as clever like themselves and so responsible. They forgot part of humanity. I think you and I, as God, would admit these poor retarded and greet them with kindness and consideration. As God I would also open their interior so that they might finally see All, just as I would let the blind see, and the deaf hear. As God I would have trouble even being unkind to Hitler. I think I would gently send him through existence again and again, to experience pain and suffering until he woke up to the Universal Human—very like Hindu or Buddhist reincarnation. Go around and around until you see yourself as Everyone and Everything.

An odd hand-me-down from tradition is that God is male. This theory has been suspiciously propounded by males. I once said elephants should properly have an elephant God. They surely wouldn't choose a human one. My experience tells me God is male and female, both and neither, simultaneously. That is, a sexual identity for God may be necessary and useful to some, but the God I have known is either, both, and neither. So when a female priest intones, "God, she . . ." I don't blink; and I intone with her, "Most Holy is *She*." When a monk is devoted to the Virgin Mary or Kuan Yin I think how wise of the church to venerate Her. There is the joke about St. Peter, who had come down to earth for a vacation. He was pestered by people to tell them what God was like. So finally he answered, "Well, in the first place, *She* is *black*."

I am also not put off by the multiplicity of names for God. Christ called him Allaha (Aramaic for father or papa). Mohammed called him Allah, others Brahman, Buddha, the Unknown, Mystery, etc. I use God as a generic name to represent all of these. When I examine the aesthetics of the sound of the word God, it seems a little abrupt and harsh. The sound of Allah or Allaha is much softer; it opens and floats. Buddha ends in the 'ha' which is breathy, of the spirit and opening up. I am not put off by these differences, but by sheer aesthetics would choose some of the softer and rarer names. I am also in accord with those who prefer not to casually bandy about any name. I appreciate that only the camel can pronounce the hundredth name of Allah. A plain-looking camel, standing like a camel, chewing like a camel, pronounces the hundredth sacred name by simply being a camel. You would own up to his reality if he fell on you. He enables us to get across the desert of life. I have already used "flower" and "garden" as names of God. I appreciate all the names and use one of the poorer ones, God, as common currency in this culture. The attributes of God will become clearer as we get into the foundations of religious experience.

When you look at religion as a discoverable human process you find something remarkably similar across varied groups. Nearly all praying and prayer is basically communing with The Power greater than one's self. We can look into this generic process and find the uses and the sensibility of it. On this level we are more alike than different. Once you grasp this essential similarity then you can participate equally well in a Jewish, Moslem, Buddhist, or a primitive religious service. The religions that arise in preliterate cultures are not simple; many primitives have the world's most complicated religions, because everything is alive and has a sacred name and a special nature. I would be honored to participate in various religious traditions. Each tradition was carefully shaped by peoples across the centuries as the best of their vision and understanding. So when we recognize prayer as a universal process, we can enjoy it in all its expressions and, indeed, enjoy the differences of its varied trappings in different cultures.

To illuminate the experience of God, I need to borrow, mostly from ancient traditions. It is a comment on the value of the current flood of religious literature that I will usually have to go back to earlier traditions. We are in a realm where the latest is rarely the best. A friend once asked me if I had read the latest book on something. I answered truthfully that in the past year I had not read a book written more recently than the twelfth century. It is the tremendous agreement of my own experience with mystics of many ages, traditions and cultures that has given me the courage to even speak of these things. So I am a mystic who represents all the mystics of many times and cultures. I will not burden you with the names of all. But understand that even though I will speak of my own experience, it is merely to give present live examples of what has been found and experienced by many, of various traditions and cultures.

Let me close with a hilarious example. Theresa of Avila, a simple nun in the 1500s, pursued the direct path to God. One of her great spiritual works was tied up by the Inquisition. They were looking for that foul demon heresy. The work was so full of the spiritual it was really beyond the capacity of the inquisitors to judge it. Her spiritual advisor commanded her to write another for the edification of her fellow sisters. She did not feel like a writer and especially did not feel equipped to speak of the spiritual. The incident seems humorous because I feel like her in boldly attempting to write of these things. Here was her written response to the command to write.

> "Why do they want me to write things?" she would ask. "Let learned men, who have studied, do the writing; I am a stupid creature and don't know what I am saying. There are more than enough books written on prayer already. For the love of God, let me get on with my spinning and go to choir and do my religious duties like the other sisters. I am not meant for writing; I have neither the health nor the wits for it."
>
> —St. Theresa of Avila, *Interior Castle* (5)

I don't in the least feel this is excessive modesty on her part. You don't deal with the All Knowing without coming to feel pretty stupid. In her book one could see her start out saying she knew nothing, then she would be given an idea she would elaborate. She was being led by God. Her feeling stupid was an essential element in the process. It meant she was wide open to whatever was given to her. She was as a child. In addition to the busy round of a nun's duties she dashed off *Interior Castle* in a few weeks. It has since been a classic for four hundred years. I wish that I could do as well as this simple nun who preferred to do her spinning and go to choir.

Those who have explored the ultimate nature of existence come upon a unique joy and a marvelous unity of experience and understanding. These are the mystics, which means simply those who have been given the direct experience of God. As a mystic I am a recent example of this ancient tradition and way. I draw upon the experiences of mystics of many times and traditions, upon mystics I have known personally, and my own experience.

The direct experience of God is everyone's potential. My method is the direct description of human experience without theory. This is essentially a project lying in both human psychology and religion. Fortunately all the paths to this transcendent experience are handy, in ourselves, not in some remote and arcane mystery to be solved. We are working in the very human foundations of religious experience, quite below the level of cultural and religious doctrinal differences and disputes. The One sought is fortunately common to us all, and seeks us all.

We will begin with a first simple look at mystical experience. From there we will explore little shifts in outlook which make the experience more likely. Then we will explore deeper shifts in understanding which are part of the way to the experience. With this understanding we can then look at the direct experience of God in its broader aspects.

In this I cannot promise the direct experience of God. That can only be given by God. But there is work we can do to clear away the rubbish of our misunderstandings to prepare to meet the One common to us all.

Dogs Barking

As a teenager
I'd go up on the roof
Of my flat.
In the gathering dusk
I could collect
Myself.
It was on the roof
That I came
Into the full flower
Of being a mystic
Having met God.

There was
A little incident
That sticks with me
Over a half century.
So small
It will seem odd.

It had become dark
I was about
To give up

And climb down
The ladder
To our flat.
Suddenly
Nearby
A mother called her child
A screen door banged
And a dog barked
And the whole universe
Opened up.

This moment
Was so momentous
It remains with me
Even now
A half century later.
Let me try
To open it up
For you too.

In these evening
Quests
In peace and quiet
And aloneness
I just open
Myself
To all there is
Being instructed
By existence.

I had been there
Some time.
It had grown dark
I was about to quit
And climb down
To the house again.
Almost as a last minute
Afterthought
The universe
Opened up.

The calling of a mother
For her child
Opened up heaven
Which is like a mother
Calling her child
To come home
Where it is safe.

The banging
Of the screen door
And the bark of the dog
Little circumstances
Said
See, it is here
In the commonplace.
Bang
Right here.

Years later
In another
Very high moment
I penned,
"Perfect enlightenment—
Dogs barking."

You see
People think of
Perfect Enlightenment
As uncontaminated
By dogs barking.
But it is the other way
Round.
Dogs bark
In the commonplace
Which is where
Enlightenment
Takes place.
Where else
Could it be?

Listen for
Dogs barking
And the bang
Of a screen door
The life
Of the commonplace.

How absolutely wondrous
And alive
It all is.

2

A First Look

Once you have become familiar with it, there come
    four experiences:
Everything that is presented (to the mind) is (felt)
    to rise in pleasure;
Day and night, you cannot be torn from this reach
    and range of pleasure;
Tribulations like attachment and aversion do not
    upset you;
There is born an appreciative understanding that
    brings together words and meanings;
By further cultivating this there arises, like the sun,
    in your mind,
Unfathomable capabilities such as visions and high-
    er cognitions.
This, then, is instruction in the most profound.
        —Longchempa, *Kindly Bent to Ease Us* (6)

I have puzzled for some while how best to present this. If I
began with many chapters on different aspects of the experience of
God, some readers would become impatient to know what the
whole experience is like. So first I would like to present the whole
experience, particularly in its more common and recognizable
attributes. There is a fairly classical mystical experience which I
believe every human being on earth has enjoyed at some time: the
beauty of nature. You are in a beautiful setting, perhaps with a sun-

set. You are relaxed and simply taking in all the natural beauty. The mood is one of patience and a relaxed perception of what is there. You suddenly and unaccountably feel as though you are a part of the immense, living, creative life before you. On a dark night in the country, the vastness of myriad stars easily brings on the same experience. It is as though you feel and enter the wonder of it all. Awe is a very basic element of mystical experience. With a very clear sky and an utterly dark place at night, I have been quite overwhelmed with the starry heavens. I have even used binoculars and marveled at the fabulous number of stars in the Milky Way.

As you gaze into the heavens the main feeling is of reverence and awe at the size and wonder of it all. The subject/object division of you versus the stars disappears. There is just awesome wonder in which you are immersed and a part of it all. There is peace and harmony, and the experience feels therapeutic, as though balance is restored. You may have little sense of time passing, or how long you were in awe.

Why do I say this is a mystical experience? A very rational doctrinaire person might say the experience has to have the label God somewhere. What rational speculation teaches often departs from what experience reveals. For me the experience had the right label when I said wonder. If I said the experience is of Wonder, with a capital W, perhaps it gets more recognizable. The experience of God has to do primarily with feeling. This simple truth is widely overlooked in religious doctrine. Feelings inform and teach by an avenue that is broader than the rational, affecting the whole life and outlook of a person more than any rational teaching can. It is often so broad and full of wisdom that it is then difficult to explain to others. This most common of all mystical experiences reveals the nature of the Divine without a God label. For some God is felt as present, but for many it is simply wonder. Though the experience is felt as a great gift, it is the opposite of anything that enhances ego or makes one feel superior. One becomes a harmonious part of all.

All of us have had this experience; where we really differ is not so much in the experience but rather in how well we remember it, and in how central the experience is to our understanding. My earliest experience of this type was at age one in a crib. I was staring at motes of dust floating in a sunbeam. As they floated and turned and emitted rainbow colors, I went into ecstasy in the incredible beauty. It apparently became central for me, for I remember it vividly even seventy years later. There are many who have had this experience, but as their attention turned elsewhere they have mostly forgotten it, and it teaches them little or nothing. Since everyone has probably had this experience, the mystic may simply be one who remembers the experience and for whom it became central to their understanding.

There are even smaller experiences which are like the rapture of nature, but they are so little they are often not recognized. Often they seem like a brief pleasantness, in which we just feel in harmony with our situation, feeling like a temple of respite in the midst of our day-to-day experience. It is a mild joy, another element that runs through all mystical experience. It is for me the greatest pleasure. In no way does the experience divide—either person against person or even person against creation. It always unites into a harmonious whole.

While admiring the sunset you could open whatever religious text you have and read it while in this mood. In this mood understanding opens up and is revealed. Words have greater depth and speak to you personally. It is as though the text has joined with the sunset and your mood to become harmony. This is the proper mood or feeling for encountering mystery.

But even without a religious text, or the label God, it remains the same, a place of pleasant harmony in the midst of one's experience. These experiences restore sanity and balance. Ideally we would structure some time for them every day. I had so many, and was so intrigued by them, that by adolescence I had worked out the way back to them. I suspect my findings are universal. If you want more experiences of wonder, learn to relax and appreciate what is before you. Just let yourself be.

I sometimes wonder if we are not each like a shallow pond. The slightest breeze or disturbance of the water scatters the light and our understanding in all directions. From my early sunset experiences I learned to leave my pond alone. Slowly it stills, and particles settle out. Then I see to the bottom, and in the night the moon and stars go their accustomed way in my pond. One cannot by any clever manipulations of one's finger still the water. Yet left alone it stills, and the depths may be seen.

In Buddhism this has been referred to as "mirror mind"—we are the mirror, reflecting the universe. In Zen there is a story of an abbot who wanted to select his successor. He asked the monks how to keep the mirror mind clean. The monks, anxious to advance, came up with much about meticulously wiping every mote of dust off the mirror. But there was a kitchen servant who had looked into the mirror so long he described it as the absolute, beyond dirtying. He was made abbot because he had looked so long as to see its very nature.

There is a lesson in this. On one level it appears that we could clean the mirror, and some get into all sorts of obsessive acts. "Perhaps if I do this or that, or was less sinful, fasted, etc., the mirror would come clear." We dust and clean, and it seems to work for a moment. Then we must dust more. But the image of mirror mind can lead us to understandings that are not useful. A mirror is man-made, it is rigid, and it can easily shatter. Let us return the image of the mirror to its source, the surface of the pond, which is of nature and reflects the nature of all things. Dust settling on its surface is slowly absorbed and sinks to the bottom; no need to remove it. The mirror surface can be disturbed but never shattered. When the reflection is disturbed, it is because of the agitation of the pond itself. Quit stirring it up. Leave it alone, and watch it become clear and reflect the universe.

I am also speaking of meditation, which in this imagery is learning to sit quietly by one's own pond and watch it become clear, and eventually to reflect all there is. After a long acquaintance it steadies and becomes a mirror. I don't know whether it would be out of place to describe glimpses I have seen in the mirror. One has come back to me so many times that I fully expect to move into it one day. I see a city in the near distance, in a wonderful soft rosy glow. There is an overwhelming feeling of harmony, so it must be heaven. I see buildings and spires, and I get the feeling of harmonious life. It always has the same sunset color. The feeling is so fine I would move in and take my place without a second thought. I have seen it countless times as though it is my place. It is as though I am seeing my own eternal ideal.

But I have drifted from a small scene into a higher one, an accumulation of harmonious experiences that perhaps makes it easier to recognize others. I have been dismayed to talk to religious leaders who recalled with effort one or two such experiences from childhood. They should be far more frequent. I would encourage people to recall and honor any and all such experiences. As one savors these experiences, they become easier and easier to return to. Though there is a familiar sameness to them, they are so full of meaning and life that it is always like finding a treasure over again. It feels familiar, like returning home again, yet it is always as fresh as the first time. It is a comfortable place, where there is no stress, the peace of heaven. It is where the mind is centered or "one-pointed." One not only experiences unity but *becomes* unity itself.

For some it may include a sense of beneficent presence. This presence is usually not seen or heard, but known with certainty nevertheless. It seeks nothing, demands nothing, but is peace itself. I often have a sense of this presence when I am in a place where many have truly worshipped. It is as though their combined spiritual efforts remain palpably present, and this presence is always in me as well as surrounding me. Omnipresent. Inside or outside, it is the same. I cannot separate them.

This feeling is also very elevating, as though everything has been lifted up into a higher world. When I leave the pond/mirror mind alone it just appears. It is given, a grace, for which one is deeply thankful and grateful, another essential element of the experience. This presence is in everything beautiful. And the more one relaxes in the beauty, the better the unseen presence can be felt. I know of no mental gymnastics, no asceticism, no posture or breathing that can bring it about. It rather seems to be the pristine nature of things, when we just let them be as they are. I used to work up lists of questions to solve in this state, but when in this state my questions looked ridiculous. Still one can solve heartfelt problems in this state, which I will deal with later.

If we take seriously that God is omniscient and omnipresent, then we are speaking of learning to recognize what is already present. I cannot fashion omniscience or omnipresence. It just is. But I can learn to remember it and find it again. I am one who collected these states and the remembrance of them, when so many others just got too busy to notice. I fell in love with it as a child, and became a collector of this preciousness. Later I was cheered by reading of many other mystics, finding that I was not alone in my discoveries.

There is another extremely important aspect of the direct experience of the Divine. It does not make you feel superior to others who don't know about it. Perhaps in the first few minutes of it some get carried away and want to tell the world, save others, etc. But steady experience of the Divine produces *profound* humility. One becomes the equal of all else. And like a good mystic, I mean this in a double sense. In one way the Divine fills one so one becomes like the All, even though this is incomprehensible. But, in another way, one is the equal of all other people, animals, plants, and even the stones and stars. I was pleased to see in the Eastern Orthodox doctrine that when they say all will be saved, they mean even the stones. A first brief experience of the All may disturb some, and make others feel superior, but the more seasoned experience leads to a deep humility. In this humility it is not unreasonable to think that any creature that comes for your help may be the Buddha or Christ. Many saints lived with this idea in mind for years.

There is a Zen story of a monk who had his meager cell broken into by a thief who took everything. The monk sensed the thief's desperate need, so as the thief turned to go, the monk asked if he didn't also want his cloak—the only thing that he had left. The thief was later caught, and while in prison he reflected on this peaceful, selfless man who was so generous. After he got out of prison he came to study with him. How much the gift of his cloak accomplished! The seasoned experience of the Divine makes one humble and the equal to all else. So pride and vanity are a sure sign that someone has not been graced with this experience. God is very like water, seeking lowly places and people.

So these are the signs of the everyday experience of the Divine. They probably have been known by everyone, and need not have the label of God or religion on it. The lowly experience of God shades down into all the wisdom, harmonies and joy of life. It is only given to some to see the Maker's label on it. It is all things of beauty; indeed beauty is like the tracks of the eternal. It is all things of love and harmony within ourselves and with others. It is marked by a joy that feels elevated, lifted up. It leads directly into wisdom. It is a primal, omnipresent aspect of reality which we cannot make or manipulate in any way. It is like the settled pond that reflects all else.

We would do well to savor these experiences which all have known, and study how we can return to them. If they are remembered and treasured, they can come to color the whole life. With practice it gets easier to find your way back to what is always present. These experiences are brought on by relaxed perception and appreciation of whatever is present. The experience is primarily a feeling of joy, wonder, and awe at what is present. This might be called a foundation experience because it has all of the basic elements of the experience of God, even though some may not see them. It introduces one to the unity of all there is. Its unifying nature contrasts with the scattering effect of most daily life. The Lord is like a shy friend who will wait around forever to be invited in. But with easy familiarity he fills the house with his love and wisdom, becoming a most welcome guest. Look at the lowly beauty and wonder of the world and become one with it.

Over the years I have met with many mystics. Because of my writings and reputation they often sought me out. None of these people were rich or famous. They were ordinary people. They came to me primarily because being a mystic can be a lonely journey; there are so few who will understand. In these encounters with other mystics there were a number of consistencies which I have come to regard as signs of the genuine experience. All were hesitant to speak, even though they already knew I was sympathetic. Why? Unknown to most people there are all kinds of forces that protect the Sacred. These are people who have met the Sacred and are quite naturally its protector. When I was a clinical psychologist, I could far more easily elicit details of clients' sex lives than I could get them to speak of the Sacred. They are quite modest and humble about their experiences of the Divine. So their attitude is the direct opposite of the person who would try to impress me.

In speaking with them I try to get a direct description of their experience. I want the experience as it was, with every nuance and quality. One of the reasons they are hesitant to speak is that the experience is full of very powerful feelings. I am reminded of my own wellspring as we discover theirs; often both of us are soon in tears, as we try to get to the experience. I have *always* found the true experience of God to have this wellspring of feeling.

I have heard people describe mystical experiences which were forty years old, yet the wellspring of strong feeling is still there, as fresh as it was in the original experience. The person talking about an experience is attempting to give a simple narrative account, but the feeling breaks in because it is so much a part of the experience. This is one of the simple signs that the experience was from beyond them. Try to picture one's Tree of Life. It is at your very center, and in the mystical experience your very Tree of Life is shaken to the roots. It feels out of the ordinary, as though the very core of your life has been touched. The experience is out of time; it doesn't fade with time, but remains fresh and powerful. The tremendous rush of feelings which break through, even in the midst of an attempt at a controlled telling of the story, is one sign that one has met the more-than-self. We may be very cool and rational beings, but the spiritual is of feeling; it is of life and love.

Some people's responses are quite as one might expect if the person was touched by the more-than-self. The person may be puzzled. Why me? They may doubt and question if it is of God. Sharing with others who do not understand will raise other doubts. All the doubts and questions little ego could raise may be raised.

In most mystical experiences we have a drama of two halves. The ego remembers something happened, and can raise all the doubts or questions minds are prone to. "Maybe it was just a dream." Others are even more prone to dismiss such experience. One woman was counselled by others that her vision was probably a stomach upset. How many stomach upsets have you known that produce an intense and meaningful vision? On the other hand there is the direct givenness in the experience—intense feelings, meaning, and the clear presence of God. The mystic may simply be someone who remembers and holds on to what has been given. The real difference between a mystic and an ordinary person may only be that the mystic, by retaining and cultivating the experience, has created a new center to his or her life.

The experience of God has in it wisdom that is simply given. It is just there, and it is quite clear. If symbols are given, they are instantly known and felt in their full meaning. Whatever is given is full of meaning, and the source of the meaning is unknown. This is another sign of something having been given from beyond one's self. The ego can doubt or question the meaning, yet the simple truth of the meaning remains unchanged; the experience is full of meaning, more than one could ever describe. This givenness is quite unlike an understanding that is gradually and laboriously derived by one's own effort. The experience of the Divine is an encounter with wisdom itself; it is simply there. I have never known trivial knowledge to be derived this way. The understanding may have to do with critical aspects of one's life, or it may deal with life and wisdom in general. It is very much of the essence of life, love and universal wisdom.

The main given is the knowledge that God is present. There is some discussion in church literature of seeing light. But I have not seen anyone in the literature reveal that the light is full of meaning and the Presence of God. When light is given, it is no ordinary light such as one can enjoy with a light bulb. It is simply a given, noetic knowledge beyond doubt that God is present. "Noetic" means simply directly known without any sensory input. It is like that to suddenly know. Suddenly there is light where there had been darkness. This is what happens in mystical experience. This is not the kind of fantasy one can self-generate. If you think you can, try it. You may create a few images, but can you create one full of meaning and of God's presence, one laden with feeling for the rest of your life? The person has the feeling of having been touched by what is far beyond their ken, and it contains its own certainty. I have surprised friends by saying I could far more easily doubt my own existence than I could doubt God's. The certainty of the experience is fundamental, whereas my own existence could easily be just a play of mirrors and illusion which could vanish in the next instant, and I would not be surprised.

I think it appropriate if some question mystical experiences which carry their own certainty. We have all heard of psychotics who are suddenly directed to kill someone. Even without a background understanding of psychosis I would have designed my own check. I simply look at whether the experience does good in some sense. I use "good" in a broad way to reflect both lawful and according to doctrine. I have had people come to me bragging of amazingly complex visions. There was no strong feeling, no meaning given, and they were taken aback when I asked, "What good is it?" It was as though they thought I should be impressed by the complexity of the vision alone! It lacked any good. Their need to impress me alone made its validity doubtful.

When people come to me with a mystic experience, it is to ask me, as an experienced person, what I think of it. If it has the marks of genuine experience then I affirm that they were given this gift, and by all means I encourage them to follow its lead. One vision told a woman she was to repair her relationship with her deceased father. Her experience had an element I had never seen before. An actual friend of her father came to her and gave her the message. In that moment she knew with total certainty that it was a message from God through this friend. Moreover when she checked with the friend, he did not know of her estrangement. I asked, "Was there good in it?" No matter how you looked at it, it appeared to serve a good purpose. I had not seen this form before—a friend delivers a message from God. I concluded that though this form was new to me, it was of God. I just had to broaden my ideas as to how God might work! Incidentally she was the wife of a minister in a church that makes much of heaven and hell and the love between people. What sense could she make of all this? She went to a bishop of her church, who said revelation only comes from the Book, and this hurt her deeply. Her experience had the internal marks of a real mystical experience, including the powerful feelings. She concluded the visitor was right, and she had already started to mend her relationship to her deceased father by prayer. I took the side of the vision and encouraged her to do just that.

An older man, near death, came to me complaining of a failing memory. I found his memory was tossing out all trivia, but he had a supreme capacity to remember mystical poetry. I reoriented him to what was happening. His memory was zeroing in on what was supremely important at the end of his life, discarding the rest.

It may help if I contrast the mystic's experience to ordinary experience. The mystic occasionally visits higher planes, but they live most of the time in the ordinary, so they know both realms.

Ordinary experience is mostly limited to the here and now. Ordinary experience is bounded by a given identity, body, history, and present circumstances. The world is viewed from these limitations and must be interpreted from them. One can add what one has been taught of the world and even in a religion, yet one is bound by these too, and must interpret existence from this base of limitations. The really big questions of "Who am I?" "What is this existence for?" "Is there life beyond this one?" etc. are unanswerable in any sure and certain manner from the vantage point of ordinary experience.

The situation for the mystic is quite different. It is as though they occasionally have a vacation from these limitations. They can stand on a high mountaintop and see the whole lay of the land. They are given more answers than they have asked for. I once remarked at a social gathering that all of the biggest questions of life have been answered long ago. One guest was quite taken aback and incredulous. Only on seeing her reaction did I realize I had spoken as a mystic and that my experience was very different from hers.

One of the consequences of the limitations of ordinary experience is that it puts a good deal of uncertainty into experience. Even if we put aside all the big questions, there remains uncertainty. "What will happen to me?" I may fairly well predict tomorrow, but what of the months or years I may have left? The bounded world has so many uncertainties beyond the factual here and now. Perhaps one of the most serious uncertainties is that other people are so different and often unpredictable. "Why do they do such things?" But even within one person there are uncertainties. "Why did I dream that?" "If only I could shake off these moods." Inside and outside, in ordinary experience we are in the midst of uncertainties. Once as a mystic I projected myself into all peoples' limitations. Having done this there was nothing anyone had ever done that I could not forgive. A psychologist friend of mine coined a universal principle, "All people do the best they can." My experience was like that. Having lived through all people's limitations it was clear that they had each done the best they could, given all their limitations. So as a God, there was absolutely none I couldn't forgive and aid, even myself. Ordinary experience is caught in thoroughly limited circumstance, and out of this quite bounded by uncertainties, both inwardly and outwardly.

In contrast, while the mystic experiences this too, he/she occasionally steps beyond this into the unbounded, the unlimited. From this perspective, "It is all good, indeed very good." While the mystic comes out of limited circumstances, he also sees the design of the whole, a design which he comes into harmony with. I am fully in accord with all the mystics who have said the answer to all of life's problems is enlightenment. Seek the Kingdom of Heaven and all things else will be added. But from the bounded limitations and uncertainties of ordinary experience this does not appear to be so. The great optimism of the mystic looks like some sort of fictitious pie-in-the-sky from ordinary experience. One must have really experienced the whole to come to the mystic's position. Each of the world's wisdom traditions point toward this same end, known as enlightenment.

People with genuine mystical experiences can be seen as on a continuum. At one end are those who are beginners. Their one little experience may puzzle and upset them. I seek out and encourage whatever trend was shown them. The woman who was counselled to repair her relationship to a deceased father is one example. At a somewhat deeper level are those to whom something of their essential nature was revealed to them. One man had a vision full of music, and he became a musician in a brief time. Somewhat deeper are those mystics who come to a universal understanding that is beyond their culture and the activities of their individual lives. I picture that they have come through some forest or bramble, and suddenly come out in a wide verdant plain where all mystics meet. On this Plain of the Universal, mystics of very different cultures, creeds, and backgrounds look remarkably alike to a fellow mystic.

Scholars not grounded in direct experience easily trip over "critical differences" where there are none to a mystic. Because of this, scholarly studies of mystics are useless to me. I need the actual live experience to work with. I came into mystical experience even before I knew religion existed. Later, the struggles between different creeds and their acrimonious debates and conflicts were painful for me. So I searched for mystics I could identify with. Much of Christianity has little or no mysticism in it. But as I read mystics of many traditions it gradually dawned on me that I was seeing the same thing presented in different cultural frames. My outlook is now compounded of my own experience, mystics I have met and corresponded with, and the writings of the world's major mystics, stretching far back over the centuries. It was the overwhelming unanimity of all this that encouraged me to try to present it as a whole.

Some have viewed the Plain of the Universal from afar and are able to describe some of its main qualities. I could illustrate this with much religious poetry. Some have been to the Plain of the Universal and rushed back to describe their experience. Then there are mature mystics who lived in the Plain of the Universal for a long while. When they come back to teach, practically every word is pervaded by the experience of the Universal. All tend to reveal the Universal, but with maturity it tends to color their whole presentation.

Let me now try to describe this Plain of the Universal where mystics of all creeds and cultures meet. There is but One in the whole of creation. Nothing else exists. In Greek, *En to Pan*, "The one is the All." This One creates Itself into all things and all beings, who wander through lostness, to freely and voluntarily find their way back to their source. There are various reasons given for this—two that I like are: "Just for fun," ("lila" in the Hindu) and, "Just to pass the time." I have been shown that this creation of the whole of existence is totally effortless, and that it was totally inevitable in the design of existence—but the mystery of this inevitability escapes me. The whole of the created universe then struggles within the intrinsic and given parameters of its existence to transform the present world back into the non-dual, changelessness of the One. Being born into the limitations of creation and the return to the source is the central drama of existence, of which all other dramas are aspects.

Different creeds deal with this central drama in different terms and with differing clarity and directness. Drama is a very fitting term, because life seems dramatic, full of ups and downs. Each of us is born into our own drama. In all creeds there is every indication that the One wants every element it created to return to its Source, and is endlessly helping to this end. The possibility of knowing the One seems to be ingrained in our very nature. We humans are inclined to see ourselves as the principal elements in this drama of universal return, but it is true for all that exists, including stones.

If we compare ourselves as humans to the rest of existence, we are both at a greater advantage and disadvantage. Our advantage is that we can clearly sense our need to "find our way home again." But our disadvantage is our capacity to get lost more easily than plants, animals, and rocks, which are more able to fulfill their nature. When I am filled with doubts and uncertainties, I admire the rock that expresses what it is perfectly, without doubt and questioning.

Now how does the mystical experience relate to this cosmic design of existence? The very first and most common mystical experience of the wonder of nature introduces us to the One Life of which all things are a manifestation. Higher levels of experience can break through into our inborn nature, which is our own path back to the One. Mystics who have come out on the unifying Plain of the Universal have partly returned to the Source and have become active parts of the cosmic design. Mystics write merely to help others find their way. The mystic, in finding the One, comes to participate in the One's wish to join with itself everywhere. Creation is an exercise in which the One is creating beings that are sentient, aware examples of itself.

I once had an awesome vision from which I came back with the total and absolute certainty that only God exists. But the moment I pronounced this insight to myself as an ordinary mortal I immediately saw a paradox. How could I, as an ordinary dumb human, pronounce this, because I was saying I was God. Was I mad? I somewhat fearfully revealed to my dinner guest, the late Alan Watts, that I had been shown only God exists. He said I was very fortunate to have the vision that the Hindus and the Buddhists seek. I felt much relieved by his saying this. I was in accord with ancient tradition.

You now see something of the center of our goal, but I have probably raised many questions. If you are strictly logical, this realm has much that will disturb you. Many of these difficulties come about because we are dealing with different levels of reality, some of which transcend time and space. So on one level I can say I was shown that ultimately only God exists. But of course as one writing here, I am on this level an ordinary dumb human who happens to remember what I was shown. I ask for your patience as we gradually explore many aspects of mystical experience. I have become convinced that those who know the supreme joy of mystical experience have done so by making some little shifts in their attitude and approach to the world that predisposes them to this experience. So let us look at these little shifts.

The day was when I did not keep myself in readiness for thee; and entering my heart unbidden even as one of the common crowd, unknown to me, my king, thou didst press the signet of eternity upon many a fleeting moment of my life.

And today when by chance I light upon them and see thy signature, I find they have lain scattered in the dust mixed with the memory of joys and sorrows of my trivial days forgotten.

Thou didst not turn in contempt from my childish play among dust, and the steps that I heard in my playroom are the same that are echoing from star to star.

—Rabindranath Tagore, *Gitanjali* (7)

Section 1

Little Shifts in Outlook

Little shifts in outlook can lead directly into mystical experience.

3

Mystery and Awe

Moreover, it becomes clear that the spiritual life is not
an escape from the world but a transformation of it. It is
not a change of place but a change of manner of existing
and living.

—Nellas, *Deification in Christ* (8)

To approach mystery requires little shifts of attitude. One is to
slow down, as though we have all the time in the world. Another is to
become fully invested in whatever is before us. In a train station I had
time to wait. I sat on a bench and simply noticed all the different people passing by. Tall and short, men, women, and children of different
races. Each moved in a different way. A frantic woman with children.
Then suddenly a black man of unusual dignity. Differences. I was seeing life flowing by, showing me endless differences. I soaked up this
lesson. Each is human, yet whatever made all this likes each uniquely different. Somehow I trace my present feeling for different religions and different viewpoints to what I discovered while sitting on a
railway bench. If Existence was for differences, so I would be too.

I could elaborate other scenes and the lessons learned from
them—in the garden, or enjoying the serenity of a cemetery, in a
garbage dump, looking at an icon, in a ruined building, in so many
different places. As a child I remember lying on my stomach staring
at the parted grass. I swore I would discover all that was there. I was
surprised to find so many tiny insects, bits of leaf, rocks, more than
I could comprehend, even in a few square inches of grass.

The contrast between my ordinary daytime life with school, friction with others, poverty, and all the ordinary turmoils of life, and this finding my way to ultimate peace and beauty could hardly be greater. I studied the way back to this beauty. It was terribly simple. Find a space and time where I had nothing to do but look and enjoy. I posed no big questions. There were no exercises to be done, just relax and *perceive what is there*. It was mostly wordless. I had to come back to it over and over to begin to be familiar with it. It was as though I was being educated in some Eternal Simplicity quite willing to show itself.

It was some years before I even got a hint that this experience might be religious. Religion seemed much too shallow and inadequate to describe it, and in many respects it still does. It was only when I read the work of mystics that it finally got a name, "mysticism." Years later I learned that it is also called enlightenment. The mantra *Om mani padme hum* (the jewel in the lotus) is the Hindu and Buddhist version of the same flowering. The lotus grows up out of very wet mud—an image of the nature of our world. The jewel and its flashing lights represent our awakening to sheer beauty and wonder.

Being anywhere, relax and notice all that presents itself. Allow existence to open itself and reveal itself. It is the total openness, waiting to receive. Instead of doing anything to ourselves, or to existence, we simply let it be and look into its nature. We carry away from these experiences a kind of cosmic sanity. As a child lying face down trying to discover all in a tiny plot of grass, I learned that the smallest part of ordinary existence contains more than I can ever grasp. The same is true of all existence. If you look carefully, you see that we come up against mystery everywhere. I have looked at a single icon, a small postcard of St. Innocent of Irkutsk, daily for two years and gladly return to it again and again to see more mystery open up (4). I wondered if I would come to have seen it all and be bored. I have spent hours on the tiniest detail. The process turned out to be very rich and endlessly evolving. Some of the most pleasant and meaningful experiences of my whole life were in looking at this icon. It is quite endless.

I have deliberately tried this patient openness in a variety of settings—once while viewing a film on the holocaust, thinking its horrors would block it. They didn't. It involves a relaxed perception of what is being presented. There is no hurry, and nothing to be accomplished. You simply let things be, and notice them as they are. You need not even seek some message or lesson. But the lesson gradually appears and asserts itself. An underlying potential opens up. I suppose the potential is in us, but it seems to be in all things.

In this experience, one moves beyond a subject/object division. *I* am not observing *things*. Rather there is no difference between me and things. It is all one sea of discovery, moving toward an egoless experience where there are no self-concerns left; there is just what is presenting itself. The Buddhist refers to this as pristine awareness. When we get *us* and *our* awareness out of the way, it is just there.

In Zen there is central reference to what is called "no-mind." When I think I am running my mind (whatever that is) then I have mind. But if I leave it alone, under it is no-mind, which appears to be a capacity of existence itself. This natural mind tends to show the universal. It is not just of here and now; it is also about what always was and will be, the universal. Sitting on a railway bench I see that whatever is making this presentation enjoys making everything unique. It loves differences, in endless variations. So I was looking at a principle of existence which made me more tolerant of differences. In relaxed perception I not only accept what is presented, but it tends to affect my very outlook and nature.

When I want to really see a person I use the same relaxed perception. I once met a master of this in the late Fritz Perls. The first time I saw him do it we were in a group of therapists, with him as the leader. A psychiatrist spoke up, and of course we all listened to his words. Fritz relaxed and listened to the emotional tone underlying the words. Fritz broke in and described the underlying plaintive tone. The man was crying out. Suddenly I heard it too. It totally altered my perception. The psychiatrist was speaking of his problem but suddenly I really experienced it as an agonized crying out. If one doesn't become too caught up in words, you can sense the real person. I look at gestures, listen to the voice quality, and let my own inner imagination run free. A common experience is to think, "Oh, this person is like so and so," revealing aspects of this person's nature. Often I have had strong images come to me that were almost an extra-sensory perception of the life of the other. All images received in this state are revealing.

Relaxed perception takes in all that is there. At the very least you will learn something. We are embedded in a mystery that is ready to enter a relationship with us. It isn't talkative, as we are. It rests in pure experience. It is perhaps like resting with one's dog. If I invite a dog on the bed to sleep, there are some messages exchanged. "You can trust me and I trust you. We are different but we are equally life." The dog learns to avoid my restless feet under the covers and finds where he can be undisturbed. And I enjoy where he presses down the covers and provides warmth. The relationship to mystery is like that. I learn from it, and perhaps it also learns from me. It is a tacit, feeling relationship. The dog and I don't need a written contract. Our contract is written in habit. He remains dog and I a person, but we can still come to know each other better.

Religion is basically familiar with mystery and comfortable with it. Beyond a few knowns and certainties, the religious is always in the territory of the mysterious. It would give it a name; it would represent it in ceremony, and the mood or feeling is one of approaching mystery and dealing with it respectfully. One can define the spirit that finds religious joy as one of friendship with, and respect toward, ultimate mystery.

The most common opposite attitude would be either to deny that mystery exists or, worse yet, have no capacity at all to notice it. "It simply doesn't exist; it is all hogwash." Let me directly contrast the experience of mystery with its opposite. I sit here writing. In the anti-mystery spirit it is no surprise. I was trained to write in school. My occupation as a psychologist required me to write reports. My professional life was about one-third writing. So why shouldn't I be able to write? There is no mystery in that.

Now let me look at this same situation as mystery. Without knowing why, I become intrigued with a subject, and I read. Then I find that somewhere in me words are forming. When I find myself going over and over a crucial line, I take it as time to write. When I sit down, words form. I have often wondered what the end of a line would be when I was setting down its beginning. I feel dismayed when I look at the size of a book I propose to write, but someone in me is full of enthusiasm and thinks it will be easy. Writing seems to be mostly listening to my spirit and taking dictation like a dutiful secretary. When I have written for hours and I'm tired and hungry, I just want to go to the kitchen to eat and relax. But I know my writer hasn't quit, so I bring pencil and paper when I go in to eat. I am about to bite into a sandwich when he suggests a change of phrase here, or a clarification there. Worst of all, he comes up with a whole new idea I have to fit into the manuscript, all in the midst of my desire to just relax and eat.

You can see the contrast between the two attitudes. The first assumes it has the *explanation* and doesn't look at the *actual experience*. The other looks closely at the actual experience and finds it surprising, paradoxical, and plain mysterious in every aspect. Poor writers tend to have the first attitude. They assume that writing is simply a rational exercise they must carry out. When they sit down with a pen they either go blank, or the writing plods like a poor beast of burden hardly able to carry the load. It is no surprise that their writing lacks life, for they have cut themselves off from the living source of writing.

Under this attitude we find no surprise in writing and we can wrap it up neatly as "nothing but." It all seems very sensible and rational. However, my school training in writing was actually very meager. The super-rational aspect of scientific psychology did much to damage my writing. Under the second attitude we simply look closely at the actual experience. It wasn't until I looked closely at the process and discovered that it is a mysterious given, just as it was to St. Theresa, that my writing started to loosen up and flow. Tagore's literary experiments suggested to me to be free. When I thought of the poor beast of burden above, the image was at first a horse pulling an overloaded cart. But I wanted the burden on the horse, so the image quickly shifted to a thin, weak, overloaded pack horse.

The writing is richer and flows better when I assume I am not its real source! As you will see later, the problem of getting ego out of the way is pretty nearly *the central barrier* to the experience of God. Buddhism is very explicit about this. The acceptance of mystery is an attempt *to take it all in and to be very honest about what we discover.* I find myself to be mystery, embedded in mystery. Mystery is pleasant and I am comfortable with it. A little inquiry again stirs up the awe of it. The spirit of anti-mystery doesn't really inquire and look closely and respectfully; it cuts off, limits, and assumes that everything is just as we say it is. Friendliness to mystery looks, explores, discovers—endlessly. It becomes accustomed to sudden insights out of the blue. It feels. It delights in paradox. It is full of life. It is far richer than our limiting assumptions.

Some see an antagonism between science and mysticism. Many religions react as though scientists are tearing down the structure of religion, block by block. But I enjoy the same mystery in science. I am a trained scientist and gravitate toward precision measurements. I have done research in navigation and ballistics, and I love statistical analysis. When I learn from astronomy of the immense age and size of the universe, it simply adds to awe. At present (and science, too, is always in the process of discovery) our visible universe appears to be fifteen billion years old since the "big bang." Bang, and the universe expands. Forever? Or will it go to a maximum expansion and then contract again? We don't know yet. In Hindu mythology one expansion and contraction is called a breath of Brahman. I am betting on the ancient Hindu vision—that scientists will find there is enough matter to limit expansion and bring about an eventual contraction. We are talking about one breath of Brahman as incredible eons of time—and we can assume that Brahman has been breathing some while.

As a mystic, I see God designs science and scientists too. I wonder why? Perhaps it is just to keep us busy, to give us something to do. Science is adding to the scope and incredible interconnectedness of the universe. The solvents in some spray cans can damage the ozone layer and lead to blindness and skin cancer in us and animals! Good heavens. Those who haven't discovered the interrelatedness of all things just haven't looked closely enough. Science has discovered a new virus in AIDS. It hides in cells and replicates with them. To add to the complexity, it is very able to mutate. In trying to control it, we are learning intimate details of the virus and about our immune system. Yet at each discovery we come to new mysteries. It has been that way ever since the birth of science and the effort to figure it all out.

I see marked similarities between the effort of science to deal with mystery and that of religion itself. Scientists do not say, "This is beyond me"; they try to figure out a reliable way to find out. They have their doctrine (the scientific method) and their rituals (experiments to test hypotheses). A scientist who proclaimed he knew it all would be a fool and no scientist. Theirs is a most friendly attitude toward mystery. It intrigues them. They must try to approach it, very like religion. Go right up to mystery, and try to make its acquaintance, but be respectful. One will get nowhere putting mystery down as nothing and scoffing at it. Scoffing doesn't limit mystery; it only limits our experience of it.

At the same time, the direction of science and religion is quite different. To figure out things science must delimit and test repeatedly until truth stands clear. Priests, ministers, rabbis, and shamans are people who have ways given them by the traditions of their people for dealing with mystery. Unlike scientists who must try to isolate and limit the mysteries they deal with, our priests deal with whole mysteries. For instance, in the ceremony of the Eucharist we are instructed to partake of the body and blood of incarnate God. We are to take this within, that we might enter upon deification, becoming God-like. We are back with Christ and the disciples, partaking as one of them. Will the ceremony do us any good? Everything depends upon how we relate to mystery. Stand back and question if a wafer is actually the body of Christ, and it is missed. Enter into it wholeheartedly as a direct participation in mystery—open to all its meaning—and you can be transformed. In religious ceremony whole mysteries are dealt with. Reflections just on the meaning of the Eucharist ceremony already fill a whole library. Yet both science and religion deal with mystery and make discoveries.

The shift here is simple enough. Seek mystery. You should be able to find it everywhere. And then respectfully find ways to become a friend to mystery. The basic feeling is awe and respect toward the all. Those with awe and respect have the basic key to a special joy.

There is a current controversy between Biblical fundamentalists and evolutionists. Fundamentalists take the Old Testament history as a literal history, which really limits it terribly. They add up the ages of people from Adam and Eve, and conclude this world is about five thousand years old. They feel that the picture of man evolved from other life forms is demeaning. But when you study geology and fossils it is obvious the earth is nearer five billion years old. When I look at the fossil record I am in awe. "My God, you have a patience far beyond anything I can understand." When I learned that the chromosomal pattern is basically the same in us as in all plants and animals I was amazed and pleased. I went into the garden and said, "Cousin fern, I am delighted to be related to one as old as you and of such a graceful form."

Contrast the picture of a creator who intervened a mere five thousand years ago to create Adam and Eve in the garden, to one who took ten billion years up to the creation of the earth, and then worked five billion more on our earth itself, before getting around to us. It appears we humans are literally a last-minute affair. I am far more impressed by the latter scenario. The One behind this has a leisurely pace which is far beyond my capacity to know or emulate. There is far more wonder in a Creator whose footsteps are five billion years long, and who spent vastly more time with trilobites and dinosaurs than us. The spirit that is friendly to mystery opens up to *all that is given* and is ready to feel the total wonder of it. It is an attitude that profoundly respects existence just as we find it. It enters into and enjoys existence as it presents itself. It need not eliminate or avoid anything.

Our bodies are made of material elements. Not many would argue with that. All of the heavier elements were blown out of supernova explosions long, long ago. Isn't it marvelous that we somehow got gathered up into life forms that can enjoy this immense show? In Buddhism there is a fundamental doctrine that we humans have a rare and transient opportunity that is not given to all other life forms. We can take what we are given and raise it to its ultimate.

I have on the wall above me a Tibetan painting of the Wheel of Samsara (becoming), which I put near me as a reminder. In a dramatic painting it tells of our responsibility not only to try to elevate our life, but all life, that we have got just this little brief life in which to accomplish much. The wheel of life above my head is held in the jaws of Yama, the Lord of Death, representing ultimate urgency. Around the wheel it shows all the stages of life—being born, childhood, being sexually active adults, old age, and death. It is more complex than my description. I love it when so much mystery is painted for me to reflect upon. It is a very gutsy doctrine. Instead of pretty angels on clouds, it shows our life as a wheel of change and a limited, brief opportunity to figure out what it is all about. Doctrines like this prod us from behind, while the joys of opening mystery pull us forward. It took fifteen billion years to get blown out into space and gathered here, and we have this brief moment as humans to understand it. That is our life. It goes round in a limited little circle. Our lives are a window of opportunity, and all religions imply that in this world we set our ultimate destiny.

If you run out of mysteries then you can look at the most central and primal one. We are consciousness, but precisely what is consciousness? Here is the root of all experience to look at, your very consciousness. Look closely. Do you make it? If so, how? Closely analyzed, it rather looks like consciousness is some sort of mysterious given whose nature transcends our understanding! In the hypnogogic state, between sleep and waking, you can watch ideas form. How long have you had consciousness that you haven't stopped to look at it? Have you experienced even one mental event in detail? And then can consciousness see consciousness? Or put another way, can you not see it? If I just accept consciousness as a given, it works quite nicely. If you run out of mysteries look at this primal one of consciousness on which all others rest!

When I see the very process I am engaged in as a mystery, it flows better. I am mystery, embedded in mystery. I partake of mystery and it partakes of me. We are friends; we get along. When we come right up to mystery, we still don't comprehend it Yet, as we become familiar with it, it gradually reveals itself. It isn't so alien or removed; it is intelligence. When we gradually work with mystery, and find it guiding us, it opens us out to a whole new dimension. We are not only never alone, but we are in the bed of existence with an Intelligence like ourselves, but far more patient than ourselves. What is it? A mystery that we are, and are embedded in. Can we deal with utter mystery? Yes, of course, but respectfully and patiently.

So the first shift is away from a prideful attitude that basically puts down everything as nothing, toward an attitude that opens up to all and everything, respectfully, experiencing awe. In this mood we can come right up to Mystery, and patiently learn. It is not a mystery totally beyond our grasp, since it also includes our effort to grasp. Many traditions say we cannot even pray but that God wills it. Is the mystery attempting to join with us? Yes, of course. There is no joining without it.

If you have followed thus far, look at all the religious efforts of all people through time. Look at the primitive addressing the spirit of a tree, the Eskimo praying to the Polar Bear Spirit, the Christian receiving the Eucharist, the Buddhist lighting incense in the temple. Seen from the perspective of friendship with mystery are not these all of one spirit?

I even find that when I give mystery a friendly nudge, it nudges me back. In Zen Buddhism a koan is a paradoxical statement given to a student to reflect upon to find enlightenment. Mystery was in a joking mood one morning. As I awoke someone said to me, "Here is a koan for you," and I awoke wide-eyed to the world. Joker gave me the whole of existence as my koan, my paradox to meditate on. What delighted me most was that a joke had been given to me out of the blue. And the joker understood me so well. He knows not only that I would understand a koan, but that I would be delighted to be given my own koan, which is the whole of existence itself. And you see me here, years later, like a good student still working with my koan.

But if mystery sometimes gets too much for you, you can use an idea I learned from some saints. Whenever you find yourself or someone burdened with the weight of mystery, just enunciate an ancient truth. "It is not given for us to understand everything." And thank heaven for that.

Across the top of my rolltop desk I arrange quotes I like. Here is one from a great Orthodox Christian saint, St. Theophan the Recluse. "All troubles come from a mental outlook that is too broad. It is better to humbly cast your eyes down toward your feet and figure out which step to take where." I laughed at that one. St. Theophan was well acquainted with Mystery, and mystery makes one humble. One becomes less and less presumptuous.

The capacity to experience mystery and awe is simple. It is available to us by a simple shift of attitude. It is the difference between narrowing our existence as "nothing-but" or remaining open to all. In this openness we easily find ourselves mysterious and embedded in an awesome and mysterious universe. This openness is good for our own understanding and development. We can approach mystery and gain from it, while never mastering or fully comprehending it. Mystery is friendly, and though not exactly like us, it is somehow related to us and is our source. Even science is not antithetical to mystery, for all our busy gathering of knowledge opens out to yet more unknowns. Even if we were given total comprehension of the universe, we would still have ourselves to confront. Openness to mystery makes the experience of God inevitable.

In some respects the experience of mystery and awe is like being filled with all there is. I have sensed that what I am doing now is my eternal role. I so enjoy discovery and setting it down, to make it available to others. It is as though this moment opens out to all similar moments. I enter into all of them, so I experience my eternal place in the scheme of things. What I am doing here is what I will always do. It is very like finding yourself accepted in the very job you most wanted. What fun to endlessly discover and make available to others. Even when I read of the work of other mystics, suddenly here and there I find myself. This experience settled down in me almost like a job title: "One who is a representative of the mystical tradition." The words came to me, "A living representative," but I hesitate to say a *living* representative. Why? Obviously I am alive, but there is something sacred about being a living representative; it is a higher stage. Contain my joy. Being a representative of this tradition is quite enough. To find what your life was meant for and to come to express it is the highest joy. We have our greatest sense of freedom in doing what we most enjoy. It is a time one would say, "Thank you. This is plenty. This is enough. I am quite content."

Yet I experienced the like of this long ago. I was in a particularly dark place, outdoors examining the Milky Way with binoculars. Discovering a myriad of stars, I entered into it. My world expanded into an awesome potentiality. They were not stars "out there." Suddenly my world had expanded. Some city dwellers rarely see stars, or just one or two bright ones. But here was the edge of our whole galaxy spread out. The one who enjoys wonder opens to the extent of this wonder. My world acquired an ancient galaxy of stars, billions spread out, showing themselves, to be known and enjoyed. What is a star but something showing itself? And shining in my life I see and enjoy. And I was almost inclined to say, "It is quite enough," being so filled with stars.

Wonder and awe accustoms us to shattering our little selves into endless joy and wonder. We can journey to infinities, to ultimates, and come back again. We survive bearing the impress of all there is, and becoming wiser. But lo, the myriad of stars are still in me and I am a representative of this tradition. What we really experience becomes permanent; it becomes us, the eternal, the solidly real.

There is an ancient religious theme of a chorus of angels gathering to sing the endless praise of God. When we examine this scene with our ordinary intelligence it sounds boring. Endless praise? And is God so vain as to enjoy this? But with a little shift of understanding the scene becomes meaningful. Praise of God isn't correct. There is actually an exchange of feelings of love between God and the angels, each loving the other. And isn't love like an endless wonder? The scene is actually a representation of a common experience. When you simply appreciate your existence as it is, it is as though the chorus sings. Appreciation is singing. It is an inner spiritual description of the situation. My wife and I have met a few people whose lives were so good that we remarked to each other, "I heard the choir singing as he spoke." When we appreciate the wonder of things just as they are, there is conjunction between the creator and the created, and the choir sings. I thank mystery even for the power to write this.

> The boy raised his eyes to the sky and long gazed in silence. His bewildered mind sent abroad into the night the question, "Where is heaven?"
> No answer came: and the stars seemed like the burning tears of that ignorant darkness.
> —Rabindranath Tagore, *Collected Poems and Plays* (9)

4
Time and Eternity

> When in affection or love one takes no note of time, for then he is in the internal man. By the affection of genuine love man is withdrawn from corporeal or worldly things, for his mind is elevated towards heaven, and thus is withdrawn from the things of time.
> —Emanuel Swedenborg, *Arcana Caelestia* (10, #3827)

The shift in understanding from time to eternity is quite simple, yet subtle. Even though all have experienced the eternal, they may not have realized it and fixed it in mind as one of the potentials of our existence.

Roughly categorized, we live in three kinds of time. The first and best-known is the outer *clock time*. The second is the inner landscape of the time we experience, which has been called psychological time. I will call it *personal time* because the fact of its being our own time is quite central. The third time is *the eternal*. This is probably the least-recognized, known, or understood, even though all have a wide experience of it. Here we will see the real value of a careful description of human experience.

Clock Time

Clock time is of the outer world. It is measured by changes in matter—whether it be a candle burning down, or the swinging balance wheel of a watch, or the vibrations of a quartz crystal. Time is actually the fourth dimension of space—length, breadth, depth, and change. Two cars reach the exact same three-dimensional spot. Do they collide? Not if they arrive at different times. Time is an intrinsic property of the outer material world. Things change and age. We can date old organic deposits because their carbon 14 was ticking away like a clock and decaying. The absolute mark of clock time is change in material things, and it has a given direction called time's arrow. Clock time is an intrinsic property of matter, whether in the world or of our body.

In the modern world we find more and more restrictions due to time. The big clock is the earth's rotation around the sun, which gives us our day. From this we have daily papers, the news, TV schedules, etc. To many people clock time is like an alien presence that somehow enslaves and commands us to get up, work, do thus and so, regardless of how we feel about it. Our vacations last only so long and then we are commanded to return to work. Our bodies age. Die at any age and lie in the ground and someone can dig up our bones and estimate our age at death. We have become incredibly accurate in clock time.

Personal Time

Actually clock time hardly exists. Like dutiful physicists we sometimes forget the observer, who looks at clocks and reacts to them. This reaction is from our internal personal time. We live in our personal time. It is *our* time. We apparently have a biological clock ticking in us which may agree with the outer clock, more or less. But when we fly across time zones and arrive in a new country, our internal clock may be out of sync with the surroundings. Our personal clock has a rhythm of its own. Time flies when doing pleasant things. When bored and waiting we experience a terribly slowed pace. "I looked at my watch, did lots of things and looked again, and only a minute and a half had passed."

It is at the boundary between clock time and personal time that we can best discover the difference. The alarm clock goes off while I am in a warm pleasant dream. It is a rude shock. I suddenly have to adjust to a whole different world. Time is short; I must get up and go to work. One of the most fundamental aspects of the human is that we exist at the boundary of different worlds, in this case at the boundary of a warm sleepy dream and the raucous sound of an alarm clock. Those who only believe in clock time are overlooking themselves.

Personal time is the time of the inner world, which is so much a state of mind that pleasant and unpleasant and all human qualities and feelings are appropriate descriptions. Clock time in the outer world shifts to the state of being in the personal time of the inner world. At best one could say that personal time and clock time resemble each other.

I enjoy meditation in which I just sit and look at an icon or a Buddhist mandala. The experience is decidedly pleasant. In this practice I lose all sense of outer clock time. It doesn't exist. After meditation I found I could not tell the difference between a six- or sixty-minute period of time, so I took to using a stop watch, a thread linking me to the world of clock time.

Our internal sense of time has a great deal to do with our state. In deepest depression or in pain, a day in clock time can seem like an eternity. The internal perception of time may speed up, slow, get bumpy, or do almost anything to express one's being. The quality of personal time is really another expression of one's state. This time is not as inexorable as clock time. If I do what I feel I should be doing, and especially if it is along the lines of my deepest love, then time flows smoothly and pleasantly. But if I sleep in, instead of getting up, or get drunk, and fail to follow conscience, then I can give myself a bad time. Personal time has some freedom in it. We can make it better or worse.

Since personal time is quite manipulable, it would be well if we found the kind of time that suits us and then set a regular schedule of coming back to it, even if the world is blowing up or burning down. As a young man I enjoyed taking quiet reflective walks at night. In these the direct experience of God was often given to me. I can remember the scene when I came to a personal revelation. I said to myself, "Well, of course, I can do this every evening." The idea that I could return regularly to this most pleasant state was something of a revelation to me. Previously, it had always just happened. But I could also make it so. So now, many years later, I return to this state. Before going to bed I open the bathroom window and commune with the garden, the stars, and the orange glow of a street light. This is my way of deliberately and almost ceremoniously returning to that state. I have worked with many in therapy who have forgotten how to return to pleasant time. One doesn't have to wait until vacation time to do it. One can learn to totally let go, relax, and enjoy a two-minute break. The kind of personal time we experience has far more to do with our experience of time than it has to do with ticking clocks.

I have known people who try to cram time. They carry around lists of what is to be done and try to rush through them. But then more items turn up to be done. It is a race against the clock. It is an excellent way to waste one's whole life—dying inopportunely with lists still undone and things piled up you will never get to. Only when a person finds their most joyous way to live do they discover the way made for them. Then one dies on time.

Personal time can be much broader than the knife-edge present of the clock world. In my present world I have awareness of my deceased parents and many saints. They are still here, as far as I am concerned, even though according to the clocks they are gone. Nothing is removed from us in personal time unless we let it be. In this inner world it is love that joins, and hatred that separates, and it is of our own doing; it is personal time. Our personal time is an image of the nature and quality of our inner life. Personal time is much more like the sequence of qualities of our inner state. We have to let go of the notion of clock time to appreciate inner personal time. Our experience of personal time definitely has aspects of our nature and the quality of our life in it. It also has something of our responsibility in it for we can make it bad or good. Why these two times—of the clock, and of the personal? Because in our body we are of the material world, but we are also of spirit, or mind, of a different nature than matter. Time in the spiritual world is purely personal time. We straddle two different but related worlds, the world of matter and the personal world of spirit.

The Eternal

Some use "the eternal" to mean the whole of time. This is impossible to experience because I cannot experience the time before my existence or events in the world after my existence. If we asked a number of people "Can we experience eternity?" most would probably say no. Even most religious people would say no. For them we may have to die to experience the eternal.

I am using the eternal in the sense of what always was and always will be. If there is an always was and will be, then our present experience is right in the midst of it. This is the eternal now. The problem is to get some feeling for the always was, the omnipresent. In the shift from clock time to personal time we have shifted toward the eternal. I am always present here in my experience. Of course our constant awareness as present is a mystery in itself. It is like a given that comes into being in this moment. But because this awareness has a history that goes back in time, and an expectation of going on, it is like an intimation of immortality. Most people have had the experience of gazing at a beautiful scene and suddenly feeling a part of all life—that our life here is simply a part of all life that has always been. That, too, is an intimation of the eternal. In Sanskrit it is called *tathata*, suchness. Not my suchness, or our suchness, but suchness in general, *The Suchness* of which our suchness is an example. The sense of the eternal, what always was and will be, is certainly the central concern of religion. But it is also important in aesthetics, myth, and idealism. I believe you will be surprised how many examples I can muster of what many think we cannot experience at all.

The experience of the eternal is steady, a sense that the present is full and perfect just as it is. There is not a thing more needed. No change is called for. In the East they create a religious monument, a stupa, a concentric form from a point at the top down to the square base, that is an image of the eternal. How is a stupa, a stone monument, an image of the eternal? Well, it stays the same for a very long while. To the Buddhists who understand its symbolism it speaks directly of the eternal. If you think too much of the stone it is made of, you will miss the eternal. You may worry that someday it will fall apart and no longer represent what always was and always will be. That comes from not experiencing the eternal within. The worshipper who wants to experience it walks around the base clockwise, just as we walk around the eternal, and when back at the origin you are where you started. The beginning and the end are the same, alpha and omega. You yourself are eternal. Grasp that and you won't worry about the stones. The outer material stupa is only a handy reminder of the eternal within. We might forget our eternal if we did not have the stone stupa. Then, like a good Buddhist we can pray to it, make offerings, and walk around both stupas, the one outside and the one within. Any religious statue or image can be used in this way. Outwardly it is material and will be greatly altered someday. But if the Buddha or Christ is within, then the outer one is a reminder of the *eternal living presence* within. If you are aware of it within, then the outer one comes alive. If the inner one is dead for you, then the outer one is merely a meaningless statue. We need the personal inner time to approach a sense of the eternal.

Some religions condemn the respect shown to paintings of religious figures as idolatry, not realizing that the worshipper doesn't revere the wood and paint, but the saint represented. The icon only becomes of value to the person insofar as it reminds them of a saint or principle that has meaning to them. The religious who condemn it as idolatry should be embarrassed to admit they have lost the internal feeling for the icon. Orthodox churches are full of icons. One is surrounded by saints, apostles, Christ and Mary gazing down at us. For me they are present and it is quite an experience to stand among them in sacred time, the time of the beginning and the end, in the eternal now.

In general, art also steps out of time and immortalizes it. I live near the western coast of the U.S. where there are forests of pine trees, and there is a lot of coastal fog. I have a silkscreen print that exactly captures the coastal trees hazed out in a fog, in tones of blue and grey. A moment which was fleeting in clock time was seen by an artist and painted so it can last, perhaps forever. The scene is framed, set apart. If we have in us a sense of eternal wonder, we can look at what the artist saw and experience it with him. Because we have the sense of the eternal we tend to collect, and repeatedly enjoy, those things that remind of this. The quiet, pleasant quality of my trees in fog is the quality of the eternal. All beauty is at least intimations of the eternal. But, for me it is even stronger; the eternal is here now. Beauty reminds me I am free to experience it again and find respite in it.

This sense of the eternal is fairly easy to see in some poetry. Although the following is a scene in Bengal, described by Bengali poet Rabindranath Tagore, we can also empathize with it. This is just an excerpt from a longer poem. He is in a big city in India, in a cab speeding to the train station in the middle of the night.

> Through gaps between the trees in the dark mango-groves
>   The morning-star could be glimpsed,
>   Honouring the brow of silence
>   with the mark of infinity.
>   On the traveler went,
>   Alone among sleeping thousands,
> While the car that hastened him echoed far and wide

Down the empty streets,
Callous in its sound.
—Rabindranath Tagore, *Selected Poems* (11)

A moment becomes representative of all moments. It is as though we are the car, callous in its sound, hastening down empty streets, while the morning star honors the brow of silence. I could easily provide many other poetic examples.

Between Personal Time and the Eternal

I can imagine that some might not be accustomed to stepping right off into the eternal, so let me illustrate aspects of our experience that are in between the personal and the eternal, and which provide both familiarity with the eternal and a path to it. In every religious drama we see the sacred portrayed in a story, as though in time, and yet in sacred time, a time worth guarding and treasuring because it is for everyone whose understanding permits them to enjoy it. Here we are in something of the appearance of time, but this appearance tells in story form of the eternal. Time spread out can become a drama of the eternal.

The Jews were put through a long drama recounted in their Bible. That sequence is re-enacted yearly in their religious observances. Christians do the same with the life of Christ. Hindu festivals also live out the life of the Gods. These events occur in sacred time. It is good for us to live through this drama, which represents our life and all life. Very simply the sacred pertains to everyone, everywhere, in all time. That is why it is sacred, and worth keeping and treasuring. Religious drama enlarges us in several ways. It extends our life back in time to the countless people who came before us, and forward to eternity. It is a pure image of the eternal that is accessible to us. We can literally move in sacred time by living through it. Year after year we can gradually find more and more meaning in it.

Myths are a classic example of the eternal in story form. Myths are particularly used in pre-literate cultures. The stories of the creation of the world, or how mountains were made are entertaining and memorable. They are what Mircea Eliade calls *in illo tempore*, they tell of the time of the beginnings. They occur in sacred time or time out of time, the eternal. They are not history as we know it, but rather humanized and animalized editions of the eternal. A key to understanding a living myth is the situation in which it is exchanged. A wise and more-experienced member of the group speaks of the eternal in the form of a memorable story. It is very like religious ceremony which is a sacred event. It is remembered, and lived through again. It is the linear and laid-out experience of the eternal in the present. Myth is an experience of the primordial essence of things. As we become involved in the story we enter the eternal.

Religions present this as a big drama, but I can also show lesser images of a similar process. Many cultures honor their ancestors. Through respect to ancestors, and prayer to them, people continue to live with the ones they love. Although the ancestors are now in a spiritual world, they are still close to us. They have entered the eternal, and ancestor worship is a way of remaining in contact with the eternal. Genealogy resembles ancestor worship, but it has only a faint aspect of the eternal. Some people are excited to collect bits of information about their ancestors, which is at least a small attempt to join with what went before. The archeologist who wants to discover the nature and quality of ancient lives is similar in his search for the eternal.

The everyday experience of the eternal is one of respite, as though one has reached a shelter away from the world of flux and change. The steady, perfect changelessness is like a Japanese garden with beautiful things all about that one can leisurely enjoy. One can sit beside a stream and enjoy the changing rhythm of water splashing over rocks. All that ever was is here. It is beyond all dualities. Debate is not appropriate. It is all here, and it is indeed good. All there is, is present. Is it not quite enough? All experience of mystery is of the eternal. Fortunately mystery is everywhere. In the experience of mystery the eternal intersects and fills the present moment.

Ideals

Those who live by ideals are involved in the prospective, looking-forward aspect of the eternal. Our ideals are our "always" which we can actively live and realize even if only little by little. Saints who honored each stranger as though they were the creator were realizing the eternal. Human wisdom is of the always. There is a story of a man who went to visit a Jewish holy man. He was surprised to find that the holy man had so few possessions and remarked on this. The holy man asked about the visitor's things. The visitor answered "Oh I'm a tourist. I won't be here long." The holy man answered, "Me too."

In our ideals we make our eternity. What we choose as ideal tends to shape our future. Act by act we build our eternal. Look closely at one's acts and you can see their eternal. When I need to understand someone, I like to visit their home. How people shape the space around them is an image of what they are internally. In Pakistan I looked at the home of a poor family. They lived all in one room, with a well-swept dirt floor in a house made of discarded building materials. In their "garden" they had a single well-tended little tree. Though terribly poor, the atmosphere was of great dignity. What people are spreads out around them and shows.

At this point I need to introduce you to Emanuel Swedenborg (1688-1772), a profound mystic who wrote of his findings more fully and explicitly than most. In his early years, Swedenborg was a stuffy scientist who mastered all the science and technology of his time. His scientific works are super-rational and dull. He felt the need to break out of this mold, so he wrote a totally new kind of work, *Worship and Love of God*, in which he entered upon direct spiritual experience. He let his feelings and imagination run free in a totally new kind of work. He thought little of it, and scholars seldom pay it much attention, but in its free fancy and rich imagery it is like a sketch of his later theology. His next published work was to be the *Arcana Caelestia*, a 12-volume spiritual blockbuster. It was as though he had suddenly become a new person who was very different from the former scientist. There is also a lesson here. The stuffy scientist wasn't a proper vessel for his spiritual discoveries. Swedenborg went on to spend decades in exploring heaven and hell which he carefully described. I read his *Heaven and Hell* and found it astounding, because the cosmic other-world structure Swedenborg was describing is also the very same structure as the individual human mind. Based on his direct experience of heaven, he describes how in our ideals and our acts we construct our eternity and are already living in it. His thinking appears very condensed here, because I have left out the extensive preceding development in his writings. So it is best to read him very slowly and reflectively.

Since angels and spirits are affections of love and thoughts thence they are not in space or time, either, but only in an appearance of them. Space and time appear to them in keeping with the states of their affections and their thoughts thence. When one of them, therefore, thinks with affection of another, intently desiring to see or speak with him, the other is at once present. . . .

Space and time have nothing to do with their presence, for affection and thought therefrom are not in space and time, and spirits and angels are affections and thoughts therefrom.

—Emanuel Swedenborg, *Divine Providence* (12, #50)

Spirits and angels are not people like us. They are seen in their essentials, and in this sense they are affections of love. Their thoughts flow from their affections and reflect them. Because they are affections of love they are not in time and space—but in their world there is the appearance of time and space. In other words they are in personal time which has everything to do with state. Love joins in this world, so when they desire to see someone they are present. It is heavenly to live in a world of love. In the next paragraph we see directly how our concern with the eternal now leads into the understanding of God.

From these considerations it may now be plain that the infinite and eternal, thus the Lord, are to be thought of, apart from space and time and can be so thought of; plain, likewise, that they are so thought of by those who think interiorly and rationally; and plain that the infinite and eternal are identical with the Divine. So think angels and spirits. In thought withdrawn from space and time, divine omnipresence is comprehended, and divine omnipotence, also the Divine from eternity, but these are not at all grasped by thought to which an idea of space and time adheres. Plain it is, then, that one can conceive of God from eternity, but never of nature from eternity. So one can think of the creation from nature, for space and time are proper to nature, but the Divine is apart from them.

—E. Swedenborg, *Divine Providence* (12, #51)

Swedenborg spent decades in the spiritual world while living on earth, and he reports it in a straightforward and matter-of-fact way, ". . . the infinite and the eternal, thus the Lord"—of course these are one. We are in the eternal and hence apart from space and time. It is "plain that the infinite and eternal are identical with the divine. So think angels and spirits. In thought withdrawn from space and time, divine omnipresence is comprehended." The always was and always is, the eternal in the now is omnipresence. Then he comes back to a central idea, ". . . but these are not at all grasped by thought to which an idea of space and time adheres." Hence the shift from clock time to personal time (which has much of the character of life in the spiritual world) is a preparation. But even our small, limited and brief experience of the eternal is of the divine omnipotence—the ever present, always was and always will be. "Plain it is, then, that one can conceive of God from eternity (because eternity is of God's nature), but never of nature from eternity." From the viewpoint of eternity the endless change in nature has a different nature. Finally Swedenborg sums it up. "So one can think of the creation of the world by God, but never of its creation from nature, for space and time are proper to nature, but the Divine is apart from them."

> What is infinite and eternal in itself cannot but look to what is infinite and eternal from itself in finite things. By what is infinite and eternal in itself the Divine itself is meant, as was shown in the preceding section. By finite things are meant all things created by the Lord, especially men, spirits, and angels. By looking to the infinite and eternal form itself is meant to look to the Divine, that is to Himself, in these, as a person beholds his image in a mirror.
> —E. Swedenborg, *Divine Providence* (12, #52)

In effect the Divine sees itself in all things, so it sees the infinite and eternal in things. When we look to the infinite and eternal it is as though the Divine is seeing itself in a mirror.

The shift from clock time to personal time is relatively simple. Clock time is outside of us and it is an intrinsic measure of the material world. Our bodies are in clock time. Personal time is our experienced time, which resembles clock time, but is full of our nature. Personal time is actually a bridge between the material clock time of the world and the eternal. It is useful to get a strong sense of our personal time and particularly how we have some responsibility for the quality of our personal time, making it bad or good. The time of the spiritual in this world and the next may resemble clock time, but it is really personal time which has everything to do with our state. The eternal exists in the sense of the "always was and will be" that is present here, the eternal seen as *always*. It is the sense of the omnipresent. It looks beyond change, even change in us, to the peace and harmony of the changeless. We have some taste of this in our experience. Our ideals reach out to the eternal, and the direct experience of it is of peace, joy, a respite from the flux of the world. It is the peace of heaven. In the eternal, everything feels right, in harmony. It benefits to find it, and to learn how to return to it. If you look for it, you will experience it more frequently. Many in the grip of Samsara, the wheel of change, forget there is a way to peace. Seen from the viewpoint of the eternal, our personal lives are a laid-out, sequential drama of the eternal, very like sacred myth and ceremony. All the varied details of our life drama are present in the eternal now. We always have the choice to become trapped in clock time, expand in personal time, or come to know and enjoy the peace and respite of the eternal. Of course the eternal is alone real and true. We ourselves transcend time. Our body is in time but our inner life easily transcends it.

Like our eyesight, we can converge our consciousness upon a point, or extend it to a vast field. It is interesting to see how the span of consciousness affects our sense of the present. This illustrated by the difference between the worm's eye view and the eagle's eye view. The blade of grass left behind by the worm appears to him as belonging to the past, whereas the hill flown over by the eagle may still be in sight and therefore present after twenty minutes of flight. The "here" widens and the "now" lengthens, until they become "everywhere" and "always."
—Pir Vilayat Khan, *Samadhi With Eyes Open* (13)

5

The Microcosm

It is to begin with, all inside us. But because we are all miniature versions of the universe, it is also found far beyond. And because we are all biologically and spiritually part of the first man, the place precedes us. And because we all carry within us the genotype and vision of the last man, the place is foretold in us. There is no surprise in any of this. We have all known it all since before we were conceived by our most recent mother and father.
—Rabbi Lawrence Kushner, *Honey From the Rock* (15)

We walk here as little universes and carry both heaven and the world. This is a very ancient idea, one so old we cannot trace its origin. The essential idea is that we are a small universe (microcosm) which is made just like the great universe (macrocosm). The idea of the microcosm in the West has been linked to Socrates, but I am sure it was common currency even in his time. It is also widespread in Eastern literature. The microcosm is exactly like the macrocosm. It isn't just a little image or picture; it is a little universe that is just the same as the bigger universe. That is the design. Each is the whole. This is characteristic of anything the Divine designs. Seen properly, you find it is the same everywhere. I introduce the idea here because it is an insight one can use to enter the experience of God. Without the idea of the microcosm you can easily fall into the mistaken belief that we are cut off from all there is. We are internally, into our very depths and nature, a representation of the whole.

Nevertheless these are not mere representations, but we really here live and walk, as little universes, and carry both heaven and the world, consequently the kingdom of God in ourselves. The Supreme Deity, Our Most Holy Father, is actually in our souls with His life; His only-begotten, or our Love, is actually in the mind itself which we inhabit.
—E. Swedenborg, *Worship and Love of God* (15)

What Swedenborg describes as heaven and hell is also an image of our life here (16). I can point to people who here and now live in a heaven and some who are in a hell. Their heaven or hell is not quite as sharp and clear as Swedenborg's description of the next world, but it is of the same essential nature. Moreover, Swedenborg said what determines whether we go to heaven or hell is essentially habit; what we are accustomed to. If we are forever making a hell here, we choose to go on with it in the next world. God does not condemn us to hell; we choose it. Some theologians strongly object. They think God would condemn the evil, but Swedenborg's experience was more psychological and like our own.

Our life here is a small sample of our eternal life. Swedenborg also says that only what is done in freedom becomes eternal. So I assume that some mentally ill, who for unknown reasons, suffer as though in hell have a fundamental lack of freedom. I would assume they would be given freedom in the spiritual world and then could work out their own fate in freedom. But the idea that what we get used to and choose in this world affects our eternal destiny has a familiar ring to me. It leads right into the idea that we ought to work on our microcosm since it is an exact representation of what we may always know.

I love and respect tradition. People of all churches, in all times, and all cultures have been finding God. The idea that only one church or way can know God is of human vanity, not God. The omnipresent works through all times and places. I need the help and the wisdom of tradition. This is especially true because I am dealing with what is universal. I use my friend Swedenborg in part to represent tradition because I don't have time enough to refer to all the different sources. But there is another reason. There are many mystics, and each provides something, but I don't know of any mystic who explored so far and came back with such a detailed description. Fortunately Swedenborg was forbidden by God to study other theologies or to ever speculate. One gets an impression of a very responsible person trying to describe all he was shown. So, in effect, even in my writing, I am here creating a microcosm, and this one on the page reflects the one in me. In this microcosm I will use whatever I can to get points across, making enough reference to tradition and churches to emphasize that I am trying to describe the always was and will be.

> The higher or spiritual region of the human mind is also a heaven in miniature, and the lower or natural region is a world in miniature. This is the reason why man was called by the ancients a microcosm or a little world. He might also be called a microuranos, a little heaven.
> —E. Swedenborg, *True Christian Religion* (17, #664)

It is said that man is made in the image of God. Deification, or enlightenment, or the experience of God comes out of improving the image (ourselves) until it is very like God. We experience God insofar as we become Godlike. When we come to more frequently enjoy the experience of the eternal, we are becoming more Godlike. When we become Godlike, it is a natural consequence that we experience God. So the idea of the microcosm also has in it the implication that we are responsible for our universal, and that the universal design contains the potentials of our experience.

The fundamental use of the idea of ourselves as a microcosm is to realize that all there is can be discovered through ourselves. Even if one is locked for decades in a tiny cell, it is still a rich opportunity to explore all there is! In a fundamental way we are not cut off from all there is; we contain it. And, of course, the opposite is also true. All there is contains us. And these two are the same. We are made in the image and the likeness. This is a doctrine that can be found in nearly all religions.

Besides its religious implications, this idea also has very confirmable psychological implications. As an existential therapist I see people as rather different worlds. I don't approach each person as deviations from the norm, like an ad agency which addresses the average consumer: I expect differences when I look at each person's design. People came to me as a psychotherapist because their design wasn't giving them satisfaction. So I had to figure out their design and then try to help them align it with their own aims.

In a profound way we have long come to see each individual as a unique example of a world. As members of the same species, all people have broad similarities. Yet each is a quite unique example. As one who has long worked with schizophrenics I have seen some individual worlds so different and strange as to be difficult to understand. But one easy one I remember is that of a woman who acted silly and demented in a medical conference. All the experts seated around the table had examined her briefly and were about to give her the diagnosis "hebephrenic" after she left the room. Just before she left, she turned and carefully counted out loud the number of people in the room and then said, "And I don't count." She hit the situation on the nail head. Was she silly, or wise, or both? I started seeing her, and it came down to a debate between us. Here I was in suit and tie, behind my desk, working. I told her benevolently that if she gave up this silliness she could get out of the hospital. She looked at me seriously and said, "Then I'd have to work like you?" I remember stumbling and feeling awkward when I said, "Well, yes." She had me. As a silly demented woman she had free board and room, a permanent vacation. She had a certain brilliant wisdom in her demented silliness, much like the Russian "fools for Christ" who so turn against immodest vanity that they appear as useless crazies. It is useful to see people as little universes in which some become comfortable in especially unusual designs.

The idea of a microcosm also implies that each part of the microcosm also contains the whole. In each gesture and voice intonation the whole person is also shown. I once had the job of teaching beginning clinicians to really see the person—to go beyond words and labels to experience the underlying person. A patient would be interviewed before a one-way mirror. Both the patient and interviewer knew we were watching in the next room. To get the students to pay attention to gesture, I made them formulate the main features of a person with the sound off. At first they would complain it was not possible, but I would point out details and start them guessing. "Examine how he holds his cigarette and smokes; make guesses about that." Gradually, haltingly, they would come to a consensus which we could then confirm by turning on the sound and listening to the words. Not only are we a microcosm, a little universe, but each aspect of us is also a microcosm. Any three spoken words of the poet, Rita Dove, and a perceptive student should be able to hear, "Here is a woman of deep feeling who loves words. She very carefully crafts them into something harmonious and pleasing." And there you have an image of the whole person. She has loved words her whole life and is a major poet. Swedenborg says that in heaven the angels can see the whole quality of the life in a facial expression or in a few words spoken. The whole of the person's life shows in every tiny aspect of the microcosm.

I once worked with a whole series of women who had killed their children. Basically the marriage had gone bad, and they were people of few resources. They sank into a depression in which the world wasn't good enough for their children. It was an attempt at murder/suicide in which they happened to survive, charged with murder. One was a woman in her thirties who had strangled her children. She had a delusion that she was the composer of love songs, all of which had been stolen by others. I reasoned that in her world design there were strong feeling elements (love songs) that were not accessible to her (stolen). This angry and schizophrenic woman couldn't experience her tender side. Love songs on the radio proved she was being deprived. Assuming that missing feelings were the source of the delusion, I worked to help her regain them. I totally emphasized feeling in our relationship, with no reference to the delusion, and she became a very warm and tender person. When she could experience her own feelings, the delusion disappeared. Just before she was discharged I asked her what happened to the idea that she wrote many love songs that were stolen? She thought for a moment and answered, "I guess I was just a silly woman."

It is typical in psychosis that the design of the person is turned around backwards. It is a very serious matter when we miss our own design! Some need help in finding their own design, but most of us are the God of our universe, and under most circumstances we have the power to create it better. When the personal design is improved, then the whole world we look out on is found to be improved.

One of the most extreme ways of missing our own nature is paranoia. The paranoid very much needs others. But something went wrong in their relationships, and instead of forgiving and getting on with life, they develop a grudge. They gradually fall into using their fine intellect to build a case against others. Detail by detail they build up this case, proving they are correct and all others are wrong. It is somewhat satisfying to come out with all this proof that you are right and others are malevolent. Of course as they become obsessed with this injustice they must tell it to others, and this drives them away.

Then people's sudden unfriendliness proves that they are part of the conspiracy. Paranoids *experience* a hostile universe, which of course proves them right. They act out a self-fulfilling prophecy, and easily get locked into this design. Their world of friendships gradually shrink to a universe of one in which they are the God that has figured out how everyone else is wrong. They unintentionally designed this entire negative universe, piece by piece. The little pleasure of being supremely right is at the terrible cost of all loving friendships, which is what they most desire.

This whole negative design could have been reversed early on if they had forgiven their trespassers. I was pleased to see that some leaders of monasteries forbid giving the sacrament to anyone who bore any grudge against another. It doesn't matter who is right or wrong. They were to meet and forgive before the sacrament was permitted. Once I was to train a young man for a knighthood. He brought up an ancient grievance he had against a priest, and I could see this was holding him back. Finally I used my authority to suggest he forgive and pray for the priest. In this way a hurt was removed. It doesn't matter in the least that the priest was at fault. The grudge was hurting the man I was working with here and now. I think it would be good to have a ceremony for young people in their twenties and thirties to sum up both the good and bad of their parents and to totally forgive and pray for them! In this way we improve the design of our own world. "Forgive us our trespasses as we forgive those who trespass against us." I had a sudden illumination one day, realizing that this was Christ's own prayer which he had used many times. He gave us what was his own.

In this way it is possible to discover flaws in our universe, and then to work to overcome them. One cannot only *be* a universe but also create a better or more harmonious one. A person friendly with their own mystery should be able to describe their worst faults and what they can do to overcome them. A large part of religious ceremony is an effort to improve one's design, but people with dissatisfying designs can also go to a psychotherapist to change them. In the secular world most people have the idea that we are a small given, in a surrounding alien world. In psychotherapy we open up and even attempt to modify a person's world, as a way of altering their experience of the world. Our inner world, our microcosm, is the avenue to the nature and quality of our own experience.

In both religion and psychotherapy our inner microcosm is seen as the foundation of our experience of the world. Both work at the foundation, but most psychotherapy conceives of the foundation in secular ways. Religion conceives of the foundation in broader world-making ways. In recent decades there has been a considerable growth in transpersonal psychologies which respect and consider the religious element. We once had a rural Mexican girl who was very upset in the alien atmosphere of a California mental hospital. She was wisely discharged to seek relief with a *Curandero* in her own culture.

When you realize that you are a microcosmic image of the whole, as God of your universe then you might decide to improve it. As you begin to improve yourself, you are likely to encounter the most central trap of the whole spiritual realm—ego. First let us see how the trap works. You decide to do something worthwhile—exercise, improve yourself, advance in income, etc. You succeed! But if you separate yourself from those who have not improved themselves, you become impatient with all the others who have done less. Your ego appears to get bigger as your world becomes smaller, because egotism cuts you off from existence as a whole. Some people find you a bore, ever touting your success. You are always telling, like a TV pitchman, seldom listening and learning. You have risen to the top of your own little mounded-up universe, but you have missed the larger world. Egotism cuts you off from awe, wonder, and mystery. Swedenborg called ego *proprium*, Latin for being for ourself alone. I could give many examples where this is seen as *the primary barrier* to the experience of God, particularly in both Hinduism and Buddhism.

If we become for ourselves alone we have shrunk to a very small universe of one. Like paranoia, there is some satisfaction in it, but it also creates a profound limitation, and an absolute barrier to the experience of the All. In egotism we have made a very small world in which we see ourself so clearly but the world poorly. In a sense it is like finding some wealth and having to build fortifications to protect it, because the egotist comes under the marauding assault of others who are not nearly so impressed. It is a small and seriously limiting victory. Over and over in the Hindu literature it is said that the little self is the barrier to the experience of the larger self, or the life of the universe.

The way out of this trap of isolation and exclusion is by *inclusion*, to expand out beyond the self, the little ego, to the All. As I improve myself and notice that others haven't, I can see how we are similar in our struggles, and feel compassion for their situation, at the same time that I see what remains possible for us both. Since the microcosm perfectly reflects the macrocosm, then each microcosm must also perfectly reveal all other microcosms, and I can also find myself by embracing and expanding into them.

Every true expansion of the self leads this way, whether one opens to the mysteries of nature, or to the mysteries of the internal, or if one expands into what one really loves doing. Any journeying beyond the limitations of the ego will serve. In these terms the experience of God is to receive back confirmation that we are embedded in the More. It is permitted for us to expand into the More and come to know all there is, coming into harmony with our surroundings. In both friendship with mystery and in the eternal we journey far beyond ourselves to the More, and the whole of creation welcomes us. The pleasures in this direction are very great and ultimate, against which a little wealth and success for the ego is as nothing. Ego is a temporary way-station on the way to self-discovery. The infant and child need to develop an ego to differentiate themselves from the primordial void. But in the journey further on, ego must be left behind like clothing that no longer fits.

Within the trap of ego there is yet a further trap hidden. Some, recognizing ego as a barrier to spiritual development, attempt to control and limit ego, not realizing that it gives substance to ego to work at killing it. Any efforts to control ego withdraw attention from the all, and further diminish the small world of ego. For it is also of ego to control ego, as can be most clearly seen in those who are proud of their self-control.

As before, the useful path is simply to turn attention away from ego and embrace the all. "Energy flows where attention goes." Expanding the viewpoint leaves ego behind. Expand and extend the journey until ego is simply lost from view. We will deal further with this central drama later when we speak of heaven and hell, for it is what distinguishes them. This drama is so central it is woven into all the rest.

Perfection is in coming into accord with the whole. No little world can be greater than this. And in this state you can see from your microcosm to the macrocosm, the whole, for they are the same. But there is a proviso. You must perfect your microcosm in order to see the inherent perfection of the macrocosm. Perfection may seem like an impossibly long task, but there is a shorter way. Look deeply into your microcosm for all the perfection already there. This transforms and undoes faults from within.

Let me give an example of the process so you can get a sense of how transforming from within works. I chose my icon because St. Innocent of Irkutsk's somber face felt like me. I chose a religious icon of a saint to anchor me in the spiritual. I timed sessions because I lost all sense of time in them. I also wrote down ideas as they came to me. If I was given anything in this process I wanted to keep it and treasure it. After many adventures I found the intensity of the saint's face was too much for me. I found my gaze drifting down the icon to a very tiny dot at the bottom. I found my spirit becoming terribly heavy. It was as though I hardly had the energy to breathe. This went on for some sessions. I was puzzled as to what was going on. I felt drawn to read the *Philocalia* (18). In its description of humility I recognized what was happening. The puzzling state I was being led through was profound humility, which is the opposite of ego. Humility is said to be the key to virtue because it is the relinquishing of ego which permits illumination. I was also pleased that ancient tradition had provided the answer. I had been a braggart, ready to broadcast all my accomplishments. Humility is a corrective. I ran into this over and over again, so that I came to respect that I was face to face with wisdom. In many ways the wisdom of the spiritual appears to draw us to precisely what we need. This is one example of seeking the perfection already there and allowing yourself to be transformed. Your microcosm contains the highest wisdom and perfection. It is already there. It is God within, or the pristine awareness of Buddhism. Seek it and expect to be altered by it.

Many traditions suggest that you find a guru or master to guide you. Although the Eastern literature often says one must have a guru, there is also reference to an internal guru. In a culture where there are many spiritually-advanced people available, I can see it as appropriate to seek a guru or to come under the discipline of a superior you can trust. But one can also work on one's own. I had no guru without, so I tested the idea of the microcosm within. It was immensely satisfying to find myself in the hands of Gentle Wisdom. Swedenborg also had no external authority but God within. A few of the great mystics pointed to someone who was critical in their development. But most often it was done from within. I have often thought it would be enough if a teacher set one on a path that leads to the experience of internal guidance. The advantage of a path within is that it is one's own, designed for the unique person. Natural wisdom perceives what needs to be done. I have often sought an answer to something, only to find I first had to be put through internal changes to even perceive or understand the answer.

The thesis of ourselves as a microcosm sets the expectation that whatever higher one might want, it can be found within, and mystics of all times and traditions agree on this. Just for a moment let us look at all the forces arrayed against this simple idea. There is external church authority which implies that it has the answer, not you. There are limiting expectations. You may not remember having met anything higher within. There is the whole captivating multiplicity of the external world. Some extroverted persons who have only looked outward have a big fearful blankness about the within. On the other hand, introverted people can so easily dream up all sorts of fantasies and get lost in them. It isn't fantasy one wants from within, but something substantial that actually transcends one's own powers. Perhaps the worst obstacle is a clever, wordy skepticism which "nothing-buts" everything, including the subtleties of the inner life. The inner does not stand up and argue with the clever skeptic. I love an image from Sri Ramakrishna on how God is within.

> Do you know how God dwells in man? He dwells in the same way as ladies of wealthy families do, behind a latticed screen. They can see everybody, but no one can see them. God abides in all in an exactly similar way.
> —*Teachings of Sri Ramakrishna* (19)

It is very like this. She is a shy lady. Busy people can go by the latticed screen for decades and not even suspect her presence. You almost have to suspect she is there and speak to her softly and gently to draw her out. The image of an awareness behind ours and looking through ours is central in mysticism. The lattice screen is our ego awareness. There is a consciousness looking through it. But it doesn't advertise on TV, loudly announcing itself. No, she is more like a discreet and gentle lady, waiting for your interest and welcome.

The idea of ourselves as a microcosm is not just one paradox but contains a whole nest of them. If we are an example of the

Whole, why can't we see it easily as we did in the awe of nature? One of the paradoxes is that we have been made king or queen of our little universe without training or experience. The One who is also present respects our freedom. We are free to make things better, or worse, or to go within and find perfection already there. The great value of religious tradition is that it suggests there is more. But tradition often says too much, obscuring the supreme simplicity of the inner design. Though we are essentially incompetent and ignorant rulers of a universe we have confused notions about, yet we are left free to do well or ill. Still there is guidance if you take the time to look for it. When we rule badly, we get all sorts of hints from "others," including our own body. When we find the right way, it is as though we have found a flashlight to illuminate the darkness.

I have been speaking of ourselves as ruling ego. Yet it is when ego steps aside that one finds there was a Ruler there all along. In the Bible we are described as a steward, one given certain powers and gifts to administer, but we serve the head of the house. And even our freedom is a paradox. It sounds so nice, but how often would we like to give it over and let someone else do the work? When we really examine paradox it always offers a way of seeing things anew from another perspective. I recall a Sufi poem, in which the author wanted a whole series of things, but each time he got one, something went wrong. The last line was, "I must be very careful what I want from now on." He suddenly saw that even wants should be examined.

The ancient idea of the human as a little universe made in the design of the whole is a profound insight in both Western and Eastern religions. It is a useful little shift in understanding, for we can look within at the whole. It replaces the idea that we are simply an entity cut off from the whole, having to find what is far beyond our reach. Our little universe is embedded in the larger universe, and totally reflects it. The small shift in outlook to one's self as the microcosm is one of the shifts that make the experience of God likely.

As God of our little universe we have some capacity to improve it. There are basically two ways to create our situation. In one we work to "succeed" and rise in our own estimation and egotism. Whether large or small, ego is the main impediment to seeing from the microcosm to the macrocosm.

The opposite path is to expand in discovery and understanding, daringly venturing to discover our world / the world. The most direct way to this is to seek the perfection that already exists within. In this approach ego becomes more tenuous, and eventually vanishes like a trivial fiction that once had uses, but is now outgrown. There is intense satisfaction in this direction, as though the whole universe planned and welcomes this discovery. This way is marked by joy. My icon is simply a way of permitting the wisdom within to teach me humility. It was a great relief to me to discover this greater wisdom within. I no longer had to be the great clever one, climbing mental Himalayas. Humility and patience were enough. To see yourself as a microcosm is a little shift that is a way to the whole.

Let me end with an incident. I said Swedenborg shows signs of being a mature mystic in that his writings are full of the One. Swedenborg is in hell and he meets a difficult spirit who says, "Where is he who speaks and writes about the order to which the omnipotent God has bound Himself in relation to man. . . . Are you the man who thinks and speaks about order? Tell me briefly what order is. . . ." Swedenborg replied:

I will tell you the general principles, but not particulars, because you cannot understand them, and I proceeded to enumerate them as follows:

(1) God is order itself.

(2) He created man from order, in order, and for order.

(3) He created man's rational mind according to the order of the whole spiritual world, and his body according to the order of the whole natural world. On this account man was called by the Ancients a heaven in little, and a world in little.

(4) Therefore it is a law of order that a man from his own little heaven or little spiritual world should govern his own microcosm or little natural world, just as God from His great heaven or spiritual world governs the macrocosm or natural world in all things in general and in particular.

(5) It is a consequent law of order that a man ought to enter into faith by truths from the Word, and in charity by good works, and so reform and regenerate himself.

(6) It is a law of order that a man should purify himself from sins by his own labor and power, and not stand still, believing in his own impotence, and expecting God forthwith to wash away his sins.

(7) It is a further law of order that a man should love God with all his soul and with all his heart, and his neighbour as himself, and not wait in the expectation that these loves will be put into his mind and heart in an instant by God, just as bread from the baker's is put into his mouth. And there are many more laws like these.

—E. Swedenborg, *True Christian Religion* (17, #71)

There is so much here. It is a summary of Swedenborg's decades in the spiritual. But it is enough to grasp that we are made "from order, in order, and for order." What is from order, in order, and for order is not at all alien to the universe, but rather is an intimate part of the whole. We are from order in all the events that created the universe, and then the earth, and then ourselves. We are made in order both in our physical bodies and in our internal life. And what is from order, made in order, is also for order. That is, our lives contribute to the order of all there is. When you feel very cut off and out of sorts, repeat the mantra, "I am made from order, in order, and for order" and reflect on what it means.

Outside my study window there is a camellia bush with lovely pink blossoms like a pink crowd looking at me. It is made from order, in order, and for order. And it is part of our order to recognize, enjoy, and honor the order of which we are a part. This may well be our highest function—to recognize, enjoy, and honor order.

Being the Key

It came to me
One day
"Existence is
One thing repeated"
Right out of the blue.

Oh, I know
What it means.
But it is hard
To explain.

Have you not noticed
That each life

Is a whole universe
In itself?
A microcosm
That images the all,
The macrocosm.
Each a complete universe
One thing
Repeated.

But it has so many meanings.
How well
Is your universe
Going lately?

We are each
A mini God
Of our universe.
Do it good or ill
One thing repeated.

It is a secret
That you really are
All that exists.
The whole universe
Rests on your doing.
For there is only
One thing.
The repetition is
Multiple images
Of yourself.
So mean people
Have a completely mean world.
Meanness perfectly imaged everywhere.
And the good person
Finds goodness
One thing repeated.

So you would bestow
Love and goodness
On all.

The quickest way
Is to come to the root
Of love and goodness
In yourself.
All the possibilities
Await your doing.
You are the key
To all there is.
This is called
"Being the key."
Or
Turning the Only Key.
Turning this key
Honors the designer
Of the lock.

Section II

Shifts in Understanding

In this section we come to some fundamental shifts in understanding of ourselves and of the larger universe in which we are embedded. These shifts lead toward mystical experience.

6

The Feeling Root of Our Existence

A knowledge of the human mind is important to the life of religion . . . It cannot be otherwise, because the inner world of the mind is the real world in which we live. The real objects of our world are not the material things in our natural environment, but rather the ideas we have concerning them, the way we feel about them, their significance to us. . . .
—George De Charms, *Imagination and Rationality* (20)

We have already looked at three fairly simple shifts in outlook which predispose to the possibility of the experience of God. Mystery is really the most central, since it prepares one to approach and attempt to understand anything which is more than our limited understanding. We open to mystery and in the process we open to learning and change.

The discovery of eternity in the present gets us out of the limiting conception of clock time, and is a further advancement over personal time. When you sense the eternal now in the midst of personal time, you may glimpse something of the ultimate.

Finally, the idea of the microcosm prepares us to find the all anywhere. The highest we would look for is always present in us as microcosm, in the eternal now, and as mystery. These three prepare us to experience the greater-than-ourselves.

Now we are entering upon more fundamental shifts in understanding ourselves, and through this, all things. In a real sense self-discovery is always a part of the experience of God. You need to be

75

changed to have the experience, and the experience will further change you. One simple way of describing this is that the experience of God sets a new center to our being. When we open to mystery we open to whatever is more than ourselves, and our ego, the great impediment to this experience, is no longer the center. Ego is a stand-in, a temporary actor on the stage. The experience of humility means we are ready to receive. It is a major experience to the mystic when this openness and humility is answered by what is higher and wiser than one's self. What we seek simply flows in and is given. And, upon reflection, it appears wiser than anything we ourselves could have created.

For example, when I wrote the end of the last chapter I felt that with the Swedenborg quote I had dropped something too big on the reader. How to soften it and make it more useful? The phrase "from order, in order, for order" stood out and was held before my inner vision. But what to do with it? Then I saw it needed elaboration as to what it meant. And further playing with it (and play is the heart of creativity) I came to the idea of making it a mantra, a phrase the seeker repeats. But it still did not satisfy me. I turned from my desk to the camellia bush. Here the pink flowers stood out, like a crowd looking at me. Then an idea came to me which was at first largely a feeling. It was of the camellia's order to create blossoms which attract bees by their color and scent. Perhaps the highest function of our human order is to see, enjoy and honor all the order in creation itself. This idea stunned me. Its truth expanded and affirmed itself. One example of this is that God creates scientists who will discover the order in creation. But I also experienced it in its largest sense. This is perhaps the highest function of human beings and ultimately the reason for our existence. The stunned feeling I had with this discovery remained with me for some days. I had come upon a universal principle whose wisdom was simply too great to credit to my own powers. I had gone from vague discontent, to playing with what was involved, until wisdom was given to me. A further idea came to me I didn't mention. Those who honor creation are themselves honored. This is not honor in man's sense but the greater honor that is spiritual. You literally cannot honor creation without being honored in the same process.

I have been through this sequence before—from vague discontent to discovery. I have become accustomed to stumbling through mystery and having mystery show me the way. Once mystery itself takes over your instruction, you hardly need a guru. You have a quite wise internal guide to personal discovery and learning. But it is unlike schoolroom learning, where it is all logically laid out on the blackboard. It is more like getting acquainted with the deeper reaches of yourself. The expansion and discovery of what you really are and the expansion of your conception of the universe go together, for they are the same process. If you have a mean little conception of yourself, you, of course, discover you live in a mean little universe. Enlarge your conception of yourself and watch the universe expand and come into a more harmonious order. This is a teaching out of ancient traditions. It is not possible to discover God without discovering one's inmost nature.

It is time to explore the real nature or foundation of our existence. Those who think that our capacity to reason and think is the foundation of our essence are really dealing with a pale shadow, a reflection of something else much more substantial. Change a person's feeling, and you will have changed their thoughts. Thoughts reflect feeling. But feeling often doesn't reflect thought. There are many examples of this. When you are in a depressed mood, try reviewing your memory for all the wonders you have experienced, and see if they don't all look small and have a gloomy cast to them. Try to think of a most inspiring experience when depressed and see if it doesn't turn dark. So what rules, reason or feeling?

I remember one particularly striking demonstration of the priority of feeling. As students in psychology we tried hypnotizing each other. A young woman who smoked a great deal was told under hypnosis that her cigarette would taste bad, but she would not recall this instruction. Awakened from trance she was offered cigarettes, and it is amazing how many different rational reasons she gave for not accepting a cigarette. You could see reason busy doing its job, but reason had no idea why it *felt* that way or that feeling was even involved. Over and over in psychotherapy I see that when feeling is changed, reason follows along.

When I explored the lives of saints I read much of the heart, referring to the center of one's feelings, rather than the physical organ. My own experience with an icon opened up the heart center. It suddenly dawned on me that the experience of the Divine was far more of feeling and affections than it was of reason. I then recalled that Swedenborg very clearly said that affection and feeling was primary. I had always felt that logic and rationality was some sort of barrier; drawing on mystical tradition and my own experience this suddenly became very clear.

> . . . as all those with experience of Zen and other forms of mysticism will agree, logical thought is actually a barrier to mystical attainment. This is so because ultimate truth transcends logical thought. For example, logic demonstrates that the one cannot simultaneously be the many and vice versa, whereas during profound mystical experience it becomes brilliantly apparent that the one *is* multifold while yet remaining one.
> —John Blofeld, *The Tantric Mysticism of Tibet* (21)

This priority of feeling over thought may be a little hard to understand. Our thoughts are easy to grasp. We can put them into words and set them down. They are more discrete and formed. Our feelings are much broader and more nebulous. At times we may have difficulty even knowing what our feelings are. If you want to find your own feelings, simply take anything that catches your eye, gaze at it a while and look for hints, suggestions, fantasy. Fantasy and imagination is feeling coming forth as image. Memories that pop into our head also image feeling. When someone says, "Oddly enough I just remembered an incident," I ask them to tell it to me so that I can discover their feeling. They had a feeling which was imaged as a memory. Knowing that, I can look at their memory and understand their feeling.

I once tried to present a proposition to an acquaintance. He suddenly interrupted me, and said that a memory had just come to him. I asked him to describe it. It was of an incident long ago when other kids tried to coerce him into something. I backed off and no longer presented my proposition, because his internal feeling was opposed. The present situation felt like the earlier one which brought about the recall. We have the odd notion that memory is like a factual account, laid out in sequence. Instead it is more like a field of images which feeling uses to represent itself. When depressed, all memories are depressed. When elated, happy memories come forth. Mood and feeling is central. Thoughts, memories—everything reflects feeling. Here I will draw on Swedenborg's two-hundred-year-old writings, because his writings are particularly clear on this point.

... everyone thinks from affection, and no one without affection.

    —E. Swedenborg, *Arcana Caelestia* (10, #2480)

... affections bring forth thoughts but thoughts do not bring forth affections. There is an appearance that they do, but it is a fallacy. And when affections bring forth thoughts, they at the same time bring forth all things of man, because affections are of his life.

    —E. Swedenborg, *Apocalypse Explained* (22, #1175:4)

I have known psychotics for whom almost all feeling had been blocked and withdrawn. Without feeling, people do not look alive and real; other people look like cardboard props. Thought reflects feeling. We should put that on a sign and nail it to the wall. This is not Swedenborg's theory, because he was forbidden by God to theorize. This was his finding after a long journey through heaven and hell. This is a fundamental shift in understanding how we operate.

The love that is the life of the Will, makes all man's life. It is generally supposed that thought makes all man's life, whereas it is love that does so. The reason that thought is supposed to do so is that a man's thought is apparent to him, but his love is not. If you were to take away the love, or any stream derived from it called an affection, thinking would cease.

—E. Swedenborg, *Divine Love and Divine Wisdom* (23, #125)

I am aware that setting feeling as the root of thought is a substantial change for many. It is easy to identify with thought, but this forms a fundamental impediment to mystical experience. Thought is where we feel in control. Identification with our thoughts reintroduces the problem of ego—that little center where we feel we are boss. Some people even identify with their words, as though to say, "Of course my inner discourse is where I am really in control." There are states in meditation and in the hypnogogic experience where we can watch feeling form thought and words. There are also experiences where words are there before you've had time to think of them. Poetry is an example in which feeling shapes words. The specificity of our inner life varies, with words the clearest, thought less clear, and feeling the broad background. We have far less sense that we create our mood, which can come upon us from heaven-knows-where. If we recognize feeling as also playing a major role we are already a long way toward diminishing ego.

Putting affection as primary puts us in the territory of mystery, for both the nature of our feelings and their source is closer to being a mystery to us. Our feeling is on the borderline between what we can discover with a bit of effort and partially control, and sheer mystery. I may know if I do thus and so I will feel better, and if I do the other I will probably feel worse, but even the source of this priority isn't entirely clear.

Setting the priority of feelings over thoughts has profound implications:

1) Spiritual experience is primarily feeling. It is only secondarily something rational that can be explained.

2) This takes as central something which is only partly understood and controlled by us, and partly sheer mystery.

3) By itself this partly overcomes egotism which is *the fundamental barrier to spiritual experience.*

4) This sets the tone, mood, or feeling of all spiritual experience.

Most of the greatest spiritual writings of all cultures has a soaring emotional quality. It simply doesn't read like rational discourse. I could find a thousand examples of this.

> I only see You. I am in love
> with whatever Your Creating does. You make
> happiness, and I'm grateful. You make
> disaster, and I'm patient.
> Anyone who loves
> Your making is full of Glory. Anyone who loves
> what You have made is not a true believer."
> —Rumi, *This Longing* (24)

Rumi is speaking to God. He honors life and feeling in himself. Those who love what God made are in externals, and overlook the very stream of life in themselves.

Consider carefully, daughters, these few things which have been set down here, though they are in rather a jumbled state, for I cannot explain them better; the Lord will make them clear to you, so that these periods of aridity may teach you to be humble, and not make you restless, which is the aim of the devil. Be sure that, where there is true humility, even if God never grants the soul favors, He will give it peace and resignation to His will, with which it may be more content than others are with favours. For often, as you have read, it is to the weakest that His Divine Majesty gives favours, which I believe they would not exchange for all the fortitude given to those who go forward in aridity. We are fonder of spiritual sweetness than of crosses. Test us, O Lord, Thou Who knowest all truth, that we may know ourselves.

> —St. Theresa of Avila, *Interior Castle* (5, p. 62)

A Day of Judgment

Every one of you,
go hide among the rocks
        and in the ground,
because the Lord is fearsome,
        marvelous and glorious.
When the Lord comes,
everyone who is proud
        will be made humble,
and the Lord alone
        will be honored.
The Lord All-Powerful
        has chosen a day
when those who are proud
and conceited
        will be put down.
The tall and towering
cedars of Lebanon
        will be destroyed.
So will the oak trees of Bashan,
all the high mountains and hills,
        every strong fortress,
all the seagoing ships,
        and every beautiful boat.

When that day comes,
everyone who is proud
    will be put down.
Only the Lord will be honored.
    Idols will be gone for good.

You had better hide
    in caves and holes—
the Lord will be fearsome,
    marvelous, and glorious
when he comes to terrify
    people on earth.

On that day everyone will throw
    to the rats and bats
their idols of silver and gold
    they made to worship.
The Lord will be fearsome,
    marvelous and glorious
when he comes to terrify
    people on earth—
they will hide in caves
    and in the hills.

Stop trusting the power
    of humans.
They are all going to die,
    so how can they help?

        —Isaiah (25, 2: 10-22)

The reader might reflect how one would give a proper dramatic reading to this. If you ask yourself what kind of writing is this, it is primarily expressing feeling. Feeling governs its content. It can be explained coolly and rationally, but if you go too far in that direction, you kill off its main feeling quality, which is the very nature of mystical experience. Because of its feeling emphasis it can easily seem illogical or paradoxical. That is one reason why so many have come out of genuine mystical experience and simply felt they could not put words to it, and this is why the word mystical often means "obscure" and "unclear" to many people. It was beyond words, but not beyond feeling. I did not use Swedenborg to illustrate this emotional quality because he was a scientist who does his utmost to try to make it clear for others. Rumi, like all Sufis, tends to direct emotional expression. Poetry is perhaps the most appropriate medium for mystical experience. Much of the Bible is highly affective. St. Theresa's tone and mood is quite common in Christian saints. Highly emotional striving and struggle is common in this literature. The reports of mystics will seem strange and incomprehensible unless it is seen as primarily the world of feeling first, thought and reason second. No wonder many scientists find this literature strange. It is far closer to opera than science.

I believe that by finding feeling as primary and thought as secondary Swedenborg is simply describing the truth. But he is also setting as the foundation of our existence an area that is both within our ken and transcending it. At the same time he is also setting the fundamental quality of the experience of God. Feelings do have meaning, tendencies, and direction, but it is as though they lead and instruct in a very broad way. The affective drives towards what is larger, even universal. It can easily instruct in universal principles. It is its very broadness which makes it difficult for thought to grasp it and deal with it.

In both Eastern and Western monastic traditions there is considerable awareness that love and the heart are central. The more you go in this direction the more prayer becomes wordless and of the heart. But in Swedenborg's writing there is a clearer and more practical organization of the matters of the heart to explain all the derivative aspects of mind.

> ... the Lord never acts on one thing by itself in man, but on all things at the same time, and the other is that He acts at once from inmosts and outmosts. He never acts on some one thing by itself but on all things together because all things in man are in such connection and from this in such form that they act not as a number but as one. We know that there is such connectedness and by it such organization in man's body. The human mind is in similar form as a result of the connection of all things, for the mind is the spiritual man and truly the man. Hence man's spirit or the mind in the body in its entire form is man. Consequently man is man after death equally as he was in the world with the sole dif-

ference that he has thrown off the clothing which made up his body in the world.

—Swedenborg, *Divine Providence* (12, #124)

The Lord acts on all things in a person simultaneously! This is actually a natural consequence of the primacy of feelings, for feelings and their derivative affections affect everything else of a person. This also reflects what was said earlier that it is not possible to enter upon this kind of experience without being changed.

Let me examine for a moment the attempts of scholars to examine the mystical literature. As a mystic, their analysis seems clumsy and foolish. They try to draw out elements they can compare from one mystic to another, but they overlook the feeling heart of the experience. They grasp at bits and try to fit them together. If they go far enough, they construct a kind of unworkable Rube Goldberg apparatus which is supposed to represent mystical experience. Mystical experience is profoundly simple; all the scholarly speculations make it far more complex and confusing than it is in itself. St. Thomas Aquinas created practically an Everest of rational thought in his scholastic philosophy. Late in life he had a brief, intense mystical experience and suggested throwing his whole philosophy away! The deliberations of scholars are quite useless to me, primarily because they start by leaving out the heart of mysticism, and with it, its life and spirit.

What I am writing here is also an attempt to make sense of mystical experience, but I am trying to remain faithful to its real nature. I would like to have the pages of this book decorated like the Book of Kells, with music coming from it, and a poetic chant going on in the background, all aimed at evoking the nature of the experience. Poetry, song, dance, every feeling medium is more suitable for it than is rational explanation. I believe that many who fail to enjoy religious writing are trying to read it like factual material. You have to get into its mood or feeling before it comes alive. It is very like high drama, with the character on the stage pleading for life. Rational analysis says, "A character on stage pleads to God." But what is left out? The whole setting, the feeling, the urgency. This drama only comes alive in that magic moment when you find that *you* are the character on stage making the life-and-death plea. In setting feeling first and discrete thought as secondary we have recognized as central an area of our experience which we partially understand, but which also transcends us. We have also entered upon the very nature of mystical experience itself.

The Love of the Life

Swedenborg also went a step further into the nature of the essential order of our experience in his discovery of what he called "the love of the life." We are each given a unique love of the life which remains with us through eternity. Swedenborg wrote in Latin because it was the universal language of the 18th century. In translation, this love of the life has also been called "the reigning love," or "the ruling love." If we could see the full implications of our love of the life we would see that each person is totally unique in this respect. At best we might find people whose loves are similar. The love/feeling/affection root of our mind is on the boundary between what we know of ourselves and what transcends us. The love of the life is further over the boundary towards the transcendent. It is of our soul, our intrinsic nature. In the process of coming to know God (and hence all there is) we also come to sense our unique bent, our love of the life. And the more we open to our nature, the more we know of God. Our love of our life is also our private path to God, so the more of God we know, the more we have opened our unique nature. The love of the life rules all of our feelings, our predilections, interests, and our choices; it is the God within that really rules.

A man's very life is his love, and such as is the love, such is the life; in fact such is the whole man; but it is the dominant or ruling love which makes the man. This love has many others which are subordinate to it and which are derived from it. These are diverse in appearance, but still they are all included in the ruling love, and with it form one kingdom. The ruling love, is as it were, their king and head; it direct them, and, by means of them as intermediate ends, it regards and designs its own end, which is the primary and ultimate of all; and this it does both directly and indirectly.

The object of the ruling love is what a man loves above all things. Whatever a man loves supremely is continually present in his thoughts, because it is in his will, and constitutes his very life itself. For example, he who loves riches, whether money or possessions, above all things, is continually turning over in his mind how he may procure them; he rejoices greatly when he acquires them, and grieves deeply at their loss; for his heart is in them. He who loves himself above all things considers himself in all things; he thinks of himself, talks of himself, and acts for the sake of himself; for his life is the life of self.

Whatever a man loves supremely forms the end which he always has in view, and this he regards in all things, in general and in particular. It lurks in his will like the imperceptible current of a river, bearing him this way and that, in whatever activities he may be engaged: it is his animating principle.

A man's character is entirely such as is the ruling principle of his life. By this he is distinguished from others, and according to it his heaven is formed if he is good, and his hell if he is wicked. It is this which constitutes his will itself, and his nature, for it is the being (*esse*) itself of his life. It cannot be changed after death, because it is the man himself.

—E. Swedenborg, *True Christian Religion* (17, #399)

Swedenborg discovered this in heaven because angels are able to see one's love of the life by a glance at the face or by the quality of even a few spoken words. There the ruling love is immediately and fully known. In this world it is far more difficult to know. In Swedenborg's 33 volumes of theology he often says the love of the life is unknown, and a few times that it can be known. Over and over we find the implication that it is not fully known, but a lifetime of living should provide a good approximation of the nature of your own love of the life. The more spiritually lost we are, the less it is known.

For every individual, his ruling affection or love endures after death. It is not uprooted to eternity. Since a person's spirit is exactly like his love and (which is an arcanum) the body of every spirit and angel is an outer form of that love that corresponds exactly to the inner form of his soul and mind—because of all this, a spirit's qualities are recognizable in his face, his deeds, and his speech. A person himself would also be recognizable as to his spirit while he was living in the world, if he had not learned to simulate characteristics other than his own with his face, his behavior, and his speech. This enables us to conclude that a person remains to eternity like his ruling affection or love. I have been allowed to talk with some people who lived seventeen centuries ago, whose lives are known from their contemporary literature; and I have discovered that the same love they had then, still activated them.

—E. Swedenborg, *Heaven and Hell* (16, #363)

I took this as a useful principle in my work with people. But I see it more slowly and poorly than do the angels. I see it implied in what each person can talk about with life, vigor, and interest. It markedly affects perception and memory, so I can present many things to you and I can infer something of your uniqueness from what you pick out and remember. It is as though we all try to adapt to the world but our particular choices in all things reflect our life's love.

My own love is in the area of scholarly study and then writing about what I have found. I have so many interests that once a friend of mine read my vita and wrote a humorous piece describing me as seven different people—and he didn't even know of my extensive interest in art. Yet all my interests tend to converge towards this one, the experience of God. In this study and writing I am close to my life's love. If I were given the choice of this way of life for eternity I would say yes, instantly. There are various indications this is right. I can write with a headache or miss meals, and not notice it. I don't assume I know all there is of my life's love, but this is a close approximation. I believe it useless to try to piece together how this developed. I had a vision that I would be a writer at the age of four while scribbling on the pages of a magazine. I remember scribbling with relish, and then suddenly realizing I would write with pencil on paper my whole life. I felt startled and then thought, "Well, that's OK."

For many years I have found that this idea of the love of the life helps me understand others. My wife is very clearly in her life's love when she is working in the design arts. She can work day and night in art, and then more designs come to her as she lies in bed. It is not merely a hobby or interest. She sees many other things such as eating, sleeping, shopping, etc. as interruptions to this work. She has always tended to see the world as design. She can see a building at a glance and easily recall it ten years later. It is typical that one's memory is nearly perfect in the area of one's life love.

I have a grandson who fell in love with tools at the age of two. He collected them and took them to bed with him. No one had prompted him in this direction. He has no one around him who really cares a fig for tools. At the age of five his love of tools went underground, because kids at school kidded him for being a tool nut. But at the age of six I took him out to my workbench where all the tools are kept, and found the love still there. He says he will be a carpenter.

In the love of the life we sometimes see common interests, as in my grandson, and also rare ones. I have a friend who collects coins used in leprosy colonies. In the whole world of five billion people there may be as many as two or three others like him. We tried probing the depths of this interest. We couldn't find it; it is just there.

There are also curious mixes of interests. An artist friend of my wife's has a degree in animal behavior. She has quite a collection of animals at her home. When you speak to her of animal behavior her eyes light up, and she can speak for a long while. She loves animals and they know it. She has been known to get strange camels to nuzzle her like an old buddy. Energy flows in this love of the life. Yet this woman is also a sculptor. So what is the mix of animal behavior and sculpture? She is marvelous in quickly shaping animal figures that are delightfully full of life. She doesn't like to sculpt people. Her sculptures sell because people feel the life in them. Did she train to sculpt animals? No, it just emerged. It was there. Her love of the life is animal life; observed, interacted with, and sculpted.

The idea of the love of the life is very like finding the *leitmotif* of the life. It amazes me that even the followers of Swedenborg (both in and out of Swedenborgian churches) fail to see how central this concept is. For me it clarifies all the unique peculiarities of human likes, dislikes, our direction, and goal—in a word the central design of each of us. It is essentially a further penetration into how the affective root of our mind and experience is designed.

How different is this understanding from one which seeks the human norm. This one and that one seem normal because they are usual and expected. To them the scholar, or the sculptor of animals are a bit odd, and the collector of leprosy coins is weird. The idea of the love of the life takes an opposite view. We each have some great love buried in us. Those who find it and enjoy it are unique, or "individuated" in Jung's sense. They are the special ones who have found their way. They have found what they enjoy above all else, and this makes their lives animated and rich. It is also the area of one's skills. I wouldn't dream of competing with my wife in her memory of visual design. And she can't remember theology even if she writes it down and carries it in her wallet, while I remember theology effortlessly.

But what has the life's love to do with the roots of religious experience? Your life's love is your personal built-in path to enlightenment. It is the path you can most easily go down. This does not mean that all will go down the full length of their path to full enlightenment. The artist may get totally caught up in his or her art, and not suspect what is further down that path. My particular path leads me to want to understand all of existence. But another may exercise his life's love in laying brick walls. If I wanted to enlighten the brick layer I would offer him parables about brick walls— much as Christ did.

Most young people up through adolescence have hardly a clue as to their direction. In contrast, among the aged it would be relatively few who have no sense of their direction. The more people are oppressed by poverty and illness the less clear it is. Most adults interviewed on what they enjoy and remember best have some idea of their direction. A few people have an unerring idea of their life's love very early. You see it sometimes among performers who felt they would be prominent on the stage, even when they were children.

But how many can fully exercise their life's love? The mundane world needs a rather narrow and limited range of occupations, especially in third-world countries, while the love of the life is infinitely varied. Many have to make a living by any means, and cannot realize their own direction. The more someone is able to deliberately choose an occupation, the closer it is likely to be to the love of the life. Very often the life's love shows up in what someone chooses to do in spare time. The one whose life's love is exercised in their occupation are the ones who love their work and would just as soon stay and work extra! They also grasp the work easily and accomplish more in it. The life's love shows up in tiny details if you look for it. A friend of mine has been limited by circumstances to cab driving and clerk-like jobs. Yet when he speaks, I hear the natural love of logical analysis one sees in attorneys. He fell into clerk jobs in the service because he loved mastering the written manuals. Though he is in lesser jobs, I know he has the potential of a lawyer who loves figuring out complex legal situations. The pointers toward our love of the life are quite strong and we have to badly misconstrue ourselves to miss them. How can we misconstrue ourselves? By believing too much in what we were taught by others, and too little in what we discover in ourselves. The ways of the world are relatively narrow and limited by the culture.

Some people simply bypass their love, often for "practical" reasons. I once gave a drug to a psychiatric social worker who was head of his department. This particular drug opened up his real nature. He spent hours as an artist who had total disdain for social work. He went into ecstasy over the play of light and shade on a mop in a bucket. His love of art was supreme. He refused to even speak of social work in this state. Off the drug he admitted he had once considered art but turned to social work for a more dependable income.

I talked to an old woman in a mental hospital in whom I saw an anthropologist who loved studying cultures. I told her she was a potential anthropologist, a word she had not even heard before. Some months later I got a $100 bill in the mail from her. That insight had been very useful to her.

The idea of the love of the life opens one to the potential in each individual. I did not expect a two-year-old to find his unique love in tools. A bum who asks for coins on the street may be a considerable philosopher. The priest may secretly be a mechanic or a saint. There is no gender bias in this. I remember dining with three women soldiers in the army. They loved the life and were proud to be soldiers.

The love of the life contains the whole design of the person. It is your innermost potential, your central design. When you embrace it and follow it, it is your path back to the all. To find or clarify the love of your life, use the following cues.

1) If you search your whole life, it is reflected in those things that give you the greatest pleasure.

2) If you scan your memory, it is what is easiest to remember.

3) When acting in your life's love, it releases a great deal of energy and joy.

4) In your life's love you will come closest to easy mastery.

Can the love of the life be gotten backwards, misconstrued and messed up? Yes. Swedenborg describes us as like a glass. No matter how white the light that comes through us, some will darken it. I can think of an example so shocking I dislike even speaking of it. A man got into homosexual affairs which included strangling and dismembering his lovers. Find a lover, make love, then get a thrill as the life is squeezed out of him, then take him apart trying to get to its source. The love of life is here and acting, but he has got it backwards. He really wanted to grasp love and life. As a boy he killed and dismembered cats, wanting to see their bones. But in grasping life he destroyed it. It is a demonic inversion of love. Another common inversion of love is paranoia. Paranoids very badly need and want others. Their overconcern regarding what others are doing and saying about them is this love reaching out. But they have such poor social skills they drive others away. They end up driven into a corner, like a terrified animal that would rather bite than try trusting to friendship.

Another common difficulty I have seen in the realization of the love of the life occurs when it is thought to be dependent on others. "If only my husband were different, then I could realize myself." You see it in performers who must have a whole audience to clap, or the natural general who needs an army. A secret is that the love of the life is *one's own way;* it can always be realized on your own. As a writer must I have readers? Not really. Most of my writing no one will ever see. I write for myself, because I enjoy it. It is usually after the love of the life has been deeply realized that the world may notice. The murderer above had it terribly backwards. He could never find love in others unless he had it first in himself. When he can find it in himself, he doesn't need to see the lovers' bones. What he is looking for is over-materialized as out there, in them—somewhere. We cannot see or recognize what is not first found within. The natural general must first command himself. The natural leader must lead himself. The great lover must love and respect himself or he gets into terrible convolutions, needing others to express what he cannot feel.

The love of the life comes down to *know thyself,* an ancient dictum. We need lots of experience to finally see the drift of what is most meaningful and captivating to us, our unique bent and direction, where we could spend an eternity. We need to experiment with it to savor its real uniqueness. Then we have the drama of attempting to express our unique way in spite of the clamor of the marketplace world which only buys certain goods. Our unique love of the life is our direction, our potential, our path, the way we can meet our own greatness, our Way. Certainly it is our own path to our highest potential. The love of the life is the reigning love. Out of it derive all the little affections we have.

I see so many of our "chance" preferences and skills as affections derived from the love of the life. I am a natural scholar, so I can survey shelves of books and easily remember what is there. In my special field I am like a magnet picking up anything even remotely related. But so many other things I barely notice. This is how affections flow out and organize one's existence. Once you see the life's love, then the derivative affections all make sense. As a child I hoarded writing paper and pencils, not too surprising in a budding scholar/writer. I am quite aware of my writing supplies today, and I have even done research on the best pen and pencil to always carry.

There is a certain magic when the love of the life is found. The person enjoys what they are doing, and they are very productive. I once was given a boat with its diesel engine in pieces all over the place. I gave the job of putting it together to a man who turned out to be a Zen mechanic. I was dismayed at pieces all over, but he patiently picked up and examined each. It was as though a love affair was developing. I watched him work and was made aware of my impatience as he carefully cleaned and fitted each piece. Rusted nuts yielded to their master. In the end the big old engine had a pleasing "chunk, chunk, chunk" of a powerful being. Derivative affections make sense in view of the life's love. Out of this Swedenborg comes to a most illuminating conception of freedom: we enjoy the highest sense of freedom when we are acting in our life's love.

> For affection shows itself only in certain enjoyment of thought and in pleasure over reasoning about it. . . . The thought glides along in its enjoyment like a ship in a river current.
> —E. Swedenborg, *Divine Providence* (12, #198)

> He does it from freedom when he does it from affection, for everything that flows from affection, which is of love, is free.
> —E. Swedenborg, *Arcana Caelestia* (10, #8690)

When acting in our life's love, we are simultaneously in our highest potential, our highest enjoyment, and in a feeling of freedom and openness to all. The potential uniqueness in the love of the life is infinite. Every person differs, to eternity. Swedenborg describes the image of the Grand Human in heaven—the organization of all this massive human uniqueness into a single figure, in which every part and every person's contribution is needed, just as every part of the body is needed. The idea of the life's love is also very practical. Love orders and arranges affections and one's thoughts and perception that it might bring about uses. By uses he means the total range of doing useful things from the tiniest to the grandest.

> Thus love is continually going forth and returning by means of deeds that are uses, for loving is to do, because if love does not become deed it ceases to be love, the deed being the effecting of its purpose, *and that in which it has its existence.*
> —E. Swedenborg, *Divine Love and Divine Wisdom* (23, #38)

Thus the love of the life realizes itself in useful deeds. Uses are heaven come to earth, love realizing itself. The love of the life arranges the affections, which affect thought, and all things of the mind including perception, memory, and choice, so the ends contained in the life's love will come to fruition in uses. Love needs use to realize its nature. It is not enough to be, it must also *do.*

When Swedenborg speaks of the soul and of what survives bodily death, one sees that his practical, natural-world model carries over into the next and is the essence of the next world. Friends are often startled by quotes from Swedenborg bearing on the next world, because we are not used to hearing these things.

> I have heard many newcomers from the world complain that they had not known that their destiny would be according to the affections of their love. . . . They had believed that each person's lot would be according to his thoughts from intelligence, especially according to thoughts of piety and faith.
> —E. Swedenborg, *Divine Providence* (12, #305)

Our destiny depends upon our realizing and bringing into the fruits of uses our life's love. All our pious words die, and only what is of love continues to live. The spiritual world is one of love seeking realization in uses. What we have realized of love is what we really are and what we will be. Insofar as we live out our love, and out of that our uses, we are already living in a spiritual world. In fact Swedenborg says directly that we are already associated with a society in heaven according to our loves and uses. I see so many parallels to the world's great religions that it would take too long to describe them. But here is a particularly direct one from the Hindu.

> You are what your deep driving desire is. As your desire is, so is your will. As your will is, so is your deed. As your deed is, so is your destiny.
>
> —*The Upanishads* (26)

I had considerable difficulty in writing this chapter. Love/feeling/affection is so much a central element that its implications run in all directions at once. In the midst of this chapter I felt discouraged and lay down. And here is a contrast between the discouraged me sleeping and what was given to me: I dreamed that someone was teaching me that the old couches I had still had use. I was thinking of throwing them away, but I was assured they might be fixed up and used by others. I awoke refreshed and encouraged.

You can get at the language of a dream by playing with the imagery near sleep. Old couches? Something I have used and have been comfortable with, from which others could derive comfort—like Swedenborg's writings. But others will have to fix them up and make them theirs. I have been comfortable using the idea of the love of the life. Though it is old, it still has use for others, if they fix it up to serve them. In the midst of discouragement I was encouraged to go on. Dreams are one of several guidance systems I have used for decades.

Along the path of the love of the life we can come into our highest realization of our unique potentials, especially when turned to uses. It is also where we experience the greatest sense of freedom and openness, because we are doing what we most want to do. If we ask how many people have come into some realization of their love of the life, the number is fairly great, particularly in the aged. But the number who have gone all the way down this path to the realization of God is relatively small. So we are looking at a potential development which rarely goes fully to its own end. Deep in the midst of the joy and freedom of carrying out your unique potentials you easily get intimations of the Universal, which is just a way further down the same path. Such people are prepared to receive the understanding of the universal. They have journeyed down their totally unique way to the neighborhood of the Plain of the Universal.

It is very like the artist who has developed a unique style. If they finally receive recognition, they see their work connected to the needs of others. If they continue to serve their art, rather than get puffed up in a big ego, they are then in the area of serving the Universal. Their gift is hardly something to get vain about. It came from beyond them, we know not how. They were guided down the drama of their path. The sense of working with and for the Universal may be given. The whole energy, power, and direction of their path was given. We only cooperate somewhat, perhaps, in its discovery and development, but with so much given, perhaps even this little bit is an illusion. All that leads to the Universal came from the Universal.

We are like water that finds its way back to the ocean, in which we can no longer discern the separate water that returned and merged. The ocean evaporates and rains down on land again, to go through adventures, before it returns to the ocean. This system is a mystery far beyond the understanding of mere drops of water.

> The stillness of her shades is stirred by the wood-
>   land whisper;
>   her *amlaki* groves are aquiver with the rap-
>   ture of leaves.
> She dwells in us and around us, however far away
>   we may wander.
> She weaves our hearts in a song, making us one in
>   music,
>   tuning our strings of love with her own fin-
>   gers;
> and we ever remember that she is our own,
>   the darling of our hearts.
> —R. Tagore, *Santiniketan Song* (9, p. 368)

> No one sees other ways
> Than the way of his love.
> —E. Swedenborg, *Divine Providence* (12, #60)

7

The Nature of the Spiritual

> Some, therefore, have imagined the spiritual to be like a
> bird flying above the air in an ether to which the sight of the
> eye does not reach; when yet it is like a bird of paradise,
> which flies near the eye, even touching the pupil with its
> beautiful wings and longing to be seen.
> —E. Swedenborg, *Divine Love and Wisdom* (27, #374)

I chose this quote because many people have such a vague idea
of the spiritual that it seems detached from everything else or even
seems nonexistent. In this chapter I will anchor the spiritual in
human experience so that it becomes quite recognizable, even commonplace. Here is the first little anchor. How is it like a bird of paradise which flies so near the eye it even touches your pupil with its
wings? If you take all of your deepest concerns, particularly those
that have been with you for a lifetime, these concerns are the very
flutter of the bird's wings. When they touch your eye (your feeling-
ful/seeing/understanding) these concerns can bring a tear to your
eye. These feelingful concerns are your spiritual life. One can as easily say they are your life. This is a first definition of the spiritual. It
is simply your very life, particularly *when conceived in its enduring essentials*.

Let us take a step back for a moment to look at this whole
process we are engaged in. The spiritual and the mystical are for
me the same thing. We are in a realm where everything points to the
same center. This is far different from the linear, step-by-step logi-

96

cal thinking of science, where ideas develop in straight lines. In science a hypothesis is conceived, an experiment is set up and run, and the results may affirm or contradict the hypothesis. Science also seeks eternal truths that apply throughout space and time, but it is slowly climbing stairs, gradually coming to a higher and better perspective.

Mysticism and the spiritual are quite different than science. In the spiritual we don't have to move or arrange anything. What needs to be discovered is essentially our own center. With a clearer center of understanding we see the world better. This is why great spiritual discoveries have been made while staring for months at a cave wall.

We cannot gaze at anything for awhile without projecting part of ourself onto it. If you haven't already discovered this, you need only to meditate for a week or so and you will discover complex adventures which pour out of you onto whatever you gaze at. What comes out of you is the stirrings of the life within you. I was pleased to see this described in *Earth Angels* (28) because I have long taken this as a given in human experience. We color the environment every time we look at anything. We are always filling our world with meaning. Throughout life we gradually build an overarching meaning which describes the whole of our existence. You can hear this meaning clearly when an older person describes the world they have created and discovered. We all come to some sort of overarching view and *this conditions what we discover.* For instance, my own mother, bless her soul, hated one racial group and considered them the source of the world's problems. She also thought that if there is a God, He must be unspeakably mean. My mother selected out of experience those things that reaffirmed her view.

It is as though we are a center which assigns meaning and this process feeds back and conditions what we select out, notice, and enjoy. We are a God, of sorts, creating a world. When I dealt with paranoid psychotics I couldn't help but admire how well they had done in creating a tight little world in which they were right and everyone else wrong.

Well, why don't we simply wise up and set out to create a more pleasant world? "I'll only deal with nice people and talk about nice things." But the unnice hangs around and intrudes. This is the way of repressive denial. It succeeds to an extent, but it also cuts off our reactions to parts of the real world, both inner and outer, limiting us and shrinking our world. Some of religion serves to reinforce this way of repression. The paranoid creates a world and the repressive creates a world. It is their concept, their design. It suits their ego.

In contrast, *mysticism or spirituality is the process of embracing all of our world.* From the highest to the lowest—it attempts to *include it all.* The mystic sees the possibility of discovering *the world,* preferring to come to terms with the world *as it really is.* There is an abiding empirical curiosity in the mystic, so that mysticism combines easily with the scientific outlook. The scientist sees the possibility of shading the data to prove he is right. But he would rather come to find what is true, even though it might be totally mysterious and unexplainable. The mystic is on this same quest. Real discovery is valued over making it what one wants.

However, the approach of the mystic is different from the linear, logical proving of the scientist. The scientist must arrange things just right to get a test of his hypothesis. In contrast, the mystic is his own discovery system. He stands in his center and has plenty to do to come into a total accord with both the inner world and the outer perceived world. Like the scientist, he sometimes thinks he really has it all summed up. "God is like this," and then the mystic is put through such trials by this same God that he becomes less presumptuous and becomes ready to discover again. In the lives of saints there are countless examples of this. I use the term saint both in the conventional religious sense and in a larger way to describe any of the great mystical adventurers. How often saints have had intractable pain and illness! But because they were saints, anything given to them, even illness, was included as part of the process of discovery.

The mystic's process of discovery takes place from the center outward. As the center enlightens, so does the perceived world, for these are part of the same. What is the aim of this process? It is simply to discover *it all just as it is.* If God is asleep in creation then the mystic would like to creep up and see the Great One snoring. If God has a mean, dark streak, then the mystic would ask not to be left out in the discovery of just how dark and mean he can be.

You might say this is terribly ambitious and even presumptuous, and I would agree. Whence comes such an ambition? The mystics agree that this, too, is from God Himself (or Herself). This God wishes to be discovered or This One would not have left trails all over the place in all of the various religious traditions! Take any of them, and you find that they all lead to the same end. And because we ourselves are such limited vehicles compared to omnipotence, omniscience, and omnipresence, let us just accept that the mystic's discovery is endless—just as the scientist's is. There will be moments when the mystic feels they "have known it all," but these are just moments. There is another contrast to the scientific enterprise. At best the scientist learns a new bit of information. But the mystic's experience tends to be of *it all at once.* He experiences the cosmic whole and may have trouble distinguishing the parts.

Because our model is one of being in the center and making discoveries, all discoveries are potential in our experience. All things are interrelated; as we change, the perceived world changes. At times a change will be found in the world before it is also found in ourself. The natural extrovert may almost always see it first in the world. The natural introvert may almost always discover it first within. That is simply part of our basic differences. Is there an advantage either way? Not really. Ultimately we can only work with what we are given, so it is not appropriate to think that this way is better than that, or that this person is better than that one. That is the way of the world, not the way of the spiritual. Because the spiritual enterprise is conceived in eternity, the seed of the oak tree is as great as the mighty and ancient oak itself.

Now we can place another anchor of the spiritual. One of its meanings is that life is considered in its larger and more nearly ultimate aspects. It is *the same territory* as your ordinary life experience. It is merely that same old everyday experience, but considered in its wider implications. The mystic is out to discover it all; just as it really is. And in this paradoxical center he is grasped just as he tries to grasp. If we are to grasp it all we must be open to discovering how the All grasps us. Therein is the real discovery of grasping. We must be squeezed tight in a grasp to really understand it. Hence, in this realm, meaning and understanding is always based on experience. There literally is no understanding without experience. So the spiritual is the discovery out from our present center towards the all, just as it is.

The Natural and the Spiritual

The ancient distinction between the natural and the spiritual is useful here. I recall an image I may have seen somewhere in the world, or in the inner realm as a vision. Three legs were shown like a triad coming from a common center. Though it seemed odd at first, I was suddenly given to know what it meant. Humans walk in the natural world and in heaven or the spiritual at the same time. The third leg is moving from the natural to the spiritual.

When my attention is devoted to the outer world, I find a world of things out there. In the country there are trees, rocks, streams, mountains, etc. In the city it is a man-shaped place of streets, cars, houses, stores, etc. That is the outer natural world. It is just naturally there. We come upon it. And from that viewpoint our body is simply another part of the natural world. We are not surprised to find that our body needs food, water, sleep, elimination, etc., and all the other elements our body needs from the natural world. If we limit our concept of the world to the natural, then we think that one day we will simply die, and that's that. There is nothing more.

But another world is here, even in this solely natural description. My five senses perceive the outer natural world. By my reacting to, selecting, and assigning meaning to all that my senses perceive, I create an inner world. My inner world may vary all the way from a close approximation of the outer natural world to a very unique and distorted version of it. If I look closely at it, I find that my inner world is really full of mystery. I have particular likes and predilections, but I don't really know where they come from. Though I am distinctly conscious, I don't really know how consciousness arises or what it really is. Now and then I quite surprise myself. Let me give an example. For several days I have been reading Swami Vivekananda's *Jnana Yoga* (29). It opened up the whole world of Advaita Vedanta. I felt quite at home in this world. Then I got a catalog of the whole Eastern Orthodox literature in the mail. In reviewing it I felt a longing to return again to the world of Eastern Orthodoxy. This longing surprised me. We do not fully understand the inner currents we feel.

This whole interior world is one's spiritual world. Swedenborg links the natural and spiritual worlds together by correspondences. It is possible to discover in an outer natural thing its correspondence to something in the inner spiritual world. For instance, I am looking at a pot of tulip bulbs just sending up their green shoots. I can treat it as purely natural, as just a pot of bulbs beginning to come out, or I can also see it in the inner world as life itself emerging. This second perception also includes the exact visual form of the pot of tulips, but it adds another element. The very youth and greenness of the tulips comes to represent life wanting to burgeon forth and realize itself. The natural can be used to speak of the spiritual. The natural and spiritual worlds are only separate if we try to separate them. They can easily merge and become one. The spiritual is the natural considered in its larger aspects, tending toward the universal. When I see the tulips breaking forth, it is an example of a principle in nature in which each thing, and we ourselves, want to express and realize our nature. Because I am tending to experience a universal principle I am also approaching the eternal.

There is a paradox about the spiritual and the natural. If we are wholly caught up in the natural, it can easily seem that the spiritual doesn't really exist. "Obviously the natural world is the only reality." To come to this view one has to overlook much of the spiritual. But, let us turn this around. From the spiritual world does the natural exist? Yes, the natural is the ultimate of the spiritual, where it manifests. Or, using Swedenborg's idea of correspondences, the natural corresponds to the spiritual. It is a matter of viewpoint. The spiritual includes all of the natural, just as it is. You need not cut it off or limit it. The spiritual gains from the natural. The mere pot of tulips in the natural realm illustrates in the spiritual realm each thing wanting to live out and fulfill its nature. Would that we could realize what is in us as well as lovely yellow tulips do.

There is also hidden in my little example an idea that I am sure will offend some of the religious. My perceived tulips became spiritual when I saw larger implications in them. Some would contend that the spiritual must always include a reference to God or it is not spiritual. They are welcome to put such a restriction on their world, but not on mine. I have thought about this a long while. I would open up the spiritual so widely that it includes some atheists and agnostics. Swedenborg says *all will be saved who act by the good they know.* If the good someone knows doesn't include God, they will be saved anyway.

Suppose we are God, and from our very lofty understanding we are asked to choose one of two candidates for heaven. One person professes to a full belief in God and attends church faithfully, but shows little love for others. The other hasn't the faintest idea if God exists, but in all his behavior he deeply respects others and creation itself. As a God my guess is you would do as I would. The second one's love and respect can easily be deepened into a perception of God, which is love itself. The first one has much to learn before the perception of God is possible.

So I come out in a surprising world. All those who have love and respect of any kind, acting on the good they know, are on the spiritual path. By these terms they are spiritual whether they know it or not. Acting on whatever good you know is the way to the discovery of the rest of good, which is ultimately God. They simply have not yet met the Author of the path. Or, if they have, their recognition is not yet complete. Those who love or respect anything, including themselves, are on the path, whether they know anything of God or even of the path itself. This opens out the way to most of mankind.

Swedenborg often wrote directly of his spiritual experiences in heaven. There are now many followers of his in Africa, in part because of a casual observation of his. He remarked that the blacks in heaven were favored by the angels because they were so easy to introduce into the life of heaven, while many Christians were not nearly so fortunate. The African blacks of the 1700s were primarily animists. *All* things of nature had spirits which they dealt with respectfully. This would seem further from the idea of the one God than the Christians. But the key was in these blacks endeavoring to live harmoniously and respectfully with nature. This made them easier to introduce into the life of heaven. To profess a belief in God while not bringing it into manifestation in some way puts some Christians further from God.

Uses

So far we defined the spiritual so it includes all of the inner life, especially when considered in its higher, more universal and enduring aspects, and I have also spoken of the manifestation of the spiritual in *uses*, the actions we take in the world. This wide sweep includes all those who act by the good they know whether or not they have God in mind! This means that a good many—indeed most people—are already on the path to ultimate understanding. The heart of the matter lies in loving whatever is seen as good, and in acting on whatever good you know. Perhaps I have a poor notion of good. Plants need water, so I give them all lots of water. But some die from this treatment. To do good to plants I must understand their nature, and which ones need less water. If we really intend good to plants we'll notice their reaction and learn from that. At every turn reality is ready to show us. And the problem is even more complex in "watering" humans. Existence itself acts intelligently to educate us, if one but looks and considers.

The longing for what seems good is the key. If I keep in this longing, existence will educate me. I used to be caught up in grand schemes intended to save some portion of mankind. Time made me more humble. Now I write a book simply because I enjoy writing of these things, and because it might be of some use. This writing is my good which I simply enjoy doing.

It is in uses that the whole spiritual enterprise comes to realize itself. My tulip leaves come out preparing the way for lovely flowers because that is their use. The bees and hummingbirds will appreciate these flowers, and so will I. The use of most things is clearly set in their nature. Unfortunately we humans are among the most lost part of creation. We would like to be of use, but how? We tend to think of uses in too large a fashion, as though only a few great and well-known people are really useful.

I know a man who for the last forty years has forever been involved in big ideas to save the world. He is too busy with these big ideas to support himself or his family, so his hand is out all the time for money. Meanwhile his wife has supported him, raised a child, kept house, etc. I honor her as one on the path, because she has lived a useful life. He failed in all the little uses and his big ideas have come to naught.

In uses the whole spiritual enterprise comes to earth and does some good. Think small. Do whatever uses come to hand. So many young people wonder what good they can do. They can start with putting their own room in order so their mothers won't have to do it. Think what is near at hand and needed. Just do these little things, and existence will show you greater uses. Wherever you are, whatever you are doing, do what you can, the little things that need doing.

The secret lies not in the great importance of what you do, but the attitude through which you do it. I walk through a room. A piece of paper on the floor spoils the neat appearance of the room. I pick it up and put it in a wastebasket. Think what is at hand that you can do and enjoy doing. I would rather pick up the paper than leave it there. Someone else might pick it up out of compulsive neatness, or out of anger, rather than because it is his good. There is a world of spiritual difference between these. The compulsive or angry person is inwardly forced to pick it up. The other does it because it is his good to do so. There is a cosmic secret that the spiritual effect varies with the spirit in which you act. This inner spirit is what communicates in this realm. It is the very nature and quality of your effort towards the good rather than the scope of your effort as the world or the news media might see it.

This was illustrated in the story of the Juggler of Notre Dame. A simple juggler in a cathedral wished to give the Virgin Mary his best gift. So he juggled for her. The religious considered this blasphemy. But the statue of the Virgin Mary moved and expressed her approval. The religious saw only blasphemous externals. The Virgin Mary responded to the real nature of his act, his wish to offer his best. It is in the natural realm where advertisements are shouted to get our attention. In the spiritual realm it is the innermost nature and quality of the effort that counts. It is the realm of life's essentials, the realm of Truth itself. Do you think you can manipulate and deceive omnipotence? The spiritual is life in its essentials which are partly beyond our understanding. But the spiritual is not beyond the real inner purpose in our effort.

The spiritual is also a realm of the greatest joy. Some have a very ascetic idea of the spiritual. "If it brings deep satisfaction, it must be of the devil." The opposite is true. The spiritual way is marked by transcendent joy. This joy is like a big sign planted along the way as though to say, "Yes, of course this is the way." Mystical experiences in my childhood came to shape my whole life, because the joy was so great I wanted to be able to come back to it repeatedly.

In uses the spiritual drive toward the good comes to earth and shows itself. We realize and enjoy good by working within it. Fruit of the tree. When faced with multiple goods needing doing, choose the use you enjoy the most. You will last longer in that one, and do more good. Swedenborg described heaven as a kingdom of uses. Imagine a natural kingdom of uses in which each one acts in what they enjoy doing, and each contributes to the harmony of the whole. In heaven all our uses fit together perfectly. There we don't ask whose use is greater than another's, for we regard as absolutely central the love with which it is done. Where there is love there is sufficient greatness.

Could it be that life is like a symphony orchestra? We each have to practice a lot, which is ultimately what this life is for. By coming together, we each contribute our part to the whole. Our making music together depends so much on coordination. Who conducts this music? Thankfully not me; I have trouble enough with my little part. But we all follow the conductor that there may be good music.

Use is ultimately a profoundly human thing. We can ask, "Of what use is mental retardation?" The Arabs considered the retarded to be touched by God because they didn't become clever and devious. They are examples of innocence and egolessness, examples we need. Of what use is a monk praying all the time? Near me is a Byzantine monastery. When I visit it I feel refreshed, as though I have spent time in heaven. We need the example of holy lives to show us it is possible. Show me a useful person, and I will show you one on their way to the Kingdom of Uses. "Faith, hope, and charity, and the greatest of these is charity." Charity is of use. A person may thoroughly enjoy being of use, but have no idea of God whatsoever. It matters not. They will fit in quite well in a Kingdom of Uses in which they have already been participating.

Use is not just the realm where the spiritual shows its worth. Use also leads us out of ourselves towards the realm where we join with and work with others. How to overcome ego? Be useful! That is, do good things for the sake of what is good itself. We get into trouble if we bend our good to our own ends. I picked up rubbish off the street and got in the local paper. Maybe if I do this a lot I can get elected mayor! This good has then been bent to suit my own ego. It is better for me to fail in such an enterprise. No, the reward for good should be in the act itself. Have you not spontaneously helped someone and experienced a warm glow afterwards? This is the way out of ego to what is more. There is so much more that can be said of uses. In *Divine Love and Divine Wisdom* Swedenborg describes love and use as the essence of heaven.

> Who cannot see . . . that an affection alone is not anything, it becomes something by being in a use. . . . affections are derived from love and are continuous with it, they bring uses forth in forms, and in these they advance from the first things of the uses to their ultimates, from which they return again to the love from which they come; all which shows that affection and use are respectively love in its essence and love in its form.
>
> That the Divine Love which is Life itself and which is the Lord, is in the form of the forms of all uses . . .

—E. Swedenborg, *Divine Love and Divine Wisdom* (#20, 22, 23)

In uses we see where the spiritual comes to earth and does something. How to be of use? We have answered in the simplest way. Do what is at hand, what needs doing. Given the choice of many options, do what you enjoy doing, for this lies closer to your love of the life, or your own essence and path, and in this you will accomplish more.

Centering the Attention

Now I have a different kind of question. When you have nothing to do, idling the time away, what to do with your attention? Is there some sort of internal focus which is a spiritual way? There is a vast realm of spiritual practices, each of which could easily become a book in itself. One can focus on the breath, on meditation, on prayer, on a mantra (a repeated holy expression) on the Jesus prayer, etc. I suggest one that is best described in Buddhism as *mindfulness*, because of its fundamental nature, and because it underlies all other practices.

I described the essential quest of the mystic as the discovery of all there is, just as it is. The mystic stands in the center of his/her universe and attempts to understand it all from this center. Since we are not only *in* a center, we *are* a center, mindfulness is simply the careful, patient, exploration of this center. What is the spirit behind mindfulness? We realize that we are a limited center of awareness in the midst of a great sea of possibilities. Perhaps by patient watching of *all that is present* I can learn something. Mindfulness does not solely focus on the limited things of the world. It includes awareness of trace feelings, ideas and images, everything now present. Part of the spirit of this practice is the sense that something is always being given now. Can I see or appreciate it? Existence has a greater wisdom in it; perhaps my limited wisdom can learn from what is being given to me now.

Mindfulness tries very much to stay on top of the present and the real—all the real, like a lab technician focusing in on something on a microscope slide. Among other things, it is an exercise in awareness and discovery. In my early mystical experiences I was essentially practicing mindfulness, which I described as similar to gazing into a pond. One is then wide open to discovery. I practiced gazing at an icon as a way of limiting the stimulus, because all that is presented in any moment is a bit much. But I found even the constant stimulus of an icon too much, and often focused on the tiniest detail.

Existence seems like a very complex drama unfolding before our eyes. Mindfulness is trying to really take it all in. Let's say you are upset over something that happened. If this is uppermost now, just look at it; let it be and look at it. Some separation between it and the real you develops. Trace ideas and feelings arise. Look at them. The situation can unravel and become less painful. I once entered a very mindful state while alone in my office. I pushed back from my desk (merely because I felt like doing it) and surveyed all the papers on my desk. Each was a problem, a work in progress. When I took the time to look at it, it was as though this was all nonsense, and the real me detached from it. The real me was peaceful and happy and the papers on my desk were like a joke. Mindfulness notices all that just is, here and now. In this the highest in us can be recognized and enjoyed. So much of human stress arises because we design our own trap and step into it. We can also push back and enjoy reality as a multi-level creation of very great beauty. What to do when you have nothing to do? Practice mindfulness of it all. In its highest aspect it is a form of honoring creation. It honors both creation and all that is in you to appreciate its multi-leveled wonder.

Your Spiritual As Eternal

Now we turn to the eternal aspect of the spiritual. You are a spirit living in a body, living in both the natural and the spiritual. The natural is the lower end of the spiritual. The spiritual you includes all of your natural: your sex, appearance, manner, all your ways, the real you. Your natural body and actions are the way the spiritual you manifests in the world. The spiritual you is really only a shift of emphasis away from "the merely natural" toward your real interior nature in its essentials. The spiritual is really a larger manifestation of the natural which includes all the details of the natural. There are a great many spiritual or interior states in which we tend to experience ourselves as enduring if not eternal. Vivekananda said we must be of the eternal even to have a sense of ourselves as having lived a long life and of having gone through many changes. Behind all these changes there is a Self that partakes of the eternal.

What then remains when we die and the body is put off? All of the spiritual of ourselves remains unchanged. After death we are a person as before, same sex, same age, same fundamental tendencies. It is even as though we still have a body, for we see and hear as before. Swedenborg says that sometimes angels have to convince newcomers to the spiritual world that they have died, because so little has changed. This would all seem too fantastic for some to believe, but we now have the substantial evidence of the near-death experience of those who have clinically died and who have returned to tell about their experience of the early stages of death (30, 31). Most people, whether they believed in God or not, go through an introduction to God in the near-death experience. (A few go through some demonic experience in the near death, but the demonic is really the Divine inverted.) Very different people go through a very similar drama in which they live, free of the restraints of the body, and meet friends who died before them. They meet a Being of Light and are led into the depth of the essentials of life. These are some of the striking aspects of the near-death experience. There are now thousands of recorded cases. It is remarkable how people of no faith, or much faith, of varied cultures and background, go through essentially the same basic experience. These clinically-dead people hear and see better and far more acutely when there is no respiration and no circulation. The body doesn't die in an instant; it takes place over a period of time, as irreversible changes set in. There is a growing body of evidence now that the near death experience alone can greatly shape the person's life in a positive direction.

Some say that these experiences are merely hallucinations. There are a number of ways of evoking hallucination, mainly by toxic reactions. In these cases it is amazing how infinitely *varied* people's experiences of hallucination are. In the near-death experience we are talking of a brain condition which should produce total unconsciousness, yet instead they enter upon an apparently intense and universal experience. It is surprising that they experience anything, but it is even more surprising that their experiences are so similar.

Although we are fortunate to have the rapidly growing body of near-death experiences, the spiritual don't really need this proof. Mystics from time immemorial have known that the spiritual goes on. Swedenborg's *Heaven and Hell* (16) is the most extensive report of the worlds beyond this one. Though he thinks in Christian terms, there have been Buddhists and Hindus in accord with his presentation. Eventually heaven and hell was opened to Swedenborg, and he freely explored them for decades, simply describing what he found. Though he was Christian and thought in these terms, his account is universal and he described everyone's spiritual potential.

What he found is that at death we put off the body and enter the spiritual world. The accounts of the near-death experience describe the entrance into the spiritual world. Beyond this entrance newcomers go through a period of orientation. In this their interiors are opened so they come into a deeper sense of themselves and how they prefer to live. Out of this they choose whether they prefer to live in heaven or hell.

The central difference between heaven and hell is a key theme in Swedenborg's description. Those who choose hell have had a lifetime of selfish orientation with themselves and their welfare foremost. They choose a world where this theme is central. Selfish people, all out for their own ends, lead to a world of conflict, but the Lord rules hell too and limits these conflicts.

Those who choose heaven cherish the good in themselves and others. Heaven is a kingdom of uses, in which "the joy of one is the joy of all." Those bound for heaven are not self-sacrificing; it is simply that what is good for them is also good for others. If you reflect upon these themes, that all in heaven are in uses, and all are concerned with the good of all, you can see how heaven becomes heavenly.

I have not in the least done justice to the interior wisdom in Swedenborg's description of the spiritual worlds. To my knowledge Swedenborg's account is the most detailed there is in the world's literature. The very interior design of our mind includes the whole possibility of heaven and hell. So *Heaven and Hell* can as well be read as a description of our spiritual interior *in this world*. The trend I described earlier, that we choose a world and then select and perceive evidence for our position, is amplified in heaven. In heaven angels' very clothes shift to reflect their interior state. It is less fixed than this world, and more reflective of what they really are.

Heaven is divided into societies where people of a like love and use find each other and enjoy working together. Heaven is also divided into levels in accordance with the degree of realization of God. The angels are simply people who have lived on earth, died, and come fully into their real uses. In the highest celestial heaven the angels have no real personal identity, for they essentially know only of God. Over and over one sees that this is a marvelous design. I was also struck by how much it reveals of this life on earth.

Swedenborg was severely criticized by some theologians because what he found did not conform to their dogma of judgment and punishment. They expected God to judge and punish people in hell. Instead, everyone is allowed to find and choose where they feel most comfortable. Some choose hell because a world where everyone is out for their own ends makes sense to them; it is what they are accustomed to. How awesome it is to realize that moment-by-moment our choices are bit-by-bit creating our own judgment. The central equation of Swedenborg's description is that our lifetime of choices creates our spiritual reality. When we die we come into this spiritual reality fully, and are even freer to find the essence of our self and what we enjoy doing for eternity.

So what is the spiritual really? It is quite the same as our inner life. It is not opposed to the natural world in which our body lives. Rather it is a larger view of the meaning, purpose, and direction of the natural world. Our spiritual is our very life, not a strange or alien world.

What is the ultimate expression of our spiritual life? It is in uses. Here our spirit comes to earth and is given ultimate expression. The essence of use is to do what is at hand, what needs doing and even what we most love doing. Use communicates and expresses our love. Love is communication in the spiritual. In this we do not judge uses externally, as the world does, by what impresses outwardly, but by the love which is its interior. Love can express itself quite well by even the smallest of uses.

Since our spiritual being is simply what we always were, and will be, this survives after the body is put off, just as the body survives when we take off clothes. Our present life is an excellent classroom for the life that follows, very well-designed in all its complexity. It is not a classroom for abstract lessons, but rather one in which we learn by quite practical being and doing. In mindfulness we leave ourselves open to learning from all there is in our present situation. Behind it is the assumption that we are here to learn of it all.

The spiritual begins with the Lord, and extends through the spiritual worlds, which are closely imaged in our interior life, to our uses, and ultimately into the natural world which images and corresponds to the spiritual. Must one think of God? Certainly if it is your pleasure. But the Golden Rule states that the essence is in how we treat others. The basic spiritual practice of mindfulness rests in all that is given to us. Those who really see and respect creation already honor God. The spiritual is one enterprise, no matter how many parts it may seem to have. It is both practical and enjoyable to learn to get along with all there is.

This is the view of Vedanta, and this is its practicality. When we have become free, we need not go crazy and give up society and rush off to die in the forest or in a cave. We shall remain where we are, only we shall understand the whole thing. The same phenomena will remain, but with a new meaning.

—Swami Vivekananda, *Jnana Yoga* (29, p. 249)

8

The Design of Personal Worlds

By perceiving and assigning meaning we are ever creating and shaping our personal world. We are like the God of our own world, shaping it for good or ill. We can be like a blind God stumbling about, destroying much. Or we can use the means given us and shape a well-made and ideal world. It is a lot less trouble and more pleasure to make an ideal one than to stumble, pretending we are unaware of our powers.

—An anonymous saint

My fundamental theme is that the direct experience of God can be had, and has been had, by everyone. There are designs of personal worlds which easily lead into the experience of God, and there are other designs which make such an experience very unlikely. In section one I described three small shifts in outlook that can lead into the experience of God. Each of these little shifts is available and can be chosen and experienced as part of one's personal world:

1. An openness to experience reveals mystery and awe.
2. The shift from time to eternity allows us to experience this larger realm.
3. Understanding ourselves as a microcosm shows us to be a model of the whole.

The ability to choose to make these shifts in outlook requires some degree of free will. There has been much philosophical talk of free will in the past. Do we have free will or are we constrained? We are certainly not entirely free. So much seems predetermined—our sex, race, and in a deep sense our capacities and predilections in the love of the life. Yet phenomenologically it appears that we each have *some* free will. When a friend comes to visit, I can choose to be considerate or to brush him off. We have a little freedom, probably enough if we use it wisely.

In this discussion of personal worlds we are in the midst of reflecting on our world and whether we choose to make choices to improve it. Mystery is available to all of us, in any context, and you can choose to be open to it. Just as an example, those who haven't opened themselves to art are missing one of life's greatest experiences. The ancient idea of ourselves as a microcosm can be opened and explored. Instead of dismissing the idea of the eternal as otherworldly, we can enjoy this experience and simultaneously prepare ourselves for the world to come. We have already been dealing with specific lesser aspects of our personal world.

In section two we entered upon more thorough-going shifts in our outlook and hence our experience. For those caught within the cage of reason, logic and words, we offered the insight that feeling is a broader way of understanding. When you fall deeply in love you suddenly understand much of love, without books, words, or theories. I have a friend, a follower of a Sikh tradition, who has a very feelingful relationship to plants. I discovered to my amazement that he practically has a love affair with plants. When he visits he often brings a plant, to introduce me to one of his friends. He has difficulty putting this into words. He would never convince a rational person of this. He is able to work all day in the fields tending plants lovingly, and he considers this more recreation than work. This is part of his love of the life and it is a distinct part of his uniqueness. I have just traces of such feeling, but my world is enriched by having met him and learning that this is possible. I thought love affairs were all with people and animals. When you find another's real uniqueness, it is as though you have been shown a whole new path that you didn't know existed.

When I dealt with the spiritual I was also dealing with the design of a personal world. The spiritual is ourselves in our essentials—what we really are. When you are concerned with what you really are, you are in the spiritual. It is what is of ourselves that is quite eternal and immortal, hence it is well worth getting acquainted with it.

Now after these preparations we can deal with the design of our world more directly. But in talking of the personal world we really need to confront what we mean by this. Do we mean the outer, objective world circumstances a person is embedded in, or do we mean the inner world in which we have some little autonomy and capacity for choice? Religious traditions all deal with both worlds almost without distinction, but this is not carelessness on their part. Your inner personal world so conditions your perception and experience of the so-called outer objective world that they turn out to be the same thing. When shown a section of rural land a businessman sees the potential profit on a business deal. My wife, an artist, finds its beauty. For myself it is a potential retreat for a contemplative. Same stimulus, three different worlds.

The Eastern Orthodox Christian mystics would often take whatever circumstances were given to them, inner or outer, as from God. They felt that since God is omnipotent and omnipresent there must be some reason and use in whatever God brought to them. St. Serphim of Sarov was sleeping on a sack of plain rocks as part of his spiritual struggle when he was set upon by robbers who thought that he slept on the sack of rocks because they were gold. They beat him so badly that he was hunched-back for the rest of his life. He, of course, forgave the foolish thieves and reflected on the uses God gave him in this experience. Saints often had serious and painful illnesses, and reflected on their uses. Often they would take treatment if something was available, but if not, reflect anyway on what God was showing them. When so used, illness at the very least teaches patience and humility, which is nearly the most direct way to God. Contrast the average person who bemoans their bad luck with illness, to the saint who takes the same illness as a lesson from God, a gift to be learned from. These saints made no real distinction between outer circumstances or inner circumstances. All were treated as from the same source, from God. They learned from circumstances that most would regard as of no use.

When we turn to the Eastern religions, particularly Hinduism and Buddhism, we see much the same understanding that the mind makes the world—both the outer "objective world" and the inner world. It is a consistent finding among mystics that these are seen as ultimately one. We are world-makers. When you look long and hard at how much the design of the inner personal world conditions perception and outer experience, then the objectivity of the external world begins to fade. But if I were asked what is the principal source of our experienced world I would have to say the outer personal world, the world of meaning we live in. The personal is more powerful than the so-called objectivity of the outer world. If the personal world is right, then you can feel rich beyond your wildest dreams, regardless of outer circumstances. But ultimately mystics don't distinguish inner and outer. In some sense both are maya, an illusion to be penetrated to see the One behind it all.

Different Personal Worlds

It might help clarify if I illustrated with a number of personal worlds I have discovered in others. As a clinical psychologist I have had to examine a great many criminals. A criminal is usually someone whose whole life is a game directed against others. A phrase from a text on projective tests comes to mind, "An alert and pretentious front." Life has been reduced to a sort of contest between them and others. They are out to get theirs. They are exceedingly alert to my responses as an examiner, as though they are constantly adding up their score in the interview. Once I thought I had one of these types, I could then play out the game on a more subtle level and see how well they followed. I would indicate subtle disapproval of the way their cigarette ash was messing up my desk. In an instant they would clean off my desk. I could hint at an interest in any topic, and they would pick this up and elaborately describe their abiding interest in this same subject. The contrast to a normal person is profound. A normal person has a certain set of preferences and ways of doing things. They cannot adapt it in an instant to my subtle cues. The criminal world is sort of turned inside out, with no center, no source, no inner basis. Life is a contest in which you have to be very alert and ready to dissemble to win your end. Even when they win a sum of money it is soon lost, because they don't have an inner way to guide them in using it.

Another personal world is one in which felt illness becomes central. I say felt illness, because in ordinary terms they may or may not have a real physical illness. Their life revolves around their illness as though it is the whole center of their being. They want to tell others all the details. They hope the listener will be like a mother and take them in their arms and cuddle the poor bereft child. They look so closely at illness as to magnify it, and so many other aspects of life are lost from their view. Their entire being has become sick and is dying and crying out for help, and in some respects this is true. But they have it projected onto the world. They don't realize that as world-makers they have made themselves a sick world, and they expect the outer world to get alarmed and care for them. Any of us could dwell on every least symptom, and magnify symptoms into some sort of serious case. It is typical of the less medically-aware hypochondriacs to have symptoms that wander around the body like a meandering ghost, quite unlike any known disease.

In contrast, the normal person is disappointed at illness, but does whatever they can to overcome it, or live as fully and joyfully as they can without it dominating them. It is quite another matter to dive into illness as though it is all there is. Hypochondriacs are like small boats that have run aground on their perceived ills. As unconscious world-makers they have chosen to invest their attention and activity in a sick world. In each individual's world design there are also a host of details that make them unique, even though they may have fallen into one of these more common world design traps.

I am sure some were bothered when I said design a world you enjoy. What is to prevent us from being totally selfish? A totally selfish world is really much like the hypochondriac's; by focusing only on what comforts me, it too runs aground. The myopic search for comfort and pleasure devours itself, resulting in a personal world full of *dis*comfort and *dis*pleasure. In contrast, embracing all provides a pleasure that dims all others and cannot be taken away. I am reminded of a movie star who became terribly upset if the bath water wasn't within a degree of her comfort zone. This comfort zone is such a knife-edge that her world is closely surrounded by the possibility of discomfort. She spoils her relationship to her servants she lives with. She creates and lives in a mini-hell which is a poor preparation for eternity.

In contrast, the world of a gifted or individuated person is both unique and broad-ranging. They present themselves in dress and in manner as an individual person with their own way, not a slave to the marketplace of fashion. They are alert and aware both of you and how they may seem to you. In an interview they are aware of both themselves and the interviewer. In conversation they can quickly spot your misunderstandings and gently correct them. They are aware of the whole world, but may have chosen to overlook most of it in favor of what most interests them. They give one a strong sense of having consciously chosen their world and created a center, a firm foundation that serves them well, particularly in times of outside chaos. They also give one the feeling of being in command, and yet they are able to shift from the trivial to the profound, freer to see many aspects of things. You can talk of their personal world with them and they will let you in to see some of the joys and challenges of their world. In contrast it is a delicate and difficult matter to even broach the matter of their real world design to the hypochondriac or the criminal. The personal freedom of a gifted person is a hundred times greater than the criminal or the hypochondriac. All psychopathology results in a serious impairment of freedom to choose. As a clinical psychologist I am mainly against psychopathology for its loss of freedom. I would like to see all free to find the way that is best for them.

When I read the lives of saints I had a strong sense that they had chosen to live in a spiritual world, and to make this the center of their living. The choice was not easy; it was a path that led through its own difficulties. But they were world-makers; they wanted a spiritual world and gradually created a joyful one. Some have wondered if one perhaps needs to be crazy or neurotic to have mystical experience. I have known very psychotic people to have giant religious visions. But the marked contrast to normals was in their inability to make use of them. What good is a great vision in the midst of a fever? When you get well, both the fever and the vision are lost. In contrast, the saints were like spiritual athletes who could keep, safeguard, and use a vision.

Karma

Karma is the Eastern doctrine which teaches that somehow it is a part of existence that sooner or later we get what we give. The Golden Rule, "Do unto others as you would have them do unto you," is a similar expression, and is a part of all of the world's major religions:

What is hateful to you, do not do to your fellow man. (Judaism)

No one is a believer until he desires for his brother that which he desires for himself. (Islam)

Do not do unto others what would cause you pain if done unto you. (Hinduism)

Hurt not others in ways that you yourself would find hurtful. (Buddhism)

Regard your neighbor's gain as your own gain, and your neighbor's loss as your own loss. (Taoism) (32)

However, the Golden Rule only says this is the proper way to live. Karma, on the other hand, describes a retribution that is an integral part of existence itself. As a mystic the doctrine of karma feels like a profound truth, because at the highest levels of mystical experience the individual discovers they are the same as the All, and through that, ultimately they are everyone else. As a mystic, what I do to others I am literally doing to myself, *right now*. As a merely practical person I would be inclined to say that if karma isn't an actual law of reality, then it ought to be. When I have heard that some dictator made off with millions, I may envy their life of luxury for a moment. But I would rather be a poor homeless person than to have their load of karma.

I see great use in both the Golden Rule and the idea of karma, because it presupposes that all of existence is bound together. Ultimately I cannot cheat another without being cheated and lessening myself. If the Lord is omnipotent and omnipresent, then there is no possibility of really getting away with anything. Yet even for a very moral person there are events that try one's soul, for instance whether to assist a loved one to die in the face of a painful and hopeless situation. Here I think the internal of one's real intent is everything. If I assist the suffering person because it will be more convenient to have them out of the way, or refuse to assist because it offends my righteous doctrine, then there will be a karmic burden. But if my intent is to help without thought of my convenience, then there is no debt. One's love, the very center of intent, is everything in this realm.

My wife was driving her beloved and very ill brother to our home. He died in the car on the way. He was a recently converted Catholic and might well want the last rites. Yet my wife knew terribly little of them. She tried her best to administer the last rites and asked me later about it, concerned whether she did it right. In a spiritual sense I could see a beautiful, golden intent, which is supreme. So I assured her that no matter how she did it, she had done it right. How well we do is measured by the very spiritual center of our intent. Our world hinges on that. God knows the limitations of our circumstances better than we do. Do what you can for the world, and the world will do what it can for you.

In both the Golden Rule and karma there is also hidden the deep issue of understanding ourselves and others. Do I want others to be unfailingly nice to me, or would I prefer you to occasionally show me my faults, even though it might be painful? What does "nice" mean? I must decide this to decide how to give to you what I would like to receive back. Karma implies that nothing is ever totally hidden. I can hide from myself that I am mean to servants. Still *I* have to live with this mean master within, twenty-four hours a day, while the servant can escape to his quarters for respite. The person who is mean to servants is likely already deprived of the pleasure of closeness and understanding, whereas the berated servant may have this closeness with others. I believe if we could see the real quality of the lives of all those who ripped people off and got away with millions, we would see something like this. Though they live in luxury, they cannot enjoy it because their inner life is so deprived we would not trade with them. The retribution in karma can be subtle and direct.

In contrast I have known saints who lived in the meanest and poorest of circumstances, yet whose life on earth—not counting the life beyond this—was of incredible richness. When St. Seraphim of Sarov was saying mass, others saw angels serving with him (33). He was sometimes criticized for losing track of the ritual when conducting the mass because he had fallen into an ecstacy. Karma is true, not just in some far-removed sense of other lives, but here and now. We get back what we put into our world design. It is as though we are junior Gods playing at world-making, to learn what it is all about. Thankfully there is a teacher who will guide us when we stumble, and that teacher appears as inner and outer circumstances. The world is a classroom. Above the blackboard it says, "Karma— All Is Known And Accounted For!"—a statement of omnipresence and omnipotence. If you are a good person you love looking at this sign and reflecting on it. If you are not, you would probably rather not see it. One doesn't fool with an inexorable law like karma. The difference is both here and in eternity.

Karma is usually described like some exact heavenly accounting system. Do so much against others and suffer just that amount. I find this such a socially useful doctrine I would not disturb it. Yet in all the traditions that deal with karma there is an agreed-upon way out. In spite of what karmic debts you have, all this can be erased by finding God. People in the Western world may not immediately recognize the familiarity of what is called God's grace or forgiveness. In Buddhism this is directly represented as Buddha's Infinite Compassion. As a mystic it makes immediate sense. The experience of God transcends all things of time. How could you carry a burden accumulated in time into this experience? Yet you can't simply behave badly and accumulate karma, and then suddenly escape this way. You are dealing with an Omnipotence which knows the very heart of your intent. Only God gives the experience of God and God can withhold it for a kalpa of lifetimes. (The Hindu kalpa is one breath of Brahman, or the time from the big bang to the total expansion and then contraction of the universe.) There are no games in this realm, no legal loopholes. The wise person realizes they are totally at the mercy of God. That is how it is.

Reincarnation

The doctrine of reincarnation can be found in both Eastern and Western religions. It is usually understood in the simple and limited sense that the individual might be recycled again through life as a person or some other being. The problem lies in thinking of the person, the ego identity, as though it is a fixed and real thing. Ego is one of those ultimate mysteries which we often take for granted as though it is fully understood. How mankind began rests in evolutionary processes that preceded us, and which themselves partake of mystery. In spite of all our knowledge of conception and genetics, the creation of our person from a single cell still contains great mysteries. Most of our early development and even our basic outlook and ways of doing things formed under the influence of others. But we finally arrive on the world stage sure of ourselves as to what we are—or are we sure? The concept of the spiritual points to essential aspects of our life which we barely understand. Our feelings and our love of the life are also mysteries given to us. We are embedded in mystery and participate in mystery, all of which has much to do with what we are. To represent this, let us use the term ego (?) with a question mark.

Do I have an ego (?) like I have a wallet or a purse? Who am "I" to have such a thing? In a few instances people have walked directly into mystical experience merely by asking who they were, because they came to sense the total mystery in which they were embedded. One Hindu sage recommended the persistent questioning of "What am I?" as the way to enlightenment. Such questioning reveals the I as shorthand for the confluence of so many unknowns in this moment. The idea that I am a clever ego puppeteer pulling strings is a little ridiculous. Where are the strings? They connect to what? I tend to experience my own ego (?) like a kind of accident, a convenient fiction, useful for signing checks or finding my luggage at the airport. This body has lived for a time and has a history labeled with my name for an identity. Yet even my body has ways and needs I don't understand. I have never really met memory, though memories have come to me often enough. When I read in the Eastern literature that ego (?) is maya, an illusion, something the personal world created, I can see this as true.

If I were very concerned about myself, my reputation, and my property, I can see scenarios in which I would get into a lot more conflict with others than if I don't take my ego (?) too seriously. A major barrier to the direct perception of God is precisely this hanging on to an ego (?). If I am a separate ego (?) then either God has to break down the artificial walls of this conception to get in, or I have to tear down the walls to get out.

All the processes that lead into the experience of God involve a reduction or a letting go of ego (?). I used the image of a still pond earlier. Disturb the water of the pond and you have a representation of ego rippling back and forth, seeking itself. Just leave the water alone, and ripples die out. It gets calm, and you can see into it. In Zen this has been represented as seeing the moon in a bucket of water. The bucket is the microcosm. It has to be very calm to really see the moon in it. All things come and go in it. The whole of life may be seen in it. What is the greater—the bucket ego, or all there is coming and going in it?

No ego. Only all there is! When someone takes their ego as a real, substantial thing instead of as a mystery, they will also have a limited understanding of reincarnation. They are thinking that me, this personal ego, will come back. They ask, "Will I return as a person again, or as a dog or cat?" Well, no, because that ego is really an illusion. A better question is will the One return as this, that, and the other, and the answer is emphatically, yes, or existence would cease. The One reincarnates, and literally takes on a body again. Personal identity is something of an illusion to be overcome, a barrier to seeing the One. But if you plumb to the depth of self-identity it is fundamentally the One. Even Swedenborg describes it this way.

Behind all consciousness is the One. If the One was not looking, we would not see. All awareness is from the One. And yes, thankfully, the One returns endlessly.

On the other hand, some people have described an experience of their past lives. Buddha himself became aware of past lives on the way to his great illumination. I have had people in experiments with the drug LSD also rediscover past lives. I was totally startled when I first found this. Later in the midst of a therapy session I recalled a past life of my own. It was very real and powerful. I had been a Mayan priest who had ceremonially killed himself, and this experience has the quality of a true personal memory. I now take it as a given that these experiences do occur; the real issue is what do they mean and how are they to be used? In Buddha's case and in several I have known, the discovery of a whole succession of past lives was a direct path to enlightenment. Discovering that they have been this, that, and the other set in motion a process of loosening up self-identity, a preparation for the discovery of the One that has always existed everywhere. One of my patients went through a series of reincarnations down through all life forms. After reaching dark primal ooze she found herself as the One; the One was all these lives.

When the experience of reincarnation does not go all the way back to the discovery of the One that really does reincarnate, it still creates an amplified image of the present life. What you were in the past has to have the same core as you have now. Let me use my own discovery of my life as a Mayan priest as an example. I had been selected from other youths for training as a priest because I had an intuitive understanding of religious matters. Over time I had been elevated to be a priest over warriors and over the ceremony of cutting out living hearts. (The role of the heart in theology still fascinates me.) I came to question this whole procedure. As priests we were sending these sacrifices as messengers to the ultimate. I myself would be a better messenger. So, in a feathered robe, in the midst of a high ceremony, I cut and sacrificed myself. The area I cut has hurt me for 50 years in this life! My current work is the process of getting the answers I set out looking for in that past life. Was I ever a Mayan priest? I don't know, and there is no way to really tell. But in any event this is an image in-depth of my present life. As a priest I worked with warriors, and in my present life I've been associated with the military in one way or another my whole life. It is at least an image of my present.

It loosens ego to experience the possibility of identifying with other lives, and the doctrine of reincarnation does that. People wonder if this creature might be her deceased mother, or will I become one of those creatures? I'd better treat them kindly. Yes, to some extent you are already one of these creatures. My wife sees when plants are thirsty. I felt so remiss that now I begin to notice too. Are we part of all life? Yes, of course. Part of all life in the past and in the future? Yes, of course. Reincarnation leads this way. Like karma, it is such a socially useful doctrine I would not tamper with it. Seen rightly it leads beyond limited ego to all life. It is a door that opens to the possibility of identifying with all life, just as God does.

Ego is an illusion to be penetrated if the One is to be known. And of course, unless the One reappeared as all things, including us, existence as we know it would not be. Like karma, reincarnation points toward a great truth which we can put up on the wall in our classroom. "Reincarnation is part of the chain of discoveries of who we are, back to the One who so generously enters existence." Some will be disturbed by this, fearing their precious self will one day be lost. But ego is not lost at all; it expands to its real and full scope as Everything. Each is the Divine struggling for awareness. The Hindus say, "Tat tvam asi." *That* thou art. *That* is the ultimate creator of all there is.

The general formula for those traditions that use the idea of reincarnation is that ignorance leads to reincarnation. Another way of saying this is that ignorance leads to being caught in the web of existence. If you think you are a fly, you can be caught in a web and a spider will eat you. The more limited your concept the more you are caught in circumstances. Liberation from being caught is to discover God, identifying with a level that is no longer caught. The doctrine of reincarnation is basically a pointer toward the value of enlightenment. Even in its simplest form as the understanding that the personal ego reincarnates, I see it as a doctrine whose social use, like karma, is to get people to reflect on their life and to try to better themselves. Even on its lowest level of understanding I would not care to disturb this. Deeply understood, reincarnation has beautiful truths within it—that there is truly something which enters creation endlessly with the highest intentions. Were this not so, all creation would end. This position is quite far from the common idea of reincarnation of the personal identity, but it is in accord with the highest Hindu/Buddhist understanding.

I might comment on the Tibetan Buddhist practice of looking for the reincarnation of a great and revered spiritual leader, such as the Dalai Lama. A revered spiritual leader is one who has taken on the vows of a Boddhisatva, one who will delay their entering paradise until all sentient beings are enlightened and can know God. This is a vow of such lofty spiritual idealism I would not feel up to it. Because the great leader vows to return endlessly, until the task is done, his followers look for his reincarnation. The returned one is identified as an infant, and then trained for his role. If you think of the great one as an ego, the whole thing looks very questionable to a Westerner. Does their ego go on with this endless struggle? But this whole process is not odd at all if you realize that taking the vow of a Boddhisatva is precisely what God might do. This wish for all to know God is from God, and not from ego. Taking the vow of the Boddhisatva and living a life sincerely working for the enlightenment of all, is a way to identify with God, and is itself a way to enlightenment.

Seen spiritually, searching for the reincarnation of the Boddhisatva is rather beautiful. When a great one, who took the vow to work for the enlightenment of all, dies, why not then look for him to reappear? Search for him and aid him in this role. It is a way of creating a spiritual continuity from one teacher to others down through the centuries. It is not ego or ordinary self-identity that is reborn, but the divine impulse. Hopefully this impulse will grow and flower everywhere endlessly.

Ideals

Ideals are signs of what is trying to emerge in the personal world. For some years I selected and trained adults to be knights and dames in a modern version of the ancient chivalric tradition. Those who came for the training were usually adults who had solved most of life's problems, and now had a little time and money and were exploring deeper yearnings. This is comparable to the Hindu who has raised a family, and now wants to go the way of yoga to reflect on the deeper issues of life. These candidates were hungry for something more, but were not quite sure what it was. About half were religious, but the religious and non-religious appeared to have much the same hunger. People have such varied and inaccurate ideas about knighthood and chivalry that it takes at least a half hour to get people to understand what it is all about, so let us simply talk of ideals, which are the same thing.

My task was to introduce them to the world of ideals. Ideals are tendencies toward one's own future design. They are signs of the love of the life emerging. But how to get at the ideals of adults? I didn't want them to speak abstractly of ideals; I wanted their real, experienced, ideals. So I asked them to describe what would be an ideal way for them to live. But since they were also in training to become knights and dames, I would project them back to the Crusades. They have their present knowledge and outlook, but they find themselves in the Holy Land. They are in council and it is early in the Crusades. Another Christian-Arab battle is shaping up. How will they handle the situation? Or I could put them in the year 1100 as a new knight under a liberal local lord who merely wanted them to do something constructive. What role would they choose? I could project them into all sorts of situations, and we would learn what is ideal for them.

When your ideals become clear, then you can set about constructively working at them. There are little things you can do now to realize them. If your ideal includes ideal behavior, as it usually did in knights and dames in training, then you can look at what you can do here and now to realize it. One of my favorite examples was a librarian who set about to become a true chivalrous knight in the library. He described incidents in which he could have put off someone who inquired of him, but instead he went the extra distance to help them. He realized himself as a true and chivalrous knight in his setting and was knighted for this to confirm it.

I projected one lady in training into the time of the crusades, but with a total awareness of the history of the crusades. When she attended a council of knights she argued for a need to understand the Arabs, their language, ways and religion. She and others were selected for this duty and later became liaison between the knights and the Arabs, thereby lessening warfare. In real life she was a manager. Her hospital had a problem with the laundry. She sent hospital staff to work in the laundry (totally surprising those in the laundry) and laundry people to work on the wards. Out of this grew a conference which ended the hospital-laundry problem. She became a Dame in the Noble Company of the Rose.

I discovered in psychotherapy that people who had a very constricted view of their situation could still fantasize freely, and this gave them the freedom to experience themselves, just as the starving person visualizes food. Prisoners often discover that they can "trip out" and experience themselves in a freer way. This is almost a life-saving function—to be free in experiencing what one's real way is. In the Western world people have often been taught to look down on fantasy or imagination. Yet inventors and artists visualize how a thing should work or look, and then set about to create it. The carpenter, for instance, may visualize a project step-by-step before a board is cut. It is a way of trying out something ahead of time. My wife is bothered by all the endless designs and projects she can conceive. I have described how for me writing is primarily an imaginative process. I set the general project and then the inner process goes to work and lets me know when it is ready to write. If you want the experience of God, I would encourage imagining what it would be like. This whole process of fantasy and imagination is your interior portraying itself. It can readily come into expression, and it represents what you would like to be, your ideal.

When ideals become clear, then we can find many opportunities to move toward their realization. Ideals are a step toward the love of the life and one's eternal. It is very important to discover and move towards our ideals. Our ideals are our plans, what we will move toward, and at the very least we can realize them internally. But in some degree and to some extent they can also be gradually realized externally. It is exciting to come to realize ideals.

Imagination

I have seen religious people who were quite afraid of any process that involves imagination. It is as though if they let their fantasy go they will go straight down a road of sexy delights that leads to the devil. Such a position has to involve a failure to explore imagination. It wastes energy to suppress such a useful process, and probably lessens creativity.

When I look at the fantasies of mature adults they typically have a very unique set of choices in them. Each contains a particular style of life and work that they would like to do, and it almost invariably is some role that would be useful to society. I encourage people to take these inner trends seriously, and to do all they can to explore them and realize them. In some respects life experiences refine one's understanding of the love of the life. As a young man all my fantasies ran to being a very distinguished naval officer. Now as an old man I would much prefer to be an anonymous and little-known wise man. All the pomp and circumstance of my boyhood dreams have been washed away by time, leaving this core ideal.

Yesterday I completed the kind of task I could do for eternity. A leader of a small church felt led by God to seek my help in interpreting a long and repeated dream he had been having. I penned a careful study of his dream, which was essentially the dream of a saint struggling with two almost opposite trends in himself. One was toward a public role which involved office and status. The other was a private role seeking only wisdom. Here is my ideal—to be wise enough to be able to help others in the deepest spiritual matters. In return I would only want to live quietly in a setting conducive to spiritual reflection. Knowing this ideal, I can choose those things that aid its realization.

From this perspective I do not fear anyone's fantasy and ideal. No matter how extreme or distorted, it is their lifeline to what is in them. Only by following it and exploring it more deeply can it be fully known. An example is a person who fears the very thought of their own death. It is as though letting the fantasy come forth might kill them. But even a fantasy of one's own death can be carefully explored, for one can do anything in fantasy. Often what emerges is simply a need to let go and relax, leave the struggle of life for awhile. Or it can contain an ideal state. For instance one person found in their "death" a remarkable need to focus and concentrate. It was as though they had a master meditator in them. When this power was cultivated, all its negative meanings disappeared.

Fantasy or imagination is a natural process by which what is in our internal makes itself known. But if it is not explored, we can certainly come to very wrong ideas as to what it is really up to. The fantasies of youth are merely the rather crude and showy aspects of what life experience eventually reveals. I encourage people to follow this inner lifeline to see where it leads. In this way one can approach one's ideal design of the personal world, and eventually you can find the love of the life that has always been yours—where you fit in eternity.

It is quite appropriate to picture what kind of life you'd like to live throughout eternity. Will you do nothing, or is there some activity you'd prefer? Often we'd prefer to do nothing when we are tired, but as soon as we are rested, some activity comes to mind. Try it out in various ways, essaying exactly what you enjoy doing. Try it until you come to an image of your own that becomes very stable and satisfying. In my own fantasy I am in my study. I've become curious about some aspect of theology and start to look it up in my books.

The image stops and becomes very stable. My ideal is simple, just to be free to discover in this realm. With the stable image can come transcendent insights and joy. This practice is a way of discovering the part of yourself in eternity. It is, of course, your own way to God.

I spent a year working on the dreams of Swedenborg (33), who dreamed often of a second-floor room that overlooks a verdant garden. The room was quite simple, with a few books and papers. He could spend eternity looking out and enjoying the verdant garden. Among other things he was a gardener. His thirty volumes were, in effect, all he saw and experienced from this room, his ideal place. People sometimes speak of "finding" one's self. When you know what you were designed for, and could comfortably do forever, then you have found yourself. I have a nice quote of a very Buddhist way of saying the same thing. In this, "sublime beings" represents any ideal that is sought.

> In all the traditions of Buddhism, sublime beings are worshipped to attain enlightenment. If we think that this practice is just using our imagination, we are missing the point of view. Imagination is considered to be unreal thinking. But whatever we believe becomes true to us, so if we believe in something, it is not imaginary. Until sublime beings actually appear to us, it may seem that worshipping them is only imaginary. Yet we must realize that as long as we are deluded, everything is imaginary and created by mind.
>
> Everyone uses imagination in an ordinary way, although this has no ultimate benefit. When we worship sublime beings, instead of just using ordinary imagination, we are using our mind's ability to create pure phenomena with visualization, prayer, and offering, which have the immeasurable benefit of connecting us with unceasing, inconceivable mind. Believing in and practicing with pure deity benefits us in this life and always because it causes the pure energy of positive phenomena to manifest until we attain the infallible wisdom of Buddha.
>
> —Thinley Norbu, *White Sail* (35)

The fantasy/imagination/ideal is the prospective part of yourself emerging; what you can become. It is your design emerging. It is the eternal you: what you always were and will be. Life is an excellent place to move from the total uncertainty of infancy into knowing. That is what life is for. The vicissitudes of life are an excellent place to learn, if you pay attention. This is what Swedenborg meant when he said the purpose of life is that there be a heaven of the human race. The purpose of life is that we each fully discover ourselves, that we might find our place in the harmonious whole, where the joy of one is the joy of all. It is not all fantasy. Uses is where we try out work to see where we fit. Fantasy indicates a direction, but life and experience is the testing ground that helps us to find ourselves.

Religious Worlds

I have long used the concept of personal worlds because it allows such openness and respect in understanding others. Having worked with people from the most gifted to the strange and distorted worlds of truly mad men and women, I have seen how it allows me the freedom to discover what is uniquely there. I then ran across the gifted words of William E. Paden's *Religious Worlds* in which he presents a phenomenological approach to religions that is very similar to my attempt to respectfully discover a person's world. He argues that religions are designed to create a particular kind of world. Very clearly religions attempt to do this, and the more the religion takes root in the individual, the more they will reflect that religious world.

> In the broadest sense there are as many worlds as there are species; all living things select and sense "the way things are" through their own organs and modes of activity. They constellate the environment in terms of their own needs, sensory system, and values. They see—or smell or feel—what they need to, and everything else may as well not exist. A world, or whatever set of creatures, is defined by this double process of selection and exclusion. . . .
>
> Human cultures construct an enormous variety of environments through language, technology, and institutions. We are born and die in these systems of symbols and imagination. Among these forms, religion in particular is a great definer and generator of worlds and alternative worlds.
>
> Religions do not all inhabit the same world, but actually posit, structure, and dwell within a universe that is their own. They can be understood not just as so many attempts

to explain some common, objectively available order of things that is "out there," but as traditions that create and occupy their own universe. Acknowledging these differences in place, these intrinsically different systems of experiencing and living in the world, is fundamental to the study of religion.

—Paden, *Religious Worlds* (36)

He then goes on to examine myth, ritual, time, Gods, and systems of purity as a way of comparing possible religious worlds. His succeeding work *Interpreting the Sacred* (37) is equally illuminating. Here is an approach that delineates the variety of religious forms, with no suggestion that one is better than another. All the contentions of which is the one right way are put aside. These different designs all function for some people, and of course their individual world intersects the world of their religion.

I was left somewhat stunned by these very illuminating works. I saw that the immense range of individual worlds extends into religious worlds. They each reflect ways of living and creating meaning. As a mystic, I am inclined to see the design of a religious world as revealed by God, as each claims to be. If so, then God is shown to be far more creative than I have supposed by fashioning such a variety of worlds, individual and religious, each suited to, and functioning in, a given time, place, and circumstance. This reminds me of the plant kingdom. There are so many different kinds of plants. This tree keeps its leaves all year, while that one goes through a yearly cycle of losing leaves, going to sleep, and then being reborn. Is not variety itself wonderful? Whatever is behind all this clearly enjoys diversity. We should try to be like the Designer and enjoy and respect diversity. We are simple creatures, each determined to find the right way, afloat in a sea of diversity. If we accept this diversity, we accept each other and all the sacred ways. Yet, in the midst of this, we can still live the way we prefer, while being considerate of other lives and other ways.

9

Influx—Catching God In The Act

There is one only life, from which all both in heaven and in the world live. This life is from the Lord alone. The Lord is Life itself. Life from the Lord flows in with angels, spirits, and men, in a wonderful manner. The Lord flows in from His Divine Love, which is of such a character, that it wills that what is its own shall be another's. All love is such a quality; the Divine Love, consequently, is infinitely more so. Life thus appears as though it were within man, and not as if it were flowing in.

—E. Swedenborg, *Heavenly Doctrine* (38, #278)

All along we have been working at the boundary of the Divine and the human. We were mostly on the human side of the Divine/human boundary when we reflected on ourselves as a sort of dumb God creating our personal world. But in certain aspects, like karma and reincarnation, we slipped over the boundary into Divine territory. We again crossed over the boundary in the matter of discovering and working to realize our ideals. This crossover may not be so apparent until you realize that your deepest ideals were given to you out of mystery, and you are forever in the process of realizing them. The process of realization of your ideals is the Divine waking up. So this Divine/human boundary is not so mysterious. We have been there before, and crossed back and forth many times. When we cross from the human to the Divine, our understanding and wisdom is enlarged too much to take credit for it. Wisdom that simply aris-

131

es, full-blown, without our even having a chance to anticipate it, we credit to a source wiser than us. So the actual placement of the boundary depends in part on how presumptuous we are. If we consider ourselves terribly clever, even in our sleep, then we claim the whole territory. God would have to come in awesome thunderbolts and a great crashing racket to get our attention. Unless it is totally awesome it can't be from God. Many agnostics would believe if only God would really MANIFEST. For a mystic the bloom of a single flower is quite enough manifestation. The more humble you are, the more signs can be found. So we have a basic dilemma about locating the Divine/human boundary. The more we presume is ours, or belonging to nature as a machine, the less there appears to be of the Divine. The more humble we are, the more there is of the Divine. The boundary truly reflects the degree of our presumption/humility.

To mature mystics the issue itself is mistaken. There really is no ego, so there is no boundary. It is *all* God. Though I am some sort of partly localized process, sitting here with hands and feet, and so on, how much do I know of it? Not much. I am conscious of writing here, but how is it done? Do I make these words, or do they flow better when just permitted? This consciousness—what is it? Do I make it or does it just arise in me? When I accept the fact that it all just is, this is the egoless experience. It doesn't alter me in any way that is outwardly obvious. Those who presume the existence of ego will think I am merely writing as anyone else might. But in the egoless state the writing is just felt to emerge as does everything else.

However, there is a subtle difference that stands for a great deal in the long run. The one who assumes ego creates limits and does not expect more. The egoless person is open to it all, and comes to experience more and more subtle and heavenly experiences. This is quite a difference. In Zen the question is asked what happens after satori or enlightenment. The answer is, one chops wood and carries water; but oh, the wood and water are not the same! It would be nice if people could take a week off from being a person to enjoy the whole scope of things.

> The Lord of Love willed: "Let me be many!"
> And in the depths of his meditation
> He created everything that exists.
> Meditating, he entered into everything.
> He who has no form assumed many forms;

He who is infinite appeared finite;
He who is everywhere assumed a place;
He who is all wisdom caused ignorance;
He who is real caused unreality.
It is he who has become everything.
It is he who gives reality to all.

—Taittiriya Upanishad (39)

Influx—Watching Creation Taking Place

Influx means flowing in, what is given. Influx from the Lord can actually be discovered and experienced in daily life. Swedenborg says we are really recipient vessels. We receive life. It does much to overcome the presumption of ego to discover this for yourself. If I could give one gift to all mankind it would be about an hour of everyone experiencing this influx, because it would radically alter everyone's conceptions and attitudes. If I asked a sample of average people, few would be aware of any instance in which the Divine flows in. A few would be able to provide one or two instances in which something so remarkable happened to them that they would credit it to God. Oddly enough, ministers don't seem much more aware of Divine influx than average people. At the other extreme are mature mystics who have found that this influx of the Lord's life animates and sustains the whole of creation. So we are now at the task of learning how to recognize what is simply given by God.

Influx is the life of the Lord animating all there is. In the Western world I don't know any idea quite the same. God's grace in the Christian sense is seen as a special and occasional gift, while influx is occurring all the time. In the Hindu *Upanishads* one can find much the same idea in *prana*. Prana is the vital energy, the power of life, the essential nature of all forms of energy. And with the usual Hindu genius for categorizing, they describe five forms of prana. In the following, prana is described in the very ancient and lovely Upanishads.

But prana, vital energy, supreme
Over them all, said, "Don't deceive yourselves.
It is I, dividing myself fourfold,
Who hold this body together."
But they would not believe these words of prana.
To demonstrate the truth, prana arose

And left the body, and all the powers
Knew they had to leave as well. When prana
Returned to the body, they too were back.
As when the queen bee goes out, all the bees
Go out, and when she returns all return,
So returned speech, mind, vision, and hearing.
Then the powers understood and sang this song:
"Prana burns as fire; he shines as the sun;
He rains as the cloud; he blows as the wind;
He crashes as the thunder in the sky.
He is the earth; he has form and no form;
Prana is immortality.
"Everything rests in prana, as spokes rest
In the hub of the wheel: all the Vedas,
All the rituals, all the warriors and kings.
"O prana, you move in the mother's womb
As life to be manifested again.
All creatures pay their homage to you.
"You carry offerings to gods and ancestors
And help sages to master their senses,
Which depend upon you for their function.
"You are the creator and destroyer,
And our protector. You shine as the sun
In the sky; you are the source of all light.
"When you pour yourself down as rain on earth,
Every living creature is filled with joy
And knows food will be abundant for all.
"You are pure and master of everything.
As fire you receive our oblations;
It is you who gives us the breath of life."
    —*Prashna Upanishad* (39, pp. 160-161)

Influx is the very act by which the Divine flows in and creates.
To me it is very odd that with the incredible tons of literature on religion there is so little describing the very act of life flowing in. It
becomes quite obvious if you look for it. To me the very essence of
a spiritual person is that they have found a way to enter into an actual relationship with the Divine. They not only send messages, as in
prayer, but they get answers. Influx is this creative answering flowing in. At the Divine/human border it is all those events in which the

Divine flows in and affects the human. Each needs to experience influx for themselves. Mystical experience is simply more and fuller influx. So to discover even a little influx is a way to discover much. What happens after the enlightenment that is waiting for all? Do you then float forever on the spiritual clouds? No. Mother Meera is a living avatar (a God-like being) out of the Hindu tradition. She describes quite well what it is like after enlightenment.

> When you know you are eternal you play your true role in time. When you know you are Divine you can become completely human and individual.
>
> —Mother Meera (40)

Enlightenment is an expansion of the little self into its full identity. Afterward you play your true role in time and become more deeply human and unique. So now let us set out to catch God in the act of creating.

Dreams

Dreams are a pretty obvious first place to start. I believe very few people would be so presumptuous as to take credit for the creation of their own dreams. Some credit the unconscious, or some other natural process, both of which are names for a mystery. But what is the unconscious? And why does this so-called unconscious use a language we can barely understand? We must be very careful not to dismiss wonder by the tricky device of assigning a name. Oh, you say it is primitive. Indeed. Do you mean it speaks a primordial language we have forgotten?

Instead of discussing all the confusing theories of dreams, let me say what I have found them to be. Dreams are an innate process that is present in all life, including animals, which becomes more apparently active when we are doing nothing. Asleep in bed, with most senses shut down, we meet this innate process. After looking at thousands of dreams, their nature has become quite apparent to me. *Dreams are the Divine commenting on our life.* These comments can vary all the way from trivial comments, for instance when some bodily sensation is represented in a dream. Or dreams can vary in depth all the way to what primitives call big dreams, in which the whole essence and nature of the person's life is portrayed. Big dreams often set about to get the dreamer's attention. All

repeating dreams are big dreams, critical to the person's understanding, particularly if there is impressive symbolism and you were
awakened by it and felt moved to record it.

The most noticeable thing about dreams is that they do not
speak our language. Briefly put, the spirit *feels* the relationships between all things. From this feelingful realm it can easily call on elements of the person's own experience, or the collective symbolism
of the culture, what Carl Jung described as the collective unconscious. The one creating your dream knows you better than you do,
and wishes to represent to you the quality of your life. Because it
feels the connection of all things, it easily speaks a language of representations.

If you had a happy childhood raised on a rural farm in flat open
country, the feeling of such a setting for you is one of being loved,
secure, and in the midst of the open wondrous discoveries of childhood. Now you are an adult, in the competitive rat race of a city.
When the spirit wants to speak of spiritual peace it might then use
scenes of wide open, flat countryside. You can get back to the meaning by feeling into the imagery.

I work on the meaning of my dreams while lying still in bed, in a
state as close as possible to the state out of which the dream arose.
There you can more easily feel your way around the meaning of your
dream. Meaning gradually slips into place, and you understand what
an element means. It is a great mistake to try to understand your
dream when fully awake, or in the company of others, because you
are then out of the state in which the dream arose. You then bring to
bear all your rational powers, and you may assign clever psychiatric
insights, impressing yourself and others, but missing the felt essence.
In the state in which it arose you feel an entirely different and deeper
meaning. When you feel your way into its real meaning, a dream turns
out to be a higher view of the essential quality of your life. If you find
them somewhat critical of you, you are likely accurate. But when very
desperate and feeling quite depressed, they can also come like an
angel to support you. Who else do you know who will faithfully come
and speak to you every night of your life of the innermost personal
essentials of your life? The language dreams use is higher than your
own because it is spiritual. It is 1) based in a deeper and wider understanding of your life than you have, 2) more feelingful than you are
accustomed to, and 3) concerned about the very quality and essentials of your life. It is simply influx from the Divine.

I not only seek the meaning of my dreams, but I also speak back to the Maker of Dreams. Lately there were several references to me as a stupid donkey. Oddly enough, I felt very good about that. So I answered back, "At least I am your donkey. Compared to infinite wisdom are not we all stupid donkeys?" Somehow I felt it very kind that the Divine would rate me even that high. I also felt that even my stupidity was Divinely ordained, so I don't complain.

It is curious to me how seldom dreams are used by most spiritual seekers. Swedenborg studied his dreams seriously until he started having even more direct guidance from God. Some primitives note and study big dreams closely. Tibetan Buddhists seem to have outdistanced most of the spiritual world. They have advanced to the point of being able to consciously direct the dream process, which has been called in the West "lucid dreaming" (41, 42). The person is aware they are dreaming and can steer the process toward aspects that interest them more. But for the most part, the whole world of spiritual people pay no attention to these nightly bulletins revealing God's view of us. On average you have about eight dreams a night. To say the least the process is most generous. There is clear scientific evidence that dreaming itself, whether or not we notice it, plays a vital homeostatic role in balancing our inner life. If the dream process is blocked for even a few days, the person walks right into frank madness. It appears that we need this contact with what is higher than us, or our life literally falls apart.

Let me give a simple dream as an illustration. A young man dreamed that his left hand was seriously injured. It looked as though he had tried to cut his wrist. There was blood. He had a strong feeling of curling up his injured hand and holding it over his heart. He awoke relieved to find it wasn't injured, because the dream had seemed so real.

I unravel the dream with a couple of assumptions. 1) The source of the dream is the dreamer. 2) Dreams speak an analogical language. So I asked him a direct question based on an analogy with the dream. "Reflect a moment. In what sense have you been killing yourself?" He answered, "It is odd you should say that. My wife says I am working myself to death. It is so important to me that I impress others; perhaps I work too hard." I asked him to curl up his left hand and hold it over his heart, and to reflect on what that suggested to him. He had no immediate realization, so I left it to him as a meditative exercise. At various times, especially when going to sleep (in a state near to the one in which the dream was given) I asked him to curl up his left hand and hold it over his heart, and to look for any meanings suggested to him. In the next session he had found it. When held near his heart it was as though his heart could heal his hand. He was taking care of himself.

So we have the whole meaning of the dream. This right-handed young man is injuring himself on his left side (unconsciously). The hand is easily associated with work. He is hurting himself, even killing himself, by overworking to please others. The solution is to curl up the hand (not work it) and hold it over his heart (have regard for himself). This will heal the situation.

The viewpoint of the dream is quite the opposite of his conscious viewpoint. He could work so hard pleasing others. The dream has a higher viewpoint. In a dramatic language of analogy it says, "Look, you are hurting yourself. Here is how to heal it." Without the shock of the dream he would have hardly been aware of this. His wife had noticed the situation more than he did. The dream is often the corrective of consciousness. It represents a different viewpoint, often showing a higher concern for the very nature and quality of one's life.

The main difficulty is not only that the dream has a wiser viewpoint but that it is stated in a language which is alien to our ordinary consciousness. When I stated the early part of the dream as an analogy it suddenly reminded him of his wife's comment. "You are killing yourself by working so hard." Once the dreamer has a foothold on the general meaning of the dream then they can work out the rest. The dream said this act is healing (holding the curled hand over the heart) so I asked him to come back to this healing gesture until he could understand it. I am inclined to accept any meaning assigned by the dreamer that fits with the dream. The process of a dreamer working out a dream is clearly one of getting in touch with one's self, specifically with one's higher self. When the young man was in deep sleep, having given up all controls, the higher self could speak freely. Its concern was to correct a pattern which in some ways was self-destructive, and to show the way toward self-healing.

I have long puzzled as to why this odd language. Why not just state the truth? For one thing the Dream Maker wants to leave the dreamer free to pay attention or to forget it. For another *the dreamer must approach the very nature of the Dream Maker* in order to work it out. Dreams are a lot easier to work out in the very mood and feeling of the dream process itself.

Overall I would say these things of the Dream Maker:

1. The Dream Maker is most apparent when the individual has given up all conscious controls and functions.

2. The Dream Maker is very concerned with the real nature and quality of each person's life.

3. The Dream Maker comes from a higher viewpoint that includes both what is wrong and a solution appropriate to the individual's nature.

4. The natural analogical language of the Dream Maker leaves us free, but enables access if we approach the life of the Dream Maker.

I don't feel it is too great a stretch to say that dreams are an influx from God. Who else is ever-present and concerned with the nature and quality of our life, even when we are sound asleep? Dreams are an influx from the Divine. Unfortunately, except for a few instances, they are mostly neglected by spiritual seekers.

The Hypnogogic State

The hypnogogic state is that transition between sleeping and waking, which we pass through into and out of sleep. Everyone on earth goes through the hypnogogic state at least twice daily, yet this state is still barely-known (43). In this state we are conscious and yet still close enough to the inner that if we pause on this borderline state we can directly observe influx taking place. For many years I was so busy I could do no real research, so I took to examining events in the hypnogogic state. Very similar events can be invoked in meditation. In both the hypnogogic and in meditation, deliberately doing nothing aids the recognition of direct influx. Similar experiences are also reported in sensory deprivation in which sensory input to eyes, ears, or touch is eliminated. In experimental sensory deprivation, you float in darkness in water at body temperature. I have not had this experience, but it is reported that in minutes one enters upon intense visionary experience. It seems that whatever mind is, if it is not occupied it will quite naturally occupy itself in its own creations. If you are conscious when all doing is shut off, you can then experience the inner going about its own way.

This morning I lay in bed to return once again to this state, doing nothing but looking for what might arise. After a while I picked up, "been going on." It was not really heard. It was the direct infusion of a noetic idea. You suddenly think something even though what was "said" was not anticipated, and not created by you. What you are experiencing is the sudden automatic appearance of a representation of your state. In my experience it is frequently in rather terse statements. I took it to be saying that though I was looking for the influx of experience it had actually been going on all along. This influx is very delicate. Its sudden appearance alerts one, and this arousal may result in our cutting it off or shortening it. I briefly scribble each item given, and then return to this inner state.

In this state I kept sensing unclear traces of meaning and suddenly got "catapult." I have not thought of catapults in many years. But I recognized the imagery. I was looking for something and it suddenly appears just like a catapult lobs stones over a wall. I was again observing it when I got "an actor." This one was especially surprising to me. I feel it meant not that I was an actor, but that it was. An actor portrays any assigned role. It is as though my interior set, as little as it was, was assigning it a role which it took and acted.

It is also possible to pose a question in this state and get an answer. I asked "Was God present?" and got one word, "state." This was a very condensed answer that I need to elaborate on. When I ask, "Is God present?" I am thinking in Western terms, asking if a being is present. It gave me a very Buddhist answer; not an object-like person but a state of being. I believe that the Buddhist conception of the One as a state is more accurate than the Western idea.

I can also give an example which involves both image and word. In the hypnogogic state I am focusing on the richness of what is present. Suddenly an image flashes for a fraction of a second. I see a man with his thumb and forefinger held up to a make a "U." I got the suggestion of "about to take hold of something," then peacefulness. His name is Ulloa. I know the significance of his name is in its sound quality. The "Ul" is "about to take hold," a high point "ll," that ends peacefully "oa." The name has a peaceful rising and falling that ends in the peaceful acquiescence of "oa." In the background I see a large body of tranquil water stretching away and having the quality of "oa."

I was trying to grasp the richness of what is present. This is represented in the man's finger position and also in what was represented by his name/nature. These meanings were also reflected in the peaceful body of water. I do not in the least feel I could create such a complex representation in the fraction of a second that it was simply given to me. I was led to feel the essence of grasping, including the peaceful satisfaction that follows a successful grasping, a coming to understanding.

Dreams are only a longer version of this innate capacity of the spirit to represent. The spirit is quite able to create such images endlessly. Perhaps it is the same process that creates our world experience, which is like a long dream. If you do nothing and simply leave yourself open to whatever comes, then it is possible to watch this marvelous inner process go on, spontaneously portraying your state and its nature. We can better see these undercurrents of life flowing in us when *we do nothing*. I have an example written two centuries ago by Swedenborg, showing how awareness of influx can lead directly into mystical experience.

> As often as I have recited the Lord's Prayer I have had the plain feeling of being raised towards the Lord, as though I was being hauled up. At these times my ideas were open and communication with some communities in heaven was consequently established. I have also noticed that the Lord flowed into each detail of the Prayer and so into every specific idea in my thought gained from the meaning of the things stated in the Prayer. This influx has been indescribably varying, that is to say, it has not been the same on one occasion as on another. This also proved how boundless were the things contained in each detail of the Prayer, and that the Lord was present in each of those details.
> —E. Swedenborg, *Arcana Caelestia* (10, #6476)

This morning when I was in the inner state I also noticed a parallel phenomenon. If I become conscious of outside sounds while in this state, they become mixed with inner experiences. I heard a distant motor shut off and wind down to a stop. I realized that both the motor and I were relaxing. I heard a distant hammering and the meaning came to me, "I am present." Years ago I was meditating with classical music on and fell into a state where suddenly I experienced myself most distinctly creating the music on the radio! This merging of the inner and the outer also occurs spontaneously in mystical experience. I was once in deep spiritual experience when a large moth showed up and was fluttering around. It was somewhat distracting, so I commanded it to light on the arm of my chair near my hand and stay there. It did, and stayed there. The next day I found it dead in the same spot. The feeling is one of a synchronicity or a harmony between the inner and the outer which is often not apparent.

After much exploration of this spontaneous influx within, I then began to notice the same thing in my daily experience. An idea or an insight would suddenly pop into my head. It had "been going on" all the time! Once I was carrying out the garbage when I noticed the cool moist quality of the air and went into a momentary ecstacy. The air had just the quality it had in many boyhood mystical experiences. The inner process is quite capable of suddenly bringing up a subtle memory like this. Often we take credit for this; after all it was my memory. Yet why do I recall it just now as I am carrying out the garbage? It felt like a reassurance that I was still in the same marvelous world I had known as a boy.

Let us stand back for a moment and see what we can learn from these experiences. In our interior is a very creative force. We lie down and fall asleep, "dead to the world" and are put through very imaginative scenes which vary all the way from light comments on our life all the way to big dreams which are capable of showing one's destiny. If we remain awake but simply try to be open, a very similar process goes on, as the busy inner presents representations of what is going on. In this inner world we are in a timeless sort of world where inner and outer merge. Outer sounds acquire personal meaning; the feel of the evening air can carry us back to childhood.

What in us is active even when we are not? I once picked up the statement, "The death of the ego is the birth of all else," meant as a cosmic law. It is like that. The hypnogogic is such a gentle process it will not reveal its presence until ego is out of the way. When we get out of the way, the underlying life can then be found, endlessly representing our state. It is an intelligence behind our intelligence, a shy and most gentle intelligence with apparently endless creative capabilities. It doesn't tire; when we are worn out and asleep it shows itself. It is not as though we have too little divine guidance; we have plenty. The mystic appreciates and welcomes this guidance.

Influx is the very process by which the Lord rules all. This process comes through the heavens and hells to us here in this choice point called world. Although it is a bit subtle, especially if you have not looked for it, this influx can easily be confirmed in your own experience. To me this is the greatest news ever. Considerate forces study and report to me on my progress nightly. I am not adrift if these forces are present and willing to reveal themselves to me. I can even talk with them and ask questions. Just be quiet and let them be. "Be still and know that I am God" (Psalms 46:10). Thankfully what is in us is moved by some inner drive to reveal itself. It reveals ourself to us and itself simultaneously, because ultimately they are the same. That is why we must discover ourselves on the way to the Divine.

Meditation

The key to dreaming and the hypnogogic state is that we are doing practically nothing but observing what is given by influx. This same can be true for meditation, which is one of the most fundamental spiritual methods. There are two basic starting paths in meditation. In one you concentrate on some mental content, such as love, or any ideal. In the other you find a comfortable position and do nothing except notice what happens. Swedenborg's way was to focus on some spiritual matter and then enter a state in which this matter was illustrated from within. Concentration is a difficult way, because the more you attempt to visualize one thing, the more you are likely to become aware of everything else. In much of concentration meditation the focus is lost and people wander aimlessly in inner processes.

I recommend simply doing nothing and noticing what happens. You might aid this by resting your gaze on a burning candle, a spot on the wall, or a religious object. I use my icon to anchor me in the spiritual realm. There has been much work in the East using awareness of breathing as the anchor, or recitation of a mantra; in Christianity one can use the Jesus prayer. My use of an icon is almost unknown in Orthodox Christianity, but meditation on a religious painting is widely known in the Hindu and Buddhist literature.

The various traditions tend to emphasize one approach over others, and personal preference is relevant. I discourage any dispute as to what is the best way. My answer is, best for whom? I tried all the ways and found that gazing at a picture in total silence worked best for me. All these methods are basically similar, because they all use something very simple to focus the attention, and you are doing remarkably little else. Without some sort of focus you might easily simply fall asleep, or wander aimlessly, lost in thinking.

Those who haven't meditated often wonder what goes on. A

very great deal. When the mind is stilled, then you encounter all your underlying tendencies. It is a pure voyage into influx. Things are given, out of the blue. You can then strike up a friendship with influx itself, asking questions as Swedenborg did. It can be a tremendous journey into all that exists beyond us. I have enough for two volumes on what I found while just gazing at my icon. I am quite in accord with all the ancient traditions that see meditation as a royal road to understanding. Close to meditation are the enjoyment of pure silence, and silent prayer, which has also been called prayer of the heart. Each of these ways needs to be practiced for months to really get into what is involved. All of these ways put the thinking-ego-mind on as slow an idle as possible. You might think that inwardly reciting the Jesus prayer is certainly doing something, but after it is said for days, it becomes automatic, and you find it saying itself. While the restless ego is occupied, you begin to notice what else is present. Countless times I have known a great sea of wisdom ready to answer any bidding. You find that the wisdom you seek has been seeking you. When the wisdom you seek answers, there is a wonderful ecstasy—friends so glad to find each other again. Meditation which starts out as a way to find influx can also become a way to enlightenment.

Asceticism and the Demonic

In their search for God, many somehow think they are unworthy, or that any deep pleasure is highly suspect. There are also those who are simply curious about demons. They would like to be frightened by one—but not too much—as in a scary TV show. Others believe that no great vision can be given without great suffering. The ascetic way satisfies all of these. Many of the great mystics have tried ascetic self-denial, including Buddha, and perhaps Christ in his forty days in the desert. St. Seraphim of Sarov made a major journey into asceticism by kneeling on a rock for over a year. Most mystics have tried some periods of self-denial and often have discarded it, deciding it was not a useful path. I was pleased when an experienced Roman Catholic abbot called asceticism "sportive." It is like showing off your spiritual muscle, and any showing off is of ego, not the spiritual.

Suppose someone came to me wanting to encounter demons. They were willing to follow any program which is supposed to evoke demons for a period of two weeks. My study of the lives of saints has made it abundantly clear how demons arise. I would tell my foolish friend to deny all bodily satisfaction for two weeks and he will meet very convincing demons long before the time is up. He must live naked in the cold, not sleep, not bathe, not eat or drink, and above all avoid all sex or even thoughts of sex. If he can think of other bodily denials, such as pain, add these too. It would help very much if I could lock him into this effort. To that end I would say that the Devil himself will come to tempt him out of his brave effort. But at all costs he must resist the Devil.

All this denial would evoke a host of demons. With heavy eyelids he would dream of sleeping, and demons like conscience would come to torment him awake. If denying sex is a problem, then the world would get full of suggestions of sex. He will see bees flying from sex organ to sex organ of the flowers in a wanton way. He might reflect on what a powerful spiritual being he was, only to shiver naked in the cold, knowing full well he was among God's stupidest creations. It would not be long to tormenting voices and ghastly images. If I could really get him to suspect the Devil's handiwork at every turn, then the process of meeting the demonic would be hastened. Say one dark night he is shivering and saying to himself, "I am a plain idiot to do this." Of course he is, but I want him to suspect *that this thought itself is the very temptation of the Devil* so he will turn against even his own common sense and his own nature. That will really produce demons. At the end of two weeks he is likely to be quite mad, having lost track of time and living completely in a wild, chaotic, demonic world. It might even be difficult to rescue him.

I have met the demonic many times in patients. The demonic arises when the person turns against their own nature. This splits the person into the ego self and a wild host of other possibilities which can include elements of hell and of the collective unconscious. If we fight against our own nature it will come out of the walls and attack us in its desire to also live. These alien elements are sometimes quite positive or heavenly, but more often they are quite hellish. I met an old-world German woman with a classical pitchfork devil. He tormented her genitals with an incredible itch. Her physician said there was no visible disease he could control. She was a bit old for raging sexual needs, so I guessed it was the larger womanly role she had rejected.

I worked for two years with a schizophrenic man, a Roman

Catholic, who was bent on denying sensual needs to become a saint
(44). He lived in a world alive with sensual suggestions. Meanwhile
this college-educated man was almost totally unable to work. He
even failed at a job hammering in tacks, because he got into too big
a moral issue over their exact placement. I had a woman patient
whose demons shouted at her in an inhumane way. She had become
quite mad and murdered her husband. It took some time to establish a dialogue with her demons. Just before they disappeared they
indicated they just wanted her to love her son. She had gotten into
denying this love in her futile attempt to save her failing marriage.

In both patients and in the lives of saints the equation seems
much the same. Tell me what your demons are up to, and I will
know what you have not accepted of your natural humanity. Demons tempt along the lines of our central tendencies. Buddha met
beautiful dancing girls, so sensuality probably was a problem for
him. Christ met a demon who tempted him to demonstrate he was
the Son of God. After forty days of fasting, Christ was approached
by the tempter to change rocks into bread. He answered right out
of God's word, "It is written one does not live by bread alone." The
Devil put him on the pinnacle of a temple and addressed him again
as the Son of God and tempted him to jump off and be held up by
angels. Again he answered out of the word, "Do not put the Lord
your God to the test." In both instances he was tempted as the son
of God, his real nature. In both cases he answered as the word
itself.

In all religious traditions it is written one must not try to tempt
God. The situation is ridiculous on the face of it. It is like an ant
looking up at a giant man, and pulling himself up to his full minus-
cule height, saying, "If you are God you will not step on me."
Perhaps the giant man did not hear, or heard and stepped anyway
and the ant disappeared. God might decide that such vanity is best
ended. Those who try to tempt God actually try *themselves*. If a
member of a snake-handling cult tells all his peers he can handle a
poisonous snake, he is saying, "I am spiritual, God is with me, watch
me and see." It is a pure play of vanity. He then struggles within himself: "Am I protected by God, or will I die?" If the snake does not
bite, the crowd is impressed, and he has to do more demonstrations
of his spiritual powers. He becomes elevated in his mind and in the
minds of others, but what is his eternity? Swedenborg once
remarked that if God had totally condemned a person he would give

them everything they asked for. If we get all we ask for, we conclude that we are god-like, and fill with pride. Swedenborg describes a miserable place in hell for those who would try this. There is endless pretense here, but their lives lack substance, for eternity.

One of the most foolish cases I heard of was a Hindu holy man who pledged to his followers that he would transcend the need to urinate. He didn't make it. I forget what demons came to shout in his ear. Urination is so simple, part of the natural functions of our body. Do it, get it over with, and don't get attached to it. Non-attachment is a central Hindu doctrine, yet this holy man was announcing his attachment to the outcome. As a mystic I would rather go in the opposite direction. Piss, and reflect that I am a very ordinary human being, and kin to the whole animal kingdom.

Demons are simply influx that comes to illustrate our stupidity. It is dangerous to forget our real nature, and wall it off so much that it has to come crashing through the walls. A basic part of our task, our learning, is knowing and accepting what is. We are to understand and come into harmony with it. So rather than try to transcend pissing, piss and reflect on all it shows you. It is a holy duty to care for the body/temple. Certainly you can work what St. Francis referred to as Brother Body until it falls down and dies, but this prematurely cuts off your uses in this world.

You can also evoke demons by completely disregarding your own needs for the sake of others, or disregarding others' needs for your own personal gain. If in all things we regard ourselves, our welfare, above all others, and act accordingly, we are choosing hell, because the central characteristic of hell is turning against a more natural balance which includes us with all others. I may not exclude the rights of all others for my own sake. Others will intrude, complain, come to fight with me, and disturb me, or I may be arrested and imprisoned. By making myself the sole focus, I so limit my existence as to be deprived, even if I do not appear to suffer in any obvious outer way. The way to heaven is consideration of *yourself with others*, in finding a balance between your needs and others'.

I wish we could open up lives to show their full inner qualities and essentials. Then we would clearly see that the lives of some who seem fortunate are actually barren and deprived. We would also see that some who seem to live a limited and deprived existence, like a contemplative in a cave, have experienced so much as to be among the richest of all.

General Aspects of Influx

We have looked first at the most easily identified signs of influx in dreams, the hypnogogic, and in meditation. The pattern of all of these is to suspend personal effort of all kinds, in order to open to the underlying life processes which are given to us. Most spiritual seekers rarely use dreams, and the hypnogogic is little-known. Their most common practice is meditation. There are many spiritual practices which resemble meditation, such as silent prayer, just silence, or the use of a mantra. A central value of any practice which reveals influx occurring is that it tends to dethrone ego. Any spiritual practice which shows you influx leads you to find yourself existing in, and even embedded in, processes far larger than your understanding. In general these processes lead one gently into what turns out to be both self-discovery and cosmic discovery at the same time, for these two are really one.

It would be worthwhile to discuss what happens when you discover you are in the midst of influx. Say you are meditating and you find something is really stirring in you. For instance when I practiced simply gazing at an icon I was led so deep into my own feelings the process puzzled me (4). At first I confused it with depression. Was I being led into depression? I felt led into reading the *Philocalia*, a collection of Eastern Orthodox wisdom. Through this I finally recognized the state I was being led into was humility. So then I read all I could find on humility. In the spiritual quest humility is the greatest gift. Once I understood that, there was no longer any difficulty arising out of my icon experience. I was overjoyed to be led into the very heart of humility. I had already found evidence that the icon-gazing led me into processes that were quite simply far wiser than I was.

Occasionally I have known people to go mad in the midst of spiritual discovery, but the error here seems to be too little understanding, and too little guidance by experienced others, leading the seeker to mistakenly turn against natural influx. When people turn against what is really a cosmic process, they create all sorts of difficulties.

When you are in the very grip of influx, it becomes critical to reflect, and it is also appropriate to check all that one is given. A few foolish people, the moment they hallucinate any voice assume it must be from God. Not necessarily. I have done this with schizophrenic patients, in which hallucinations contended they were God. I cured one lady by simple tests which showed that her hallucinations were wrong! She came to doubt them, and they vanished.

In an opposite way, it can be a high point of one's life to find one is in the hands of the living God. There are many signs of this, all of them generally showing that the source of the influx is much wiser than the individual. Another sign is that the source fits with the deepest religious tradition. One's tradition can be your personal guru if there are no other competent ones around. When I found that saints writing centuries ago spoke to what was happening to me, then I could accept it easily. Mystics who really find God end up not only supporting their tradition, but usually deepening its meaning. I am a mystic of all traditions so I tend to support all of them. I suggest turning to a guru of your own tradition as part of the check on whatever is given to you, using your own common sense and judgment. What God wants is that you come into the Kingdom wide awake, having experienced and freely chosen this way. When Swedenborg was asked, "What is the real purpose of human existence?" his answer was "That there be a heaven of the human race." But heaven is not just a place. Heaven is the gathering of those who have gone through life and have freely decided to seek harmony with existence so they can be in heaven "where the joy of one is the joy of all." This is the real purpose of human existence.

Having worked with the influx from God for some while, I can add other clues for seekers. What we are dealing with shows ultimate wisdom. It sees way beyond this moment and your simple desires. It can respond either inwardly or in outer events. You never know what or where. So what is the real boundary between us and it? The first approximate boundary has on one side all you deliberately do. On the other side is all that is given to you inwardly or outwardly. For example, when in the hypnogogic state, I received "catapult," I knew I had not created it. Besides, the word represented such an old idea, and it was an image of the hypnogogic state itself where a stone suddenly comes over the wall right at us. So the boundary of influx has our work on one side and what is given internally or externally on the other side.

To someone who has worked a long while with influx there is no real difference between the mysterious inside of us and events from the world. So when I am impatient to get somewhere in a hurry I have not the slightest surprise that all of the slowest cars in town are programmed to be right in front of me. I take it as a cosmic joke—a cosmic finger pointing and saying, "Here, learn patience." Similarly I have not been surprised to be given extra-sensory perception when I needed to see into someone else's life.

Over the long run the person who finds influx can find all the guidance they desire. My own deepest wish is to see into the highest nature of things, and I would say I have abundant guidance. But if you try to turn influx to lesser uses, to make money or get fame in the eyes of others, it simply will not guide to this end. Mahatma Gandhi had in mind the welfare of a whole people, so he was guided to this end. That he got fame was incidental, and of no consequence to him.

Along the path of guidance by influx *you are in the hands of a wisdom that knows you very well.* In dreams it comments on your faults and struggles. Influx provides what you need and are ready for. It is like a teacher who knows you are in the second grade in reading and knows exactly what you need to learn to reach the third grade. It is slow, patient, knowing that it has an eternity of time. It can lead you through apparently unjust and unreasonable outer circumstances into just the experiences that shape you for an eternal end. The better you can see your own nature, your real love of the life, the more you can cooperate in this process, rather than complain at every little thing that doesn't go your way. Is influx always spiritual? Yes and no. If your deepest interests are material—such as laying bricks—then influx is quite capable of leading you through everything of bricks. But, over a lifetime of pursuing one's interest, it does tend to lead into larger and larger considerations. The gifted brick layer comes into management of brick layers! The larger aspect.

Those who understand influx from God have profound advantages. If they really want to see into their nature they are aided in this quest. Coming to know themselves, they begin to see the order of things. Seeing the overall order of things, they can cooperate in the design. The general direction of all this is toward a harmony with existence. We can clearly see the opposite of this—people who have no sense of the design of things who come into a chronic disharmony. Even if they get rich and famous, their life is still essentially a ruin. The way to heaven is to come into a general understanding of how our lives are in the hands of Wisdom.

It Is All Influx!

Earlier I described the locus of the boundary between us and influx at the division between what we ourselves are doing and what is given to us. If you really explore influx, even this boundary begins to blur. In meditation you can actually look at the currents which shape your life. Precognitive dreams exist and suggest that at some level critical turns in your life are known ahead of time. As you explore your ideals you may realize that these, too, were given to you. So you are following something preprogrammed into you. At the moment I have a bluejay nest near the house outside my bedroom window. I can see four chicks with eyes now open. Clearly animals (and ourselves) are programmed for the whole process of procreation.

In the mystic's greatest vision it becomes apparent that all life is influx. There really is only God, and this Ultimate One manifests down through the spiritual worlds and through us to this world. There is really only one life. Swedenborg says we really are recipient vessels. Life is poured into our vessel selves. Along with this general influx there is also given a sense *as if* we run ourselves. I have traced this same insight in Advaita Vedanta, the Jewish Kabalah and in Buddhism and Christianity. Love wills that what is its own becomes another's.

Can you personally check on this? Yes. If you really withdraw into yourself and look really closely and long it should become apparent to you that your life/consciousness simply comes into being. Do you personally set about to create your own awareness? Moment by moment it is simply just there. None of us really knows what it is, or how to create it. Your body/senses are like a clay pot. Life is simply poured into the pot. Crack the pot here or there and life is no longer given. The near-death experience strongly suggests that the life, which is really what we are, goes on separately from the clay pot. We adjust our eyes to see something, but what is sight itself?

> From these considerations it also becomes clear how much a person is swayed by the illusions of the senses who believes that the eye sees, when in fact it is the sight of his spirit, which sees by means of the eye.
> —E. Swedenborg, *Arcana Caelestia* (10, #1954)

Influx is discovered when we do nothing and simply become acquainted with the life in us which goes on anyway. Influx is a higher guidance system in which we are led by an ultimate wisdom which knows us very well. As we come to accept that our lives are embedded in a higher wisdom, we gradually come into accord with the whole design of existence. Further along this path we find the ultimate—that there is only a God of love which created all there is, and is the Source, the Sustainer and the ultimate nature of all there is.

It is a step forward to discover the existence of influx, the larger-than-ourselves, in the midst of our living. It is a further step forward to discover in this influx a guiding intelligence which is wiser than we are. When you choose to use this wisdom to shape your life you are on the path to enlightenment and harmony with all that is. Enlightenment is a personal discovery that allows you to reaffirm the ancient traditions that there is only God. At no point in this is it necessary to suspend good judgment and common sense, for it is an essential part of heaven that it be formed of experienced people who have freely chosen to be a part of all that is.

Section III

The Experience as a Process

The individual's seeking,
and God's response,
as an understandable process.

10

Your Personal Relationship to the Divine

Religiousness means engaging the sacred. It means having a focus, a point of engagement. These points are the earthly embodiments of the gods: incarnations, authorities, priests, and a multitude of symbolic objects.

A god is not just a bare object like a statue in a museum but part of a bilateral relationship. A god is a god of someone or *to* someone. Only in the eyes of a religious person can a god be a god as such. A god is a category of social, interactive behavior, experienced in a way that is analogous to the experience of other selves. With gods one receives, gives, follows, loves, imitates, communes, negotiates, contests, entrusts. A god is a subject to us as objects and an object to us as subjects. We address it, or it can address us. Part of this relational quality is evident in the etymology of the English term *god*, which traces back to a root that means either "to invoke" or "sacrificed to."

The religious meaning of a god lies in what one does in the presence of the god. If gods are not just objects but constituted by forms of behavior between subjects, this relational universe sharply contrasts with antiseptic, demystified world of scientific language where the earth is not a place of any exchange or engagement where nothing is addressable. In this absence of dialogue, scientific language flattens everything it sees into data, but in the language of

gods, the world is experienced through categories of invo-
cation, listening, and respect."
                —William Paden, *Religious Worlds* (36, p. 124f)

I want to reemphasize that the process of the individual approaching God and finding God's response is profoundly simple. All
the varied methods that have been described, both East and West,
have certain basic elements. The individual may choose an approach that comes right out of their culture, or they may develop
their own. I have done both, experimenting in this area for decades.
I believe we are different enough that each person will likely do better in one approach than another. The method that is most suitable
for you may simply feel more relaxing and peaceful. I was attracted
to the use of a religious image even before I started systematic work
with it. Swedenborg followed several ways, including dream inter-
pretation. But when he read the Bible as though God were present
in it, and speaking to him, this approach must have suited him best,
because he abandoned every other way and kept to this way the rest
of his life (45).
    The method that is right for you will lead to relaxation and
peace from the beginning, even before you see any signs of God's
presence. Since God is present and knows what will work for you,
and is willing to lead you to it, you can trust your intuition about
method. You could begin by praying over this issue itself, looking
for suggestions that just pop into your head. I have sometimes been
led into a bookstore, to a particular section and to a particular book.
Intuition can also be mixed with some doubts. When I was first led
to gaze at an icon every day, part of me also thought, "This is a weird
thing to do." In the beginning I had some concern that perhaps I was
wasting time. I gradually, experimentally, worked out the details:
which icon, viewed where, at what distance, etc. Each of these
points was settled just by what felt right. When I found I was in such
an eternal timelessness that I lost all sense of clock time, I started
recording time just to keep track of what was happening. So, in
selecting a practice, I would recommend:

    1) looking at your tradition,
    2) praying for guidance,
    3) experimenting,
    4) following intuition, and

5) looking for a certain sense of peace and elevation as though something may be here.

These are sufficient clues for each to find a way that suits. There is no exact right way. A way that seems perfectly stupid, such as looking at tea leaves in the bottom of a cup, can work if you feel drawn to it and approach it in the right spirit. What then is the right spirit? You assume that God is ever-present and you have chosen to meet here, in whatever situation you have selected. It is very like a lover going to a street corner every night with the feeling that the beloved will come. It is unlike the human situation in which your beloved may well not know you are there. In this case your beloved knows full well you are there and is always there waiting for you.

Let us follow the image of meeting on a street corner as a representation of the essence of all possible approaches. You are going to go there and wait persistently for signs of the beloved, who knows you are waiting. There is another way in which the situation is unlike waiting for a person. In this case you really don't know what your beloved looks like, or how he/she will appear. The more demands you put on the situation, the more you will delay the appearance. If you assume that God will ride up like a knight in shining armor on a white horse, you may have to wait a long while.

A far better assumption is that you have no idea how the lover will appear, and all that is not the direct effect of your own will may well be the lover. You decide only that you will stand here and wait, and long for the beloved. Let's say a gentle fog comes up, and swirls around on the ground at your feet. You may have already foolishly said, "This is fog, not my beloved." But having nothing else to do, you study the gentle movement of the fog and you begin to feel a kind of magic harmony. It is as though the gentle swirls are demonstrating life, how it flows, spirals, turns, how it lies on the ground. After the appointed period of waiting (and you can stay longer if you want) you leave with a subtle feeling that everything is all right.

Did the lover come? Remember the dictum. If you didn't fashion it, God did. Yes, the lover came. You could put it down to mere fog and fancy if you want, but that would rob you of the gift that was given. Is it better to be a clever skeptic and put it down to fog and fantasy, or to allow even fog to instruct you? Once you learn your beloved is there, but perhaps shy and modest, and can come in any form, then you develop the capacity to see what others cannot see, and to be instructed by the least thing. The lover was there not only in the form of the fog but also in the meanings that flowed into you by influx while reflecting on the fog. You were being shown cosmic things. It is unlikely that you would come away from the meeting with your beloved with a lot of ideas you can easily spell out to others. "I was shown thus and so." Most, or all of it, is deeper than your rational wordy self. You were being shown through the inner essentials of your life. It is characteristic of the beloved to come in your deepest feelings, in your spiritual being. If you told me the next day that someone came and told you a lot of clever things, I would say that is not the way of the beloved. The way of the beloved is Gentleness and Subtlety Itself.

If you have just begun to have meetings with your Beloved, I recommend you not tell *anyone*, because your relationship with the Beloved is not yet established. It is young, delicate, and tentative. If you have any concerns about the relationship, share them with the Beloved, even though the Beloved already knows. You need to speak of them to yourself to make your concerns clear to you, and to seek the Beloved's guidance on this. Generally the Beloved is so totally considerate that you are likely to have no such concerns. But if you tell other people, they may cast doubts, and your relationship will suffer from these doubts. Persist, learn, and tell no one until the relationship is solid and secure. Others don't need to know, and they will be unable to sense the validity of your experience unless they have been through a similar experience themselves.

The Signs of God's Presence

I have had a number of people come to me when they were in this tentative stage of the relationship asking, "Is this God?" They came to me because they felt I would understand. I look for a few simple things which mark their experience as of God.

1. Have they been modest, not bragging, and tending to withhold and conceal the experience because it felt sacred to them? If the experience is not broadcast to gain recognition, vanity and ego is not involved. Often there is an inner certainty of the validity of the experience. But where the person is not experienced with the spiritual, there can also be doubt. The fact that they are acting as though protecting the sacred may be something they haven't verbalized, but it will be there. Somehow they feel that the experience involves their depth and even their life and destiny.

2. Did it mobilize their whole spiritual being, so that they easily come to tears when speaking of it? Strong feelings mobilized in depth means that this was not a construct of fantasy, something closer to consciousness, but is in depth, beyond where they have dominion and control.

3. Was the effect of their experience spiritually good? Spiritual good gently leads toward a broader and more harmonious life. It includes most of the things people would call good. God may do something totally beyond my ken, but if its effect is of simple good, you need look no further for its author.

4. Does the telling of the experience to me also mobilize my feelings and produce tears? Can I feel God's presence in it? This may not be an appropriate sign for others, but is true for me. The feeling for me is of great joy that someone else has been given an experience of God.

If the answer to all these questions is yes, I have no trouble saying, "Yes, it is of God." I came to these criteria purely by experience. I have not seen them set down anywhere else.

Once I was in the odd position of being able to give a knighthood in the Orthodox Church. I very much wanted to give it to someone worthy. The priest picked out an old woman who was always ready to help. I was left alone with her in the church kitchen. At first I asked of her and seemed to run into a block. She didn't want to speak of herself. In a pause in the conversation she looked around the kitchen at what needed doing. So I spoke of the joy of doing for others. At this she visibly brightened and came alive. Her spiritual way was the simple good of service to others. She would not consider an honor. She was already inwardly honored beyond her dreams.

I have long ago abandoned the idea that a spiritual person ought to appear dignified, handsome, or special in any way. I am quite used to finding it in anyone, anywhere. I was examining a black alcoholic burglar who had become so mentally ill he was on a back ward. I saw him staring down at the floor, and asked what he saw there. He answered that he was being shown the struggles of all minority groups down through history. This inner education had gone on for weeks. He said he was too unworthy for this revelation, reminding me he was a drunken burglar. I simply said he must somehow be worthy, and he broke into tears. My recognition triggered his own recognition, which was emotionally realized in the tears. This crazy useless drunken burglar had in him a great potential for understanding the struggle of all minorities.

I had momentary trouble with two cases which might be illustrative. I already mentioned that an old woman held back from asking me until a whole crowd had cleared. She did not want anyone else to hear her question. She recounted a short dream in which a Golden Sun came to her and asked if this was God. I was inclined to give her my standard answer that we have to study the dream. Suddenly I saw she was near death and was desperate to know if she had met God once. The experience hit me first. I affirmed it was God, and we both cried. Was it good she should think thus? Yes, of course. She was near the end of life and needed my support in the belief she had met God. Also she was a follower of Swedenborg and he describes how God appears as a Golden sun. It was merely the suddenness of such a question out of the blue that threw me for a moment. When we both cried there was no further affirmation necessary.

I have already mentioned the example of the wife of a minister who took me aside. She was reluctant to speak so I had to inquire. A real man, known to her, had come to her and said that her father who was dead wanted to reconcile with her. She cried. However strange it sounded, she knew he was a genuine messenger of God. I cried too. I counselled her to follow the lead given and pray to resolve differences with her father. Was it good? That is easy. To establish love where it is absent is always good.

Opposite experiences occur when someone comes to me basically in a bragging mood, asking me to confirm than they are quite special. Vanity is not of spiritual good. One woman claimed to see auras, but in a simple test I found her *less* perceptive than average people. I found myself just unimpressed. In the spiritual realm, status, degrees, education, all these outer things mean nothing. I found genuine visions in a criminal who experienced them in solitary confinement, while I generally do not find them in priests and ministers.

I feel it my duty to confirm even little experiences, to raise people's confidence, and to encourage them to continue to seek and find more. Most of those who come to me and ask about their experiences are beginners in the process, and the beginning experiences are the hardest of all to recognize. I especially like to see people become established in some sort of practice and enter upon a relationship with God.

I have hardly used the word enlightenment for this experience of God, because the word has acquired a meaning which I feel is a mis-direction, particularly for a beginner. "Enlightenment," "moksha" in the Hindu, "satori" in Zen, etc., all describe the same experience. The mis-direction is an overemphasis on one big experience. People expect it to be awesomely impressive. "It will be so big my whole life will be changed. People will see my radiance." Remember what I said in the introduction, "No Miracles, Please." Looking for one big experience tends to make people overlook all the tiny and almost ever-present experiences *which are the very foundation,* possibly leading to a big experience one day. The big one may never be given; that is a matter of the grace of God. The millions of tiny experiences are ever-present. They have always been with you. But you must do your work to find them, and through them to be changed and developed. How long does this spiritual process go on? It is endless, through this life and eternity. Our ignorance compared to God's is so great it will take forever.

Seeking the exceedingly rare big enlightenment can result in overlooking the beginnings of an eternal process of development that can be entered upon now. Some people also think that after a big experience nothing further needs to be done. I have had several giant visions complete with light, but I am not sure that they gave me any particular advantage. It is from that perspective that I encourage others to go the slow lowly way. Seeking one giant overwhelming vision is like expecting God to meet you in the form of a knight on a white horse, blinding you to God's ever-gentle presence and the instruction you are already receiving now by influx. What you are seeking is already occurring, and will occur forever. The little discoveries can be entered upon any time, anywhere. They also involve subtle inward changes which are integrated one by one into the very fabric of your being, opening you to more and more.

The beginnings of discovery are like finding that you have a handsome gazebo in your own garden. You had overlooked it before, because it was overgrown and off in a little-visited corner. You clean up the place and realize that here is your refuge from the stresses of the world. You can go there any time, and as you sit quietly, enjoying the life that surrounds you, you find that your inner priorities sort themselves out. What you had been neglecting is now found to be first in priority, while problems that seemed so central are now low on the list; they just don't matter that much. In your gazebo/refuge you gradually center. How? Who knows? Perhaps we are like a compass; once we quit shaking and turning the case, the needle settles down and becomes steady. Leave yourself alone, and you settle down; your direction becomes clear. The gazebo/refuge is an image of meditation or any other spiritual practice that works for you.

In your inner gazebo/refuge, problems insoluble in the world are easily solved. You are the understanding, the instrument, the means to all else. If this is destroyed, your world goes. If this is in crisis, the world you experience is all crisis. You are the way to the harmony of yourself and the world, so the first priority is to get your own life in order. There is a saying somewhere in the Bible that if one man is saved, the world is saved, and this is one of its meanings. When one person is in order, the world is in order. So though I have known big enlightenments, I prefer the little way, the slow little way of endless discovery. Each little discovery makes the day worthwhile. Each little one is enough in itself, because each little one is a reflection of the design of the whole, the all. The little way is a much more realistic picture of what anyone can easily find. When there are little gold coins lying everywhere, why seek vast wealth in some distant place, especially when one little coin is enough to enter paradise? There are quite enough for all. We are dealing with an incredible abundance.

The Paradox in the Divine/human Relationship

We may as well face the central paradox that occurs when the little human seeks to deal with God. It is very like a three-year-old asking you some question. Perhaps she asks where she came from? It seems a simple question. But does she mean her own body, her awareness, all life, ultimately, or is she asking of sex, or simply where she was born? As a parent you gauge your daughter's level of understanding, and try to answer in terms of that. You don't want to put her off. The question is quite all right, but is she ready for the whole of theology, sex, obstetrics, geography and genetics?

I find that God operates in much the same way with us, quite willing to answer, but aware of our situation and our limited understanding. At times I found that my question was met by silence and some days of internal changes. On the way to finally seeing the answer I was shown many clues, many associations, so rich I couldn't put them together at first. The answer was coming, but *I* was not yet prepared for it. When these changes were complete in me, then the answer was quite apparent. My "parent" was completely willing to answer, but had to prepare me to understand it. I see nothing wrong with individuals asking even great ultimate questions. But they should look closely at the answer they are now getting, and the personal preparation that may be required for full understanding.

There is also the paradox that God is aware of your ultimate destiny and works in time to that end. The poorest sort of asking is to pin all hope on God meeting you Tuesday morning in the bank to grant you a bank loan. Be God for a moment. You are ultimate freedom and someone asks you turn up Tuesday at 10 a.m. and grant a loan. Yes, if somehow your ultimate destiny would be furthered by this loan. But suppose you had been wasteful with money, playing too many schemes. Suppose a little poverty will be more educational. Will you, as ultimate freedom, do this bidding? Not likely. Much of God's apparent deafness rests on just this: we often desire what is not our ultimate good. Ask for things in the direction of your life's love and watch circumstances open up. At times I have been allowed to see my ultimate place in the scheme of things. Then it became quite clear why one way was blocked while another opened wide.

However, there is a kind of asking that is *always* in the direction of your destiny. It is asking for wisdom, understanding, patience, tolerance, love, all the virtues. They are in the cards for you, regardless of your path, and if you sincerely and patiently ask for them they will always be given. If you look at the contents of saints' prayers, this is their main request. Of course I am not speaking of simply mouthing words. Can you picture a God of All so stupid that he cannot tell in an instant, even before you speak, whether you mean it? I cannot. Words are not essential. The main value of words is for *you* to get straight in your head what you want. It may even help for you to say it out loud so you hear yourself saying it. In heartfelt prayer, the message gets delivered, for God is in your heart. And notice when it is answered, so that you discover yourself acting more virtuously. The process is the same as the lover waiting on the street corner. It is also important to realize when you are being answered, so that you may be thankful and learn more of the ways of your beloved.

I have had so many piddly little requests answered that I have gradually come to the conclusion that God is not too busy, and enjoys relating to me. I generally don't bother him over trivial things, but now and then I get stuck and ask God for help, and almost always he has. For example, I keep a record of all the household dues and subscriptions on a pack of about forty 3"x 5" cards. One day the whole pack vanished. It would take me two or three years to recreate it. Likely it was in my study, so I searched high and low for an hour. Finally I gave up, plopped in a chair and asked God to help me find them. It was as though a voice spoke and said, "Raise your eyes a little." When I did, I saw something sticking out of a book. It couldn't be, but yes, I had put the pack in a book as a bookmark and forgotten it. I have had so much help like this that I suspect mystery is friendly, that it wants to be remembered and called upon. I don't think the cards were the issue, but rather that I remember He is present and willing to help. Of course the whole losing, search, sitting right in front of the cards, and the answer were all designed that I might speak of it to you! All things are interrelated in this realm.

The idea that God is deaf or too busy simply is not true. It is our understanding and perception that is not sufficiently developed. Religious tradition indicates the omnipresent is always here and the omniscient knows before you speak. Your speaking your prayer is so that *you* may hear it. I would suggest diligent heartfelt prayer mostly for virtues. It is even better to rank the virtues and decide which is supreme for you. Though I would put less emphasis on asking for little things, perhaps your friend wouldn't mind.

If all your prayers remain unanswered, then it is time to work on the relationship; there is something awry in the understanding between you. If you are really turned down on something that seems reasonable to you, try to see your ultimate destiny in it. Figure that your friend has acted with ultimate love and consideration, and try to see what it is. And remember your own responsibility. Suppose a king was your close friend and would do almost anything for you. Would you ask him to scratch your back when you can do it perfectly well yourself?

Ultimately prayer is of the same fabric as your relationship to this one. Everything comes back to this friendship. I like the image of friendship because it implies two different people, yourself and God, and all of the experiences and feelings that go into it. Much is understood; friends don't need to analyze who did what. It is a very unequal friendship in a way; we are so stupid and our friend is wisdom itself. Our friend is also ever-present and has all the time in the world. Fortunately our friend launched us into existence and wants us to return home safely. It is only we who need to wise up. The main fault I would find with my friend is that he is too subtle, too patient. I wish he were a little cruder, more obvious, like me. But since my friend represents All There Is, then I will have to adjust.

A friend of mine once took the drug LSD and found he was playing cosmic chess against himself. What a hopeless game. If he won, he lost. God has all the cards, having designed me, my thoughts, all of it. This is the only game there is. And since the only way to win is to become like the Master Player, I best study the ways of the ultimate. Play with him and learn to be like Him. Since I can't make Him crude like me, I best learn to be gentle like Him, so we get along better. This is the trend of all religious traditions, that you become like the Ultimate. Why? It is for your own good, so you can get along better with all there is, including yourself.

The Relationship in a Formal Sense

If we look across religions, we see people relating to God in a great variety of ways, with ritual, ceremony, and prayer being prominent. In contrast with the formality of ceremony and spoken prayers, the simplest and most direct way is where one speaks or relates to the Divine inwardly, often right in the midst of daily activity. You speak your mind just as you feel it. This is the area of spontaneous prayer. What I will be saying on this is quite different from the bulk of texts on prayer.

Religion, and one's personal relationship to the Divine, is best understood from the top down, from its highest to its lowest level. In Christian terms I am dealing with God the father, in Hindu Brahman, in Islam Allah, in Judaism YHWH, etc. The first point is to bear in mind the nature of the One you are addressing, because this has a fundamental effect on your approach. Most of the great religious traditions identify at least three characteristics of God at this ultimate level.

1. This One is omnipresent, always present, everywhere. Inwardly or outwardly, there is no possibility of evading this presence. No matter where you are, or what is happening, this One is fully present.

2. This One is also omniscient, is all wisdom and knowledge itself. Omniscience also transcends time, knowing equally well what always was and will ever be. Again there is no possibility of hiding anything from omniscience, not even your most secret crime, or your most trivial act.

3. The third attribute that all the mystics and much of tradition accepts is omnipotence, all power. Omnipotence can create myriads of objects and beings and universes simultaneously, without effort. I once experienced everything being created, and it appeared to be done totally effortlessly. Obviously this is in marked contrast to our efforts which have trouble creating even small things. In some traditions there are more "omnis," such as infinite compassion. But these three are central when we seek to relate privately and inwardly to the Divine.

In view of these attributes, there is a tremendous difference in viewpoint between the Divine and the human. Misunderstanding this difference often gives some the impression that God is dead, deaf, or on vacation. For many there appears to be no One there to speak to. I myself felt for some years that God was gone, so my experience has included both absence and presence, and I can well understand those who feel frustrated in this area.

Often someone wants something and prays earnestly for it. They may get into long, repeated prayer, with the idea that God might pay better attention to more repetition. But this is forgetting omniscience which was already totally aware of what you will say, even before you say it. It also forgets omnipotence which created your very urge to ask, and omnipresence which is the easiest thing in the world to contact.

I have been shown some dim understanding of the fundamental difference between the Divine and human that results from omniscience. The Divine views us in our innermost potentials, what we will be in eternity, and acts towards this end. This is a viewpoint far larger than our small concerns to get this and that in the here and now. The Divine is like a parent who is ready to deny a child a toy towards some larger end in the child's eternal life. So the child pleads and even demands the toy, all the while finding it denied. The child may get angry and feel it has a bad parent. I, too, have asked for toys. After long experience I have come to a guiding principle in these cases. If something is consistently denied you, then seriously look in it for some hint and sign of your eternal. Instead of getting angry at the bad parent, look into it, and even pray to be shown the eternal uses in the situation. It is a part of God's wise compassion to firmly deny some things. Seek in it for some good.

Suppose you are given an intractable depression that prayer doesn't help. Then look for what is being accomplished in the depression. Very often the depressed person senses that old treasured values are falling down and dying. Many have gone through periods when most old friends turned against them. In the midst of this dying of old values and the absence of old friends, look for what tender shoots are beginning to grow. One or two things you neglected before interest you a little. Someone you previously paid little attention to begins to look like a real friend. Like the mystics before me, I am not making any distinction between inner or outer circumstances. It is adversity either way. Say you lost a loved one. It is all right and normal to go through a mourning over a loss of what was. It only prolongs and deepens the consequences of mourning if you don't face up to it. It aids progress if you look more deeply into it for what new is coming in the midst of it. Look for traces of light in the dark.

We are dealing with something so awesomely greater than ourselves in the three omnis that we best prepare to learn from any encounter. In my experience prayer is answered in subtle ways at the same time the petition is made. The wisdom ever-present is already answering in delicate inner states and trace inner leadings. If I were to complain on behalf of mankind, it would only be that the answer given is too subtle for most. Often in prayer I have felt my understanding opened, as though I am suddenly in the midst of new possibilities and new views of things, too rich and subtle to set down in words. What I had felt urgent a moment ago is suddenly seen as unimportant. It feels taken care of, even though it hasn't been taken care of in any practical sense. It is as though we approached our mother asking for gum. She didn't give us any, but turned and embraced us so warmly that gum no longer mattered. It is very like this when dealing with the Divine. The fundamental issue is always the love of God. In that love all other issues are solved. In view of this love the whole of life looks like a momentary educational travail, worth going through, in order to become wiser.

As you prepare to make your petition, consider that you are in the ever-presence of the One petitioned. It is you who had turned away and now turn back. Be aware that you address an omniscience that knows you incredibly better than you know yourself. While preparing to address the omniscient omnipresent it would be well to search your heart for what is of supreme importance to you and ask for this (46, 47). Why ask for gum or a toy when the whole universe is available? You are far more likely to be given what is of supreme importance to you than any gum or toy. If you take this seriously I could easily see you leaving behind all wordy petitions and falling into a reverie as to what is really, really in your heart. There are traditions in which one asks for what will most satisfy these desires of the heart even when they are unclear or unknown. It would not hurt to wordlessly dwell on this for months and years. Meanwhile, notice your heart and your experience opening up. God seems most deaf when we ask for too little. Of course this is another direct way into enlightenment. In the lives of saints it is obvious that many travelled this way. By entering into a search into your essential nature you are already on the way to the Divine, which then formulates your deepest wish, which is fulfilled. This way you open up the very source of joy which is the answer to any sort of quest. The further I explore in this realm the more I am impressed that our deepest satisfactions are a good guide, way beyond chewing gum and toys.

> When we feel ill,
> We seek health,
> Because a greater happiness lies that way.
> Similarly we try various things
> Until we find what we enjoy the most
> Drawn by the happiness it brings.
> So is it not apparent
> Happiness guides us
> On the way?
> Those who fear pleasure
> As though it leads astray
> Surely have not known
> The highest pleasure
> Which leads to
> Our place in the cosmos.

I know that Puritans and ascetics may fear the allure of lesser pleasures. They fear one might be destroyed by chewing gum and toys. Those who can be caught by lesser things have simply never felt the greater pleasure.

I will mention some personal incidents which curiously illustrate omnipresence. Years ago I was in a state where for an hour or so I was instructed that the Divine would manifest in my life in two ways. One was by light and the other by sound. Whenever I happened to be thinking of the Divine I would be shown an intense pale blue light if what I was thinking was true and a black dot if untrue. This just appeared, as it did again just now, pale blue. Swedenborg had an orange flame that appeared to affirm that the love of God was present. This had been reported a few times among mystics as "photisms." The experience is comforting, the Divine reminding of Its presence.

Sometimes it is given that when I think of the Lord, exactly at the moment when the word "Lord" crosses my mind I hear a sudden real external "crack" sound. It is not a split-second before or after. It is an affirmation and reminder that the Lord is actually present. I have tried producing this myself and have never succeeded. Of course others simply hear that pipes pop, or that the house shifts, or whatever. They lack the internal experience of perfect timing. This has been with me for three decades, yet I have not run across this presence in sound anywhere in the literature. It is comforting. I think I am alone, reflecting on God, and God cheerfully shows His presence.

The Gift of Tears

There is one sign I asked for, which now I wish I had not. At the time I was concerned with separating what was of my own will and what was of God. I asked for some internal guidance on this. Now when speaking of the Divine I may suddenly feel the whole of the Divine present, and I become flooded with tears. This has been reported in the traditional literature as "the gift of tears." I was given the gift of tears to distinguish what was of my own ideas and what of the Divine. I really wanted some quieter, less obtrusive sign! I have tried to give back this gift but have not yet succeeded! It has almost completely crippled my public speaking on these matters. I have used a whole box of tissues on a single talk. It is always the same. I am trying to speak calmly and clearly to an audience on sacred matters, and suddenly I feel the truth open up, far larger than me. In the Eastern Orthodox Church, people with this gift were sought out as the ones most trustworthy in teaching of the sacred. When speaking of the holy, the holy opens up to show me that what I am saying is holier than I understand, and I am as surprised as anyone.

Because it occurs so spontaneously, while I am merely trying to make a point while talking, I do not have the leisure to go back and reflect on what is shown. That is, I am shown an infinity of things while I am busy talking. It is too much to note. But it leaves me with the feeling that what I am saying is far more real and powerful than I had thought. It tends to occur while speaking before an audience. I have learned that a desperate effort to conceal it only makes it worse, while warning an audience about my peculiarity lessens it somewhat. I am almost afraid to ask for a lessening of this sign for fear that omnipotence will make it more manifest. I know it sounds disrespectful to try to send back a gift like the gift of tears, but it thrusts me into far more public notice than I want. Besides, many just conclude I am weird or emotionally unstable, because they are unable to sense the interior experience that accompanies it.

So I have been given three signs, light, sound, and tears. Much more common signs that countless persons have noticed are simply peace and happiness when reflecting on the Divine. In all the accounts of these signs only Swedenborg told of the inner experience which is the key to why it is given. Swedenborg sought the love of God and it was shown by an orange flame "which darted through the portals of the brain" to assure that the love of God was present. For the most part I am not one to seek signs. I have seen people become foolish in seeking a sign in every passing cloud. The real, which we each are, is really sign enough in itself.

In dealing with God consider well the implications of omnipresent, omnipotent, and omniscient. In every respect you are better off to try to become like what you address. That is the way with real friends; their understanding drifts towards a oneness. Perhaps all this will make some too reticent to speak to the One. You can always ask for virtue and understanding, for that is in the very nature of the relationship itself. But don't ask and turn away, failing to notice what is even now and thereafter being given to you. A settled, mature friendship with the Divine is the keystone to all life's efforts. A real lifelong friendship is full of the unspoken. I see the nature of one's relationship to the Divine as the very center of life. Certainly it is the core of what each person is.

11
Seeking and Discovering

As the sun, who is the eye of the world,
Cannot be tainted by the defects in our eyes
Or by the objects it looks on,
So the one Self, dwelling in all, cannot
Be tainted by the evils of the world.
For this Self transcends all!

The ruler supreme, inner Self of all,
Multiplies his oneness into many.
Eternal joy is theirs who see the Self
In their own hearts. To none else does it come!
—*Katha Upanishad* (39, p. 94)

The way to find God is very simple. The individual seeks and
God responds, what I call a personal relationship to God. Some describe this as a dialogue, but the word "dialogue" implies it is
mostly talk, and talk may have little or no role to play in it. A close
relationship can have so many implied elements. By emphasizing
the implied and wordless we are back in the area of the affective.
This doesn't bar speaking out now and then, but usually talk begins where there is difficulty. When there is harmony, little needs
to be said.

The Seeking

Both sides of the equation, both the seeking and God's response, contain mystery. Let us look first at the mystery of seeking. The most remarkable thing about the seeking is that the individual already has some idea of what they are seeking, and they have some means of recognizing when the answer is given. Many traditions point out that one cannot seek God without God's assistance. This assistance is an intimate part of the seeking. God knows your innermost trends and uses these in the seeking. If some aspect of reality has always attracted you, then God will use that. I know of a monk who was contemplating whether to become a conventional Roman Catholic monk or to go into the Byzantine Catholic order. He sought an answer to this choice. He was stunned when an icon of Jesus in a store window momentarily came alive, representing the Byzantine way. What is in you makes up all of the subtle elements of the search. You need not find precisely the right method. Start with any at hand. Experiment. The process itself will guide you as to what is appropriate. Your destiny does not hang on finding the perfect way. It hangs on the seeking itself. So get started in any way and explore the seeking itself, to be led to the way appropriate for you.

Some worry about finding just the right way of seeking. If you are in a religious tradition, then by all means give the ways of your own tradition a try. These ways have generally been developed over the centuries. They exist because they have worked for many. Often a tradition will provide guidance, all the way from the shallowest canned prayers to the deepest heart-searching. Explore all, but look closely at the deepest ways of your tradition. Among primitive traditions the proper way was often an arduous naked fast and vision-seeking in the jungle or desert. If you come from a primitive tradition, try to do at least half as much. I was quite impressed by Malidoma Some's book (56). Even though he was force-fed by the Jesuit tradition, he literally could not find his way until he went back to the traditions of his people.

If you are without a religious tradition, you can simply seek on your own, or borrow whatever approach is at hand that appeals to you and is practical in your life situation. I essentially found my own way. I did not turn to the various traditions until later. You can begin your search with the most foolish misunderstandings. Just don't stay in a way that is proving fruitless. You can begin with a perfectly dumb approach and still succeed, because the Divine is in the midst of your seeking and is already guiding you on a way that fits marvelously with what you are. Experiment, and look for the faint hunches as to a better way. It is really more like play. When we play with the possibilities in a situation we are open to learning. So the seeker is being sought and is led in the midst of the seeking.

The way to find God is to look deeply into your seeking itself. Seeking is not merely a simple decision; it contains all your internal trends and nature. Self-learning is a very proper part of the process. God is hidden in you. On the way to discovering how this is so, you learn all about what is hidden in you.

Part of the seeking includes all of the thoughts you have regarding the very nature of God. My mother conceived of God as ultimately cruel. If something like this is there, blocking the relationship, then tell God of this (to inform yourself, since God already knows) and seek to work this out. Day after day, state all your reasons for concluding this. Then seek to work out this difference, and look for signs in you of this difference being resolved. This is far better than carrying a grudge forever and never dealing with it. Deal with whatever impedes your seeking.

I was surprised when I first found that Tibetan mystics made use of fantasy. Now I also see it as part of the process of seeking God. You can fantasize what God is like, or what God's response might be. Fantasy is not entirely created by you, but draws on such subtle elements of your inner that it is really a combination of the Divine and the human. Tibetans have been experimenting with this for centuries, and have developed detailed fantasies which the learner is to practice. In one they take on the role of the creator and make the universe. You need not use these traditionally-ordained fantasies; your own are quite suitable as long as the focus is on seeking God. You can enlarge and represent this any way you want. Your fantasy is unlikely to be Divine revelation at first; it will be mostly your conception and your hope. It helps to be relaxed, and even lying down and near sleep when doing this, to be in a more interior state. Don't be surprised if the process takes over and ends up instructing you. Fantasy comes from the region where the Divine and the human meet.

Saints who have fully utilized fantasy have become very sensitive to whatever imagery arises in them. Some have evolved into seeing the future, and others' spiritual destiny. I have had traces of this. Once when interviewing a very fat woman I wondered inwardly what in her life led to her being so overweight. I suddenly saw her childhood home on a farm. She was raised in a very dull, plain setting. The peak of the family's experience was in coming together to eat. Later she went on eating without this family closeness. I then described her childhood home, even to details of the orientation of the house to the road, and she confirmed I was correct. This process of extra-sensory perception involves a great sensitivity to spontaneous imagery. We don't make these images; they just show up.

When strangers came to St. Seraphim of Sarov for his help he often knew their name and the nature of their problem. He needed this knowledge to help them, and once people saw he had this wisdom he was far more effective with them. In another incident a fellow monk had taken Monk Feofil's prayer book and hid it in his own pocket. Feofil had simply asked himself, "Where is my prayer book?" and had been shown by influx that it was in the monk's pocket, and that the monk was to die soon. He went up to the monk, touched his pocket and said, "You are playing games like this when you are to die soon?" (48) He used this incident to get back his book and to remind the monk of his spiritual state.

We know that Swedenborg knew the date and hour of his death, because he wrote Methodism's John Wesley, saying that he could not make an appointment because he was due to die. Swedenborg lived a very full life doing what he enjoyed most. A servant girl, who was with him at the end, said "The master looked at his watch and said it was time, and died. He seemed so happy you would think he was going on a picnic!" This kind of extra-sensory perception is no good for winning horse races. Since it is Divine influx, it should only be used spiritually. If not so used, it simply disappears.

Another aspect of looking within at your own seeking is that memories of your childhood may arise. When you come to an inner state you don't understand, it can be spontaneously illustrated by a memory out of the past. Look into the feelings of the memory and the affections that are being expressed there. Along the way I recalled many childhood experiences. It is not only a memory you are getting, but also the recovery of a feeling or state which you once had. It is as though to say, "Do you not recognize this? You were here before." It is a recovery of a piece of yourself. Before retiring I open a window and linger to enjoy the air. Suddenly one night the garden smelled exactly like a farm I was on some fifty years before. It was my first and only time on a farm so it represented something new. That night many new insights came to me. Visions of heaven have come to me and they seemed exactly like a memory, the recall of something known before.

At times these images may not make sense at first. Once while reflecting I saw a large bird pecking at its breast so it bled into the mouths of its young. The image was a bit shocking and made no sense to me. Years later my hair stood on end when I saw the same image in a medieval text, representing Christ's sacrifice for mankind. There is a similar image in Buddhism when Buddha recalled a past life in which he was a tiger that sacrificed itself so that its young could live.

An ideal time to examine your seeking is when fully relaxed in bed when you easily enter an interior state in which imagery is lively and it is easier to go deeper into what underlies it. Imagine what the presence of God would be like, and see if later it doesn't prove close to the mark. This whole book arose out of a simple realization that most presentations on God are rather dull and dry. Rarely is the joyous pleasure of the experience even mentioned, so I set out to correct this impression.

I hope the seeking is beginning to make sense. Out of whatever host of understandings or misunderstandings you have of God—perhaps of a grey-bearded old man in the sky—you can go on your personal and very individual search. The search, at its heart, already contains some vague presentiments of the nature of God. The search leads inward through your feelings, even through memories of childhood. In this seeking you are discovering yourself at a deeper level. What you seek is in your essential self. Being omnipresent, it isn't far to be sought. It is watching and participating in your seeking. So your seeking is a joint process in itself. The very will to seek itself comes from the Divine. All the presentiments of what it will be like come from the Divine. If you are learning anything of the real you, you are on the correct way, for the way is through personal understanding to all there is, to the great plain where All meet. You are not on your own; you are aided in the seeking. The aid is already there in the midst of the seeking. The One you are seeking is already at work in the heart of the process of seeking itself. There is no true dualism of the self versus God. This division only exists in misunderstanding.

> We have mentioned these matters so that people would
> not believe that they climb up to God on their own—it is the
> Lord's doing.
> —E. Swedenborg, *Divine Love and Wisdom* (27, #68)

In the East there is a tremendous emphasis on finding the right guru. In the West we have commercialized this idea, with gurus' books and materials being sold widely. But Buddha found his way on his own after he exhausted local tradition. He was being prepared inwardly as he worked through and discarded one traditional approach after another. Gurus make good sense if you are in a tradition with many gifted masters ready to teach. Yet even then the guru is most useful in the preliminary approaches. A parallel example is training in art. A person is led to art by a wish to create out of themselves, and a joy in that discovery. In the early stages, teachers are useful in demonstrating techniques, making suggestions, and even in pointing out mistakes. But eventually, if the artist is not to be an artificial carbon-copy of some other artist, he or she must find their own way, their own vision arising out of their love of the life.

Eventually students find their way to the guidance of God, finding they have an interior guru. It is a matter of being sensitive enough to discover this leading, which is there from the very beginning. This natural internal leading is far more sensitive and responsive to the peculiarities and trends in you than any guru or external system can be. What is in you has a sense of your whole path, and can lead you around the obstacles in that path. The ways of tradition are good approximations of what will work for the average person. A very sensitive and wise guru can be an advancement over the blanket recommendations of tradition. But there is absolutely nothing that compares to having the Divine friendship as your main guide. My guess is that when the way is found through tradition, or a guru, it is because these outer trends have led into the personal friendship with the Divine. I see individuals as different enough, and set in such varied circumstances, that ultimately only the Divine can lead you through the maze. One can begin with one's tradition, or a real guru, to go far enough to discover the leading that was there all along. Once you have this internal guidance, then external guidance is hardly needed.

The one who has found their own way usually returns greater depth to their tradition. The mystic brings people back to their tradition, giving it deeper and enriched meaning. Each religion is like a precious book that was formulated over the centuries by the lives of many. But each individual needs to personally rediscover its meaning by applying it to their life. The book doesn't speak of itself; in itself it is only printed paper. Its meaning can only be seen in terms of an individual's own life. The book only lives through individuals. It becomes a sacred book only to those who have found the sacred in themselves.

God's Response

The individual seeks and God responds. Out of a long series of these interactions develops one's friendship with God. So now let us examine the second half of the equation, God's response. At its deepest level God is seeking and guiding in the midst of our finding a way to God. This response is already there, already occurring; it is only a matter of noticing it. If you conceive of yourself as a separate being, cut off from creation, you are in the midst of a misunderstanding. There is no separation possible; separation is an illusion of the ego. We create this little ego, a lesser actor, a temporary stand-in, which then becomes the major stumbling block to spiritual understanding. What is omnipresent, omniscient, and omnipotent is there right in the midst of your seeking. Swedenborg enunciates a truth of many traditions when he says that *we are given* our sense of self-identity. We also learn from everyone else that we have an ego, or it may have just grown up because we have a body and carry around our own history. The whole path of the mystic is a journey from this little self to all else, an opening up that occurs right in the midst of the self. Our true identity is with the Divine.

One key in our seeking some indication that the Divine is present is that it is right in the midst of all we hold ourselves to be. Swedenborg and other mystics call it Life Itself. That is, if we plumb to the very root and basis of our Life we will find the Divine there as the very source of life. The Divine is not off on some distant mountain, or in some exotic place. The Divine response is best described as modest and gentle, self-effacing. This is why becoming sensitive to influx is so important. If a good idea or good impulse comes to you out of the blue, consider it given to you by influx. Unconscious wisdom does not belong to the little ego. With this little gift comes a certain peace and joy, a feeling as though all is right. The Hindu/Buddhist samadhi is simply resting in this peace and joy. When you are letting yourself just be, like our image of the quiet pool, all that is given to you in this state is from the Divine.

Once you get used to being in the presence of the Divine, the gentle guidance and leading becomes more apparent. Our greatest brilliance appears best when we do nothing. The statement from the New Testament that "The sheep shall know their master" comes to me (49). Sheep come to know their master in most subtle ways: the rhythm and sound of his footsteps, the master's voice and even smell. It is very like returning to some very familiar and favored place. Mystics sorely miss being away from it. St. Theresa of Avila and other mystics have described the dry spells when away. Yet we can prepare our house and wait for the master.

I believe that religions which imply that the path to the direct experience of God is an endless and difficult process do a disservice. The One sought is already there. The limitations in this relationship are all on our side. Don't look for awesome thunderbolts; notice the littlest thing. Some fearful people will say that it is dangerous to open ourselves to the subtle things. My answer is, "Try it and see." When they can enter the subtlest things and find joy and peace of mind, their skepticism will fade. Let them follow this foolish way until they find they are face to face with Wisdom itself, and we will see what happens to skepticism. When I found I was in the hands of Great Wisdom it was a great relief to me. I no longer had to be so clever, to save the universe. The universe had a wisdom in it that could save me. Thank goodness!

"Thank goodness" is one of a number of expressions that come out of this experience. They have become such common currency that we forget their origin and deeper meaning. In this state you thank Goodness just for being. Once in this state I suddenly realized that "holy smoke" is another of these expressions. Holy smoke is the sudden recognition of the presence of the Holy Spirit, like the scent of incense filling space in the midst of mass. "By God" is another. There are many exclamations that can be seen to arise from the experience of the Divine. In Islam there is the recognition of the will of Allah in common speech. "If Allah wills" is a recognition that despite all our plans, Allah finally determines all.

In the mystic's understanding we are totally embedded in and surrounded by the Divine. It is in the sky, the very ground we stand on, in our having a body, and our consciousness. There is nowhere we can turn where this is not. I can look within at the endless spring of ideas in me. Or I can look out at all the world and its people and things and feel quite surrounded by this Life which is equally within and without. I admire this Life which wells up in me and in all creation. It is joyous to see it coming forth. This is the egoless state, enjoying it all as it is. It is like being beside a spring issuing out of the ground in paradise. Everything is right just as it is.

Sometimes when I am asked some great ponderous intellectual question I feel like being very contrary, because the answer is in experience, not words. When someone asks me, "How can I know God?" I feel like being obstinate, and I attempt to turn them away from hanging onto my words. "Have you noticed if your seat is comfortable?" "Is the room warm enough?" Then I would ask them to focus their attention on their breathing. If they could pause and just observe their breathing for an hour or so, they would have the beginning of an answer. Words can inspire, but "inspiration" means "breathing in." We are filled with something which then rests in breathing out. In and out; a living process. We can get all tangled up worrying about it. Am I getting enough air? Or we can let it be, let it do its thing, and watch how well it goes.

The personal relationship with the Divine develops slowly out of life experience. At worst the individual gets busy and drifts away, getting lost. Some then realize that something is missing and come back to it. It is worthwhile to observe under what circumstances God is most easily sensed, so one has a way to come back to it. I have been doing this so long that I can return to it almost anywhere or any time. What makes it difficult to return to the sense of the Divine? It is stress of any kind. Stress creates the feeling of me versus the world, the sense of our limited self separate from all else. Certain circumstances enhance a return to the spiritual, especially just being peaceful and taking time to appreciate things just as they are. I return to appreciating the quiet pool. I appreciate peace itself. Remember the circumstances in which you sense God and return to these. This ultimate friendship is built out of a multitude of such experiences. Is this entrance into the experience of the Divine so difficult to find?

Aesthetics

Aesthetics, or the appreciation of the beautiful, is not ordinarily understood to be related to the mystical. I have enjoyed both the mystical and aesthetics since childhood. The relationship between these areas puzzled me until recently. Bruce Glenn, in *The Arts: An Affectional Ordering of Experience* (50), put me onto the key. He taught aesthetics in a school devoted to the teachings of Swedenborg. Under these circumstances he was bound to consider the relationship between aesthetics and the mystical.

Earlier I pointed out that the mystical primarily has to do with the affections or feelings. The rational or thought aspect is secondary. Aesthetics is also primarily a matter of affections or feeling. But the real connection is this: the art that captivates our attention is the art that represents what is in us. *When an art form embodies our innermost feelings, that is the art that we enjoy and appreciate.* Art shows forth a very lovely representation of our inner self. Since it is deeply affectional, the art we enjoy allows us to meet and appreciate subtle, inner, feeling aspects of ourselves. So through the art we enjoy, we can meet and even come to understand this side of ourselves which we could otherwise easily miss.

Some people think it must take some training to appreciate art. While training can enhance appreciation, this is a misunderstanding of the basic situation. I was once in an art gallery with a five-year-old. I said, "Let's pretend that you can have any one painting. Look at them all carefully, and tell me which one it is to be." Often children most enjoy bright colors. My wife and I play the same game. She tells me which one she would want to own and I tell her my favorite. Sometimes there is none I would particularly want. Her choices show me the quality of her inner life. After many such episodes I can almost predict what she will like.

I realized one day that I was buying art which created the mood I most enjoy. I would be inclined to fill the house with this art. When I seriously consider a painting, I ask myself, "How would it feel to live with this?" I find I have accumulated a number of very different paintings. I have one of a lonely scene in the arctic with a glacier and a whale spouting in a cold empty northern sea. Another is a detailed pencil drawing of a woman in an interesting room, staring at a wall. Another a scene in dark blues and blacks of country buildings in the evening. Everything about my choices looks different except the mood. These different scenes are all very peaceful, even reflective, with a little bit of life somewhere, so I enjoy living with them. This quiet reflective mood I keep purchasing in different forms is an expression, for me, of the mystical. I can live happily with art that represents this to me, because it has the feeling of the quiet pool in which everything is reflected. I can count nine examples on my walls that I have chosen over the years, and I have a collection of art postcards with many more examples.

Let me describe one in particular and what it does for me. It is a Jerry Schurr poster called "San Andreas Lake," which has many features similar to the cover of this book. In the foreground we see dark water with a way through the rocks to other waters, with hills and mountains stretching into the distance. There is a distant soft orange glow of a sunset. For me the scene is utterly peaceful and majestic. It is like looking into incredible vistas of the unexplored. It peacefully awaits discovery. It reminds me very much of glimpses I have had of heaven. Peace itself is there, opening up vast vistas of possibilities. It is no wonder I have lived with this one for years and still return to it with pleasure. Having the art you enjoy is like having beautiful reminders of every ideal moment in one's life. Instead of these treasured experiences flashing by in a moment, and being forgotten, I bring them home to live with me. Before I simply liked art; I didn't know why. Now it is so clear to me how art assists in returning to one's own nature.

Contrast my choices with the art my wife has chosen. As a fiber artist, the center of her interests is in design. She has several portraits of the southwestern Indians and has a natural feeling for an artist's place such as Santa Fe, New Mexico. I can enjoy my wife's art. I skim all of her fiber arts magazines and tell her what I especially like. Yet it is not my way. My way is through quiet reflection in which I can see all of life. My wife also chose a Japanese garden view in splashes of fall colors, with a marked and colorful design aspect. From the same artist, Toshi Yoshida, I bought one which is a quiet evening scene of a river with houses along the bank, the yellow light of windows here and there reflected in the water. My Yoshida has the same soft quiet mood I like. I hardly know why, but there is some magic for me in a darkened scene with the cheery light shown in the interior of houses. I am outside the house, but a few feet away is the warmth of a family scene I can join any time. My wife will recognize that this is my life situation. Why not just go into the warmth of the family situation? I lose perspective in vigorous activity. Somehow I must understand it all, so I need the quiet. This is an example of using art to come back to what is one's nature. The presence of this art is like a silent ritual, a presence that continually centers and reminds of our love of the life.

Once you grasp the connection between art and what is in us, then the uses of art become clearer. We have tended to put art off in a special realm which only some can appreciate. This is a mistake. Ideally everyone should have a clear sense of what they enjoy in all the arts, and make it a central focus in their lives. If I were asked to train people in mystical experience I would seriously consider starting with art appreciation. The way art appreciation works is quite well-known. Begin at the client's level. If they are young people who like rock and roll, start with music with a similar beat and feeling. Gradually move into musical realms they had not appreciated before. Delve into history and the structure of music, because the more you know the more you can appreciate. Begin where they are, and gradually expand their appreciation.

I had just one afternoon in an art gallery to teach a gifted friend who had no understanding of painting, or how to appreciate it. I began as I did with the five-year-old. Which of the paintings or sculptures did he prefer? Then we would spend some time opening up his feelings regarding his choice. Then we tried for others. Of course my approach was entirely affective. It had nothing to do with reason or education. By the end of the afternoon he was beginning to think of himself as an art lover. Bronze sculpture particularly attracted him. He loved the color and the sense of human strength. He was a business leader with a powerful sense of strength.

My wife and I have taken courses in both aesthetics and in music appreciation (51). As the teacher shared all of his rich aesthetic impressions of a painting, it gained scope. Somehow the course was symbolized when he spoke of Camembert cheese. I never appreciated cheese before, but he made it so delicious I'll not forget how he mouthed it! One person's appreciation easily spreads to another. I remember very well Leonid Ouspensky's description of what he saw in icons (52). His more practiced eye opened up vistas for me that would have taken much time to find on my own. Bruce Glenn's appreciation for poetry aided mine.

My wife and I attend concerts which are preceded by an analysis of the music. I would like a whole day of study of every aspect of a single symphony to approach discovery of the whole of it. I remember once going to see some minimalist art—bricks arranged in a simple pattern on the floor. I recall what looked like a dirty old mail bag apparently thrown against the wall. Puzzled, I went over to see if it had a label and an artist's name. It did! Here was something of no consequence thrown against the wall, labelled as art. Surprisingly, when we left the gallery the rubbish in the street also looked like art. Beauty is in the training and the experience of the beholder. Art appreciation is easily learned.

How is aesthetic experience related to the mystical experience? That is easy. To appreciate any art you need to learn to give yourself to it. And when it becomes beautiful for you, you are experiencing the depths of yourself. It is another way to open yourself wide and relinquish ego. In egotism we think of ourselves as a thus-and-so limited thing. But one can't enjoy a whole symphony without wandering beyond the boundaries of the ego. I have been there in the midst of the power of Beethoven's Ninth. I have felt like Tchaikovsky, and I have felt the deep religious devotions of Armenians with Hovhaness. I have known the rhythmic wonder of the ancient Indian ragas. In Rembrandt's portraits I more deeply experienced what it was to be human.

Art simply puts us in touch with depth. We discover both ourselves and the depth of life itself. Ego seems so small and trivial in comparison with this. Each artist goes as far as they can along their line. Through their art I can follow behind, going as far as I can. Following Van Gogh I became like him possessed by a remarkable sense of the power of life, so a single sunflower drove me near madness. Once you learn to give yourself to the experience you can follow into so many wonderful adventures.

While in the midst of studying Orthodox Christian icons I saw an exhibit of small Byzantine ivory carvings. I had the whole British Museum to cover that day, but I spent most of the time in that one room. The Byzantines had commissioned little ivory carvings— diptyches, and triptyches. Triptyches are tiny portable altars that open out like a book. Somehow they clicked for me. I could feel my way all the way back to the people who would commission and carry these little religious icons with them. I spent some hours as a Christian in Byzantine times. It was such a simpler age then; believe and find your way to heaven. It is so easy to enter into other cultures this way. It is very like visiting different worlds and coming back feeling like a citizen of varied worlds.

Even difficulty with art can serve as a useful illustration. Clearly I easily take to and enjoy quiet reflective art. Once in a gallery I was really put off by an abstract painting that was all splashes of brilliant reds and yellows. I could hardly bear to look at it. But I had time, so

I stood before it, determined to appreciate this garish thing. We eventually came to terms. When I left that painting, I knew I could enjoy anything; it was that much of a challenge for me. I would not buy and live with such a painting, but I left feeling it also had a right to be. Since then, a certain magic has developed for me around bright yellows and reds. They call out to me, and I must look again, for unknown reasons. All art expands your experience, leading us into experiences and feelings we don't even understand yet. That is part of its gift; to expand our experience even into mystery.

When I first spoke of mysticism in this book I wrote of those who have the sense of the More in the midst of natural beauty. Natural beauty, in all its forms, including the naked human form, is also the subject of art. It isn't only comely young bodies I enjoy; aged bodies and especially faces show a richness of human experience that is missing in the comely young. All good and beauty can lead into the experience of God. Even when it merely expands your appreciation, it opens your experience to discovery. Art can lead into expanding your sense of the richness and wonder of all existence.

The process of learning to open to beauty and opening to the experience of God are along the same path. In both you discover beauty and richness. In both you learn to open yourself to something more, an embodiment of what is in you. Both the wide experience of art and the mystical head for the wide open plain where All Life gathers, where we are more alike than different. The aesthetic experience and the mystical experience are for me the same thing. All things of God need not have a God label on them. It is quite enough that something is beautiful. All the beautiful and the ideal are along the way. At the moment I am listening to Eric Satie's early piano works. His piano compositions were so simple that some critics felt he wasn't really a musician. Among the hundred lives I could lead, one would be to play the piano this way—playing so simply but with such feeling that the composition becomes embedded in the soul. Yes, all the experience of beauty is part of the way to the experience of God. Swedenborg lays down the means by which the aesthetic enters.

> Nothing is ever able to enter the human memory and
> remain there unless there is some affection or love to attract
> it. If there were no affection, or what amounts to the same,

no love, there would not be any discernment. It is this affection or love to which the thing entering in links itself, and once linked to that affection it remains. This becomes clear from the consideration that when a like affection or love returns that thing reappears as well, presenting itself together with many others which, from a like affection or love, have entered previously. . . . This is something that experience teaches, and anyone may confirm it for himself if he stops to reflect.

    —E. Swedenborg, *Arcana Caelestia* (10, #3336;2)

Without love there is no discernment! And art appreciation is a way to love and discernment. Bruce Glenn has a fine quote from a poet that sounds so contemporary one needs to be reminded that it was written 150 years ago.

The human mind is capable of being excited without the application of gross and violent stimulants; and he must have a very faint perception of its beauty and dignity who does not know this, and who does further know that one being is elevated above another in proportion as he possesses this capability. It has therefore appeared to me that to endeavor to produce or enlarge this capability is one of the best services in which, at any period, a Writer can be engaged; but this service, excellent at all times, is especially so at the present day. For a multitude of causes, unknown to former times, are now acting with a combined force to blunt the discriminating powers of the mind, and, unfitting it for all voluntary exertion, to reduce it to a state of almost savage torpor. The most effective of these causes are the great national events which are daily taking place, and the increasing accumulation of men in cities, where the uniformity of their occupations produces a craving for extraordinary incident, which the rapid communication of intelligence (news) hourly gratifies. To this tendency of life and manners the literature and theatrical exhibitions of the country have conformed themselves. . . .

When I think of this degrading thirst after outrageous stimulation, I am almost ashamed to have spoken of the

feeble endeavor made in these volumes to counteract it;
and reflecting on the magnitude of the general evil, I
should be oppressed with no dishonorable melancholy, had
I not a deep impression of certain inherent and indestructible qualities of the human mind, and likewise of certain
powers in the great and permanent objects that act upon it,
which are equally inherent and indestructible. . . .
    —William Wordsworth, *Lyrical Ballads* (50, p. 243)

Wordsworth lived from 1770 to 1850, before radio, TV, comput-
ers, and all our present "outrageous stimulation."
    My last quote on this subject is *On Beauty* by the Greek pagan,
Plotinus, one of the great mystics who lived about 200AD. Here he
is dealing with the Good which is an ideal akin to God. Good reveals
itself to lovers of the Good as beauty.

Therefore must we ascend once more towards the Good,
towards there where tend all souls.
    Anyone who has seen it knows what I mean, in what
sense it is beautiful. As good, it is desired and towards it
desire advances. But only those reach it who rise to the
intelligible realm, face it fully, stripped of the muddy ves-
ture with which they were clothed in their descent (just as
those who mount to the temple sanctuaries must purify
themselves and leave aside their old clothing), and enter in
nakedness, having cast off in the ascent all that is alien to
the divine. There one, in the solitude of self, beholds simplicity and purity, the existent upon which all depends,
towards which all look, by which reality is, life is, thought
is. For the good is the cause of life, of thought, of being.
Seeing, with what love and desire for union one is seized—
what wondering delight! If a person who has never seen this
hungers for it as for his all, one who has seen it must love
and reverence it as authentic beauty, must be flooded with
an awesome happiness, stricken by a salutary terror. Such
a one loves with a true love, with desires that flame. All
other loves than this he must despise and all that once
seemed fair he must disdain.
    —Plotinus, *On Beauty* (53)

I am not concerned that in my mysticism I venture into realms that often don't seem religious or of God in a conventional sense. Plotinus saw the connection to beauty long ago. I am surprised we have to rediscover it. Natural beauty, which few fail to appreciate, is just the entrance to a whole vast realm of beauty. What a delight! We have a way to the mystical that is very trainable and a pleasure to learn. If I could give all mankind two practices, they would be the appreciation of beauty and meditation. Both deepen our sensibilities and are on the way. The well-rounded person should have some experience of both.

Stages in the Relationship

What we have said thus far does not give an adequate picture of stages in the relationship. We begin with the individual who considers him or herself as an isolated unit. They may or may not even have any confidence that God exists, much less see God as ready to respond to them. They can seek along the ways of their tradition that appeal to them, or be guided by a guru, or go on their own, being guided by what works for them. The earliest difficulty is in establishing the search and in recognizing the Divine response.

The path from these beginnings can be long or short. Since the way leads through self-understanding, it can be that so much personal discovery is needed that most of the time is spent on this. Issues of health or self-discovery can take time. Like any friendship, there can be ups and downs. Periods of discovery that the Divine is present and is considerately guiding the individual are up periods. Down periods occur when the Divine seems to have left. Often these dry periods are ones in which subtle changes, such as simply learning patience, are taking place.

Gradually there have been so many interactions with the Divine that the presence of the Divine is no longer in doubt. The central issue may then shift into a long discovery about how to get along with the Divine. The very famous Tibetan saint, Milarepa (54), had every reason to want God to aid him in revenge on his enemies, and indeed this was accomplished. But Milarepa spent a long time in developing beyond such a frame of mind to becoming a more universal holy person. He later saw that his success in revenge actually slowed his development.

Once the friendship with the Divine forms, one is in for personal change. When you think of a person locked in their limited world view, compared to one who feels at home in the universal, you sense something of the scope of the changes required. The Divine shows the way; it is up to you to follow. The relationship is like an evolving drama. You have ultimate wisdom leading on one side, and the free individual in considerable ignorance on the other side trying to follow. You are in freedom throughout. All religious traditions emphasize that the real sign of believing is doing. "By their deeds shall you know them." It is not a matter simply of mental assent. When the individual finds and expresses their innate love of their life they are on their way to expressing friendship with the Divine. They have finally agreed to what was ordained for them. Having come into the full expression of what was in them, they are also on the plain of the universal. The love of the life is their unique way to the universal. This is one way in which Swedenborg's concept of the love of the life is of far greater import than just aptitude and interest. Their uses to others comes out of the deep sense of the way that is theirs.

At this stage the friendship with the Divine is mature. The dualism of me-versus-God has long since been in the process of fading. In dualism was all the apparent differences, the search, and all the difficulties. As the relationship drifts towards oneness, every sense of separation and boundary is removed. All the avatars, saints, holy people, Christ, Buddha, Mohammed, and the prophets are exemplars of this possibility. There is no separate "me" or ego in the experience of the Universal. In the experience of the Universal, the whole range of existence opens up, and you can explore anywhere. Your understanding and your view of existence can open without limit. But the basic experience in the mature relationship is that It is all One. There is God everywhere. Yet, perhaps paradoxically, one remains simply a person. The ultimate identity has expanded while you remain simply a person.

In the mature experience it is as though you've always known Oneness. There was no struggle, no time of step-by-step advancement. It was always thus. It is like finding yourself home in the familiar and the very pleasant.

12

The Play of Existence

At this point I have given many hints, many leads, but the heart of the experience is still missing. There is some use in all the hints and leads as preparation; now I would like to turn to the experience itself. I can best express it in blank verse, which is like a Japanese sumi painting where a few black brush strokes suddenly become the essence of a lively creature. Verse is also like the finest calligraphy where a few apparently careless brush strokes have so much power that you feel the word represented, even though it is in foreign characters. So now my few brush strokes. Then, if you don't mind, I will elaborate what each mark means.

The Play of Existence

The entrance into the Divine,
Is always through this present moment.
It cannot be in any other time.
It is like a descent
Into the wonder of your very nature.
There is no other way.
It is to fall into accord
With the total nature of reality.
The All—
What Always was—
And will be.
This is the Homecoming

Returning where you started
Arriving home at last.

Ah, but how is this accomplished?
The All sent Itself out
To learn in the world
To rise from innocence
To wisdom.
And The All guided the return
Most eager
To return to Self.
And in the return
All the vicissitudes are forgotten—
But the wisdom remains
In the Always Was.

So there is the appearance
That wisdom can grow—
But Always Was knows better.
It is a drama
Within the Theater of Existence
Creating the appearance of time.
Entertainment—
To pass the time.

Sitting in the theater
Someone next to me asked
"How many times have you died?"
And I answered, "Never
I know not of death.
Death is an appearance in Innocence
Not in wisdom.
Yet innocence is the way to wisdom.
See, everything is useful."

So let us now go to the drama
Sit comfortably, and enjoy the spectacle.
It is a projection of Wisdom
Ever illustrating the nature of the All.
Every now and then

We fall into Samadhi
Stunned by all that emerges
Out of us.
Swaying and dancing
Lovely music
Subtle colors.
"Thus before their eyes
All things seem to laugh
to play
and to live."

The first three lines set the time framework for the experience.

The entrance into the Divine
Is always through this present moment.
It cannot be in any other time.

We are setting about to enter upon the experience of the Divine.
But where is the gate, the entrance? In the world's vast literature,
and all its speculations, there have been countless answers to this.
It is in the Temple of the Jews, at Mecca, on the Sacred Mount Meru,
while others say it is not in this life but in the next. . . . Many answers
imply a vast amount of striving. The poem gives an answer that will
puzzle some. The present is the entrance. Which present? Not the
one just past, nor the one to come. This very present. And I include
in this present everything, just exactly as it is arranged at this
moment. This arrangement is the setting of the present. But of
course, if I can once find the Divine in this present, then I can also
do so in some other present moment. These lines remind me of the
religious phrase "Salvation is now."

If my three lines create a sense of urgency to investigate the possibilities of the present, well and good. Some wonder what salvation
means. There is much discussion on this, but in the terms of this
poem salvation means simply to meet God. Then you are saved. The
third line, "It cannot be in any other time," is meant to lock you into
this time frame: the present moment is the fullness of the real. From
this real center the past is doubtful and the future is theoretical. So
another implication of these first three lines is that the very
entrance into the Divine is located in the full, immensely powerful
reality of this present, and that all other times are fantasy and imag-

ination. We are embedded in a reality which is the Entrance itself. We are always at the entrance.

> It is like a descent
> Into the wonder of your very nature.
> There is no other way.

These three lines describe what you are to do in the present. The present is a kind of booming and buzzing confusion, as William James described it. We need a direction, and the answer may seem at first a bit paradoxical. It is a descent into your very nature. Simply center in your present experience. With recognition, your underlying feelings become clearer. Someone sent me a compact disk with a Mambo as the lead piece, and it is playing now. In the present moment I feel like getting up and creating a dance to this. Without knowing the formal steps, and with a leg badly damaged by polio, I just move everything to portray the rhythm of the music. The composition uses a very low thump of a drum. By influx I suddenly see what Buddhists and others are doing with a deep-sounding drum. It is intended that each be vibrated to a very fundamental level. It thumps through me, and I am in the midst of ancient ceremonies. I worry if I can move freely enough to express this. But that is ego. Who cares? I am enjoying expressing what I feel.

This is the descent into your nature: to discover and express what is in you, even when it seems negative. Perhaps there is an underlying depression. Enter it, and try to find the root of sadness. The descent is a discovery as what there is opens up. In a university class I taught on phenomenology, a young woman avoided this descent, because she felt suicide was there. But I invited her to try anyway. She saw a snow bank. She thought she wanted to crawl in and die by freezing to death. So I invited her to crawl in. Finding herself in the snow cave, she smiled. It was so quiet, away from people, and so warm. Instead of taking on the cold of the snow, she felt her own warmth. It turned out to be not death, but a refuge. I told her it was her own refuge and she could return to it anytime. The whole episode lasted just a few minutes. In the descent into self you just relax and discover what is there.

One of the implications of the descent into self is that yourself is to be discovered and honored. In the descent you forget what others might think of you; they don't matter. You are spending a brief time looking at the raw material of yourself. You want to discover and recognize whatever is there. Often you find underlying trends that point directly at your love of the life. In one descent I came to the idea of presenting this matter by blank verse first, to show it all, and then elaborate each line. My highest experiences of God more easily speak out in blank verse. Among other things, creativity lies in this descent, because what is in you is far more creative than the outer you.

All through this book I have been emphasizing that the way to God involves self-discovery. Can you bypass this discovery and still discover God? A few have succeeded, but then they had to go back and clean up all they bypassed. There has been much debate in religion as to whether the psychology of personal discovery plays any role. Some have attempted a forced march into the citadel of religion without any self-confrontation. The result can be the terrible spectacle of a person who mouths all the right words of their faith, but their life has dark secrets they want to keep concealed. It simply doesn't work, because their experience lacks the core experience of God on which life itself rests. They are like spiritual manikins. They look like a person but they don't live. Full living involves self-discovery until you meet the source of your life itself. A scientist knows that his instruments have to be in good order before any discoveries can be made. In the search for God, you are the instrument. Ultimately you can't avoid your own nature. It is all you have, and it is the very basis of your world design. If your world is messed up and not satisfying, look to yourself as the source of the mess.

It could also happen that it is only you that you seem to discover in this descent; there seems to be no God. In this case you have much to discover of yourself. Look for God hidden in you. It is no tragedy if you only discover yourself. If you are really discovering, that is all that is necessary, and if you are to ever meet God, self-discovery is the very foundation.

Into the wonder of your nature.

I stress wonder. The earliest wonder may be that you aren't at all as you thought you were. The young woman who was feeling depressed and vaguely thinking of suicide is an example. She feared the terrible possibility of suicide. In moments we discovered that she basically just needed to find a quiet refuge in herself, away from the stresses and demands of others. She discovered this refuge near at hand, by descending into the experience. It is wondrous to discover that you aren't quite as you thought you were. The deeper aspects of yourself can also be a wonder in themselves, almost magical. You can descend into yourself and look upon the wonder of all existence. After such a descent you may discover yourself feeling more friendly to others, and even to birds, plants, and the clouds. Wonder broadens beyond your self-concerns, to life itself, and eventually to the plain of the universal. This wonder is a foretaste of the Divine. The appreciation of anything, whether it be the wonder of yourself, or the wonder of creation itself, places you in the courtyard of the temple. You are the fulcrum of your existence, a world-maker. Appreciate yourself to appreciate the world.

Some really fear a great and terrible discovery in themselves. The worst I have ever found is that I have been a total idiot. I have discovered this often enough that it now seems humorous. Being an idiot isn't so bad. It fosters humility, leaving you feeling no better than anyone else.

Like the first three lines in which the way is made emphatically in the now, the descent into your own nature is made the only way. Another implication of the descent into the self to find God, is that God is within you and is the root of your real nature, and the source of your life.

> It is to fall into accord
> With the total nature of reality.

This is an important discovery. In the whole of the world's mystical literature the implication of this step has often not been made clear. In the preceding three lines we went through the descent into our very nature. The "fall into accord with the total nature of reality" is what you can experience at this point, passing from the personal effort of the descent into yourself, to the beginning of mystical experience. You "fall" into this, because it is not of your personal effort, it is simply given to you. You "fall into accord" or into harmony with the total of reality. The mystical experience opens up, showing you the total design of reality. In your earliest experiences you may simply experience the world as though cleansed by some heavenly rain. All things seem very bright and new and full of life. It is primarily an affective experience that includes feelings of peace and harmony, and that all is right with the world. You have begun to experience the plain of the universal, where there is a kind of heavenly joy and peace. You have gone deep into your nature to the real place where you are the microcosm, the image of the all. But it was always more than a mere image. This is the way to the All, as the experience of the mystic simply opens up to

> The All—
> What always was—
> And will be.

The experience in the present also transcends time. The mystic is experiencing both what always was and what will be. The "always was" opens up ancient tradition as alive now. When I spoke of the use of a massive drum with a very low note in ceremonies, the tradition simply opened up to me, becoming full of meaning. "And what will be" opens up the future. You can be shown much of what will be, but it will only be shown if used in the same spirit in which it was given. During the worldwide concern over the atomic bomb I once asked God if mankind would survive. I received the answer that humans would always be. But I don't know if this meant that mankind on earth will always be, or mankind in a spiritual sense. Often the experience of what "will be" is of the total wondrous interrelatedness of all things, woven into a marvelous harmony. You come away from this with the feeling that all existence is in wise and compassionate hands.

> This is the Homecoming
> Returning where you started,
> Arriving home at last.

The Divine creates itself into all there is. You were launched into the innocence and ignorance of infancy. Each of us retains some sense of our home, so that when we return to the Source it feels very familiar, like coming home after being away a long time. I was startled when I first felt this definite feeling of familiarity. How could it feel so familiar if I had never known it before? But that was mere reason asking questions. It is like home, where you most want to be, where you feel most comfortable. Enlightenment is essentially this homecoming. It enlightens because you suddenly fully recall the home, the leaving, the long struggle of your journey, and now returning home, experiencing the whole design of existence. Most of the great difficulties and tragedies of life only make sense in view of this homecoming. They are difficult to appreciate in themselves. People often ask, "Why did this one die and not me?" "Why are some put through such trials that they wish for death?" The real answer to all our hardest questions is in the homecoming, an experience that answers all. Short of that there remain nagging questions and endless speculation. In "Arriving home at last" is relief and satisfaction, and time itself is transcended. One mystic said that transcending time is like being on the peak of a mountain and seeing quite well some people struggling on one path and others on another. But from this peak you know that all are going to make it. Compared to this, the question of what day and year is a small one. Swedenborg found salvation, finding God, as coming to all who act by the good they know. Some people's good is small and limited, but it is the best they can do, and good enough. The business of life is to learn more of good—a lesson of which there is no end. The entire next stanza comes out of a reaction as to how this could all be.

Ah, but how is this accomplished?

This is a review of this essential path. The questioning is answered differently, but similar to the main path laid down in the first stanza, with the universal answer, given by all mystics who have journeyed this far.

The All sent Itself out
To learn in the world
To rise from innocence
To wisdom.

The universal finding of the mystics is that the All sent Itself out into the world, to take on all the difficulties of this journey. Ultimate wisdom creates itself into the ultimate ignorance and the dependence of the infant. It did this "to learn in the world, to rise from innocence to wisdom." There is both mystery and paradox in this. In the transition from the All to the infant we have stepped into time. It will take time for the infant to grow up and return to the All. Shifts from transcending time, to stepping into time occur several times in the poem. Why create a problem that requires time to work out? Why not leave it in the fullness of the All? This theme has been treated in several different ways in religious myth. In Hinduism, Brahman would have done nothing forever unless seduced into activity, through which creation was set in motion. Time is created by this step down from transcendence into time—time, creation, activity, the spinning out of events—all this is created.

The whole purpose of this stepping into time is "To learn in the world." Stepping into the world creates existences that would not otherwise be. The Creator wants to try it out, just to assess all that could be. How else to assess all that could be but to create Itself into all there is and try out various existences? Of course omniscience already knows this. What we are doing is moving back and forth from the ultimate to creation. The omniscient transcends time. The creature is in time. In time, each goes through changes, which are the purpose, all the way from the birth and death of stars, to the evolution of life on earth, to the life experience of a person. At this moment we have a dualistic model, things changing in time, while the Divine is unchanging, transcending time. No dualism remains standing in mystical experience; they are all dissolved into Oneness. But what is the path from things spread out in time to Oneness? We are that path, the link from the world of time to the timeless.

But the transformation from in-time, to the eternal transcendence, is now only a part of what is involved. To get a perspective in time we need much experience in time. Simply having lived is not really the issue, but rather the wisdom and understanding gathered from experience. Science has done a fine job of gathering much rational understanding of the things of the world, but here we are really dealing with wisdom, which is of life itself.

Swedenborg's exploration of the education of infants and children in heaven is an adequate description of the situation of all of us. Swedenborg reasoned that if a child dies in infancy, it is then the model of innocence. Perhaps in heaven nothing else is needed but being in total innocence. He was shown that infants and children are instructed in heaven and why.

> Angelic spirits who were above and in front spoke to me in angelic language that was not divided into separate expressions. They said that their state was the state of a serenity of peace, and that they also had young children among

them, from whose presence with them they received a feeling of bliss. Those spirits too were members of the female sex. They went on to speak about young children on earth. They said that immediately after these are born, angels from the heaven of innocence are present with them; then in the next phase of their life angels from the heaven of the serenity of peace; after that angels from the communities of charity; and then, as innocence and charity diminish when they are older children, different angels again are present with them. And when at length they become more grown up and enter upon a life alien to charity, angels are indeed present though more remotely, but in accordance with the ends of life which are especially regulated by the angels by a continual instillation by them of ends that are good and a turning aside of ends that are bad. But to the extent they are able or are not able to do this, so they flow in more nearly or more remotely.

Many may suppose that young children stay as young children in the next life, and are as young children among the angels. Those who do not know what an angel is may have become confirmed in that notion by the images seen here and there in places of worship, and in other places where young children are portrayed to represent angels. But in fact it is not at all as they suppose. What makes an angel is intelligence and wisdom, and as long as young children do not possess these, though they do indeed reside with angels, they themselves are not angels. But as soon as they have become intelligent and wise, they now become angels for the first time. Indeed what has amazed me, they no longer appear as young children but as adults, for their disposition is no longer that of a young child but of a more adult angelic disposition. Such is the effect produced by intelligence and wisdom, for it may be clear to anyone that it is understanding and judgement, and the life from these, which cause a person to seem to himself and to others to be an adult. I have not only been told by angels that this is so but also have spoken to a certain person who had died as a small child and yet after that appeared as an adult. The same also spoke to his brother who had died when an adult;

and he did so out of so much mutual brotherly love that his brother who could not help weeping declared that he perceived nothing else than that this was love itself which was speaking. There are other examples besides this which there is no need to mention.

There are certain people who identify innocence with early childhood, for the reason that the Lord, when speaking about young children, said that heaven consisted of such, and that those who do not become as young children cannot enter the kingdom of heaven. But those who think in this fashion do not know the internal sense of the Word, nor thus what is meant by early childhood. "Early childhood" is used to mean the innocence that belongs to intelligence and wisdom, the nature of which is such that they acknowledge that they possess life solely from the Lord and that the Lord is their one and only Father; for a person is human because of intelligence and wisdom—essentially truth and good respectively—which people have solely from the Lord. Innocence itself, which in the Word is called early childhood, exists and resides nowhere else than within wisdom, so much so that the wiser anyone is the more innocent he is. Consequently the Lord is Innocence itself, because He is Wisdom itself.

As regards the innocence possessed by young children, because as yet it is devoid of intelligence and wisdom, it is merely a kind of plane for receiving genuine innocence, which they do receive gradually as they become wise. The nature of young children's innocence has been represented to me by something wooden and practically devoid of life but which is made living as they are perfected by means of cognitions of truth and affections for good. The nature of genuine innocence was afterwards represented by a very beautiful young child, full of life, and naked. For the truly innocent, who dwell in the inmost heaven and so nearest to the Lord, appear before the eyes of other angels as none other than small children, and indeed as naked; for innocence is represented by "the nakedness of which they are not ashamed," as one reads of the first man and his wife in paradise. In short, the wiser angels are the more innocent they are; and the more innocent they are the more they appear to themselves as young children. This is why in the Word innocence is meant by early childhood.

—E. Swedenborg, *Arcana Caelestia* (10, #2303-6)

So the innocence of infancy lies in no capacity for judgment. They need instruction so they can be in the higher innocence of actual wisdom. Our situation is much the same, for in many ways our ignorance is so profound as to resemble the innocence of infants and children. Those who live longer are instructed by life itself. We come into the innocence of wisdom in the mystical experience in which we discover the One that is the All. All this was implied in "To rise from innocence, to wisdom."

> And the All guided the return,
> Most ready
> To return to Self.

There is some paradox here. The All guides the return to Self. The feeling of this "most ready" guidance is very like a parent who wants the child to mature and go their own way, yet the parent is concerned about the outcome. Christ Himself used the image of a parent, the Father, for the One. It is the total loving wish of the parent that we, the children, be free to explore for ourselves. It is this freedom that puts risk into the grand drama of the One, creating itself into the innocence of infants, to journey back to self. The depth of our parent's concern is shown in the eight or so dream bulletins we get per night on our spiritual state. This is not a distant and absent parent but an attentive one, close at hand.

The means of guidance are many. I see every spiritual tradition as a guidance. The whole of the religious and psychological and even the practical literature on how to do things is guidance. We each have friends ready to guide us. Our senses guide us. And all our inner states and dreams are forms of guidance. There is an abundance of guidance. It might well be easier to settle on what is best to do if there were far less guidance! When mankind lived in isolated groups, before about 900 AD, each group with its religion, it was simpler. If called upon to describe the whole drama of existence, it would be in this single line, "And the All guided the return, most ready to return to Self." The implication is that the return is already complete. This is far more appropriate than implying we are each on the way, for that is the limited view in time. In the limited view of this line there is acknowledgement that the journey had anxiety in it. But in the eternal the return is already complete. It is another time shift paradox. It was an anxious journey, but it is now complete. How is it complete? If you understand this simple poem it is complete. When is the moment it is done? Now. How is it done? It is done in yourself. It is "What always was and will be." This is the Homecoming.

> And in the Return
> All the vicissitudes are forgotten
> But the wisdom remains
> In the Always Was.

The Return is capitalized here, implying the Return has solely to do with the One. The One in us, which is the very root of our personal identity, is the One who has found the way back. All the terrible vicissitudes are forgotten, or forgiven, because they were the means to the full wisdom of the return. It was a difficult trip, but we learned much. I sometimes think even ordinary tourist travel is designed to teach us to appreciate home. The worse the trip, the better the homecoming. Some might conclude that for me to come to this insight, my life must have been easy, but I have had forty-seven years of serious pain. But even this vicissitude is forgotten.

Again these few lines have an apparent time shift. We have returned. The troubles are forgotten, or really forgiven. If I carried an eternal grudge for forty-seven years of pain I would be forever barred from the Homecoming, and that would be Hell. When I recall the pain, I look to see what good was in it. It wrote into me a wish to make the way easier for others, so the brief pain had an eternal use. Among a thousand other things, it made my writing style simpler, because I don't want to cause anyone the pain of having to figure it out. The time shift is that we have recently arrived, and we discover all the vicissitudes are gone, and the wisdom remains. This is not our wisdom as ego, but it is part of what Always Was—in capitals because it is of the Divine. If I had to describe the nature of human beings in these terms I would say humans are God waking up, rousing, becoming functional. Timewise this is being between asleep and active, yet already God. See, He is stretching, getting ready for a day's activity!

> So there is the appearance
> That wisdom can grow—
> But Always Was knows better.

Now we look at the ultimate nature of this time shift. If God creates Self into all creation, to go through vicissitudes, to come back to Self, then obviously there is a growth of wisdom! *Yes, but in time only.* In the eternal this is clearly seen as an appearance, an illusion. Swedenborg himself says one cannot understand heaven unless one divests oneself of the idea of time. Heaven is really a state, just like your present feelings. In your feelings there are events like time, but your internal sense has a far greater freedom than inexorable clock time. When dying, you may carefully review every detail of your life, but someone there with a stop watch would find this review happened in a few seconds of clock time. In many places Swedenborg mentions the vastness of the spiritual compared to the natural world. A "brief" angelic thought is as myriads when compared to a natural thought.

In both Buddhism and Hinduism it is made quite clear that time is an appearance, not an ultimate reality. In fact the *maya* or illusion aspect of ego is partly because it is involved in time. The extra-sensory shows up in many aspects of the spiritual, because in time transcended there is no barrier. So there is an *appearance* that wisdom can grow, but Always Was knows better.

> It is a drama
> Within the Theater of Existence
> Entertainment
> To pass the time.

Suppose there is a theater. Last night there was a play by Shakespeare on stage. Tonight there will be a very modern existential play, such as *Waiting For Godot*. The theater itself is like time transcended. These plays and the times and events they portray are like our lives in time. People enjoy these plays; they are entertainment. I wonder how we would pass the time without them. It would be painful if there were no plays and we all sat in our seats in this theater in the dark and wrestled with our souls. I especially liked the Shakespeare last night. It was *Much Ado About Nothing*. I love the language. I like to read the play as it is performed. Then I can see, as well as hear the words, and savor them better. Leonato asks a messenger the results of a battle. "How many gentlemen have you lost in this action?" The messenger says, "But few of any sort, and none of name." A Don Pedro did very well. Here is how the messenger reports it. ". . . He hath borne himself beyond the promise of his age; doing, in the figure of a lamb, the feats of a lion; he hath indeed better bettered expectation than you must expect of me to tell you how." (Act 1, Sc. 1) Aye, Shakespeare was a master wordsmith.

One of the reasons we honor drama, is that it is a very fitting representation of life. Like all art, it enables us to experience ourselves once removed, and ably portrayed. The fundamental Hindu characterization of the nature of life is *lila*, play. I quite realize some people's lives are so hard and bitter that they would be offended to hear this. Remember that I speak out of my forty-seven years of pain. The drama is meant to seem very real and deadly. That is part of the drama. When you see it as theater you can sit and enjoy the drama, because it is not really so deadly. As the messenger said, "But few of any sort (were killed), and none of name."

> Sitting in the theater
> Someone next to me asked
> "How many times have you died?"
> And I answered, "Never
> I know not of death."

You see me sitting here in the theater. Someone who was aware of the drama of life spoke to me as one of its actors. As an actor I have died in many performances. If I died many times it must have been *me* that reincarnated and came back! The person next to me is thinking *in time*. But at that moment I identify with the eternal. So I answer, "Never, I know not of death." Once when in the spirit I asked God of death. I expected some enlightenment on the whole process. Instead God answered with this same sentence. "I know not of death." In time I may have been an actor who died many times, but from the viewpoint of the eternal this is merely an appearance. The eternal literally does not know of death.

> Death is an appearance in Innocence
> Not in wisdom.
> Yet innocence is the way to wisdom.
> See, everything is useful.

Yes, all living things appear to die. But this is an appearance in Innocence. I capitalized Innocence because this is ultimately an aspect of the Divine. For one, innocence is the order of all things. The laws of natural order are like Innocence simply and unselfconsciously doing its thing. It is very fortunate that the laws we discover in our tiny corner of the universe appear to apply everywhere through all the reaches of space. Blind nature is really innocent. I have been very struck by the way that children of the same age behave similarly. They act out of an innocent order inscribed in their natures.

Yet death appears in innocence, not in wisdom. Taking things naively at face value, all living things die. But why isn't this true in wisdom too? Wisdom is of life, of what is eternal, what always was and will be, alpha and omega, the beginning and the end. In this realm, life is continuous. This realm knows not of death, which is in the innocence of appearances. We have gone through the same shift out of time to the eternal. Yet we don't thereby discard innocence as lesser and useless. We absolutely need the innocence of the laws of nature, and the innocence written into our nature, to mature to the point of wisdom. Wisdom does not just spring up to full maturity; we needed this help. We had to go through the school of hard knocks to get it. So innocence is absolutely critical and sacred to wisdom. Swedenborg speaks of the innocence of wisdom which angels are in. He remarks that angels in the innocence of wisdom may seem small, and not of much consequence, until you notice that they are in the natural fullness of Divine Wisdom. They are also naked, because they have nothing to hide.

It turns out that innocence is the way to wisdom. When I was led through humility in my icon gazing I was being led back through innocence, to natural wisdom. When we leave the pond alone it falls into its natural innocence, and when we gaze reflectively into its mirror-like face, we experience its wisdom. Creation needs curious creatures like us, humans forever asking and seeking. We are the Divine stretching and waking from slumber. So I honor innocence in all its forms and thank it for its wisdom to get me this far. When baptized into one church I had to take a religious name. The name I chose was Innocent, though I had no clear idea why at the time— except that the icon I long gazed at was St. Innocent of Irkutsk. Everything is useful. It made me curious about innocence so I can innocently report this to you.

So let us now go to the drama
Sit comfortably, and enjoy the spectacle.
It is a projection of Wisdom
Ever illustrating the nature of the All.

After making this shift several times out of time to the eternal, and back again, we become accustomed to it, and it no longer seems paradoxical. The plain fact of the matter is that we really exist in both time and the eternal. It was only our lack of exploration of the eternal that made it seem at all unusual. We walk in two worlds simultaneously.

People have often wondered what you do after enlightenment. The brilliant answer in Zen is that after enlightenment you chop wood and carry water; you do whatever needs to be done. The master who gave this answer was in a place where wood was actually chopped and water carried. But beyond that we can also go to the drama, sit comfortably, and enjoy the show. This is the spirit of nonattachment so prized in the Bhagavad Gita and in Buddhism. It promises to be a good show.

This nonattachment doesn't in the least prevent doing things—how else will the wood be cut and the water carried in? What is meant is that once you reach this level, and see it is a show, to pass the time, then you can really comfortably enjoy it. You become less caught up in the comic/tragic aspects. People die often on T.V.; how often do you weep over them? And if you do, it is God speaking to you of something in your own nature, not yet fully experienced.

In the line, "It is a projection of Wisdom," we come to the real nature of the spectacle we can enjoy. The whole of creation is a projection of Wisdom, Wisdom being actualized. It is very like God's thought, as some have said. Only this God visualizes vividly, "Ever illustrating the nature of all things." Swedenborg refers to all existence as correspondences of the spiritual. This is the same. We are in a theater of correspondences or representations. The ultimate, having nothing else to do, lays out all its potentialities in sequence called time, to review them.

Every now and then
We fall into samadhi
Stunned by all that emerges
Out of us.

We are now the Ultimate One, sitting comfortably in the theater, enjoying the show. Now and then we fall into samadhi. I don't know of an adequate English equivalent for this word. It is a very pleasant state in which it is All One. The One doesn't always get caught up in the drama as we might, sitting wide-eyed, taking it all in. The One dozes off and lapses into its primordial awareness from time to time, and then snaps out of it, to notice the show again. Samadhi is like a stunned spiritual state—spiritually stunned by the fullness of it all. The unfolding drama adds to the samadhi, for the One looks from the drama into awareness of all its implications. When we take the position of the One, viewing the panorama of our existence, we can fall into periods of a stunned ecstacy in which the utter fullness of it all is seen as emerging out of us. The last section further describes this state of the One, having snapped out of samadhi and returning to enjoy the drama.

> Swaying and dancing
> Lovely music
> Subtle colors.

The last line is from Swedenborg. I was asked to do a piece on play, and when I read of Swedenborg getting into the play of children, one line just stood out and stayed with me because it quite perfectly described the experience of enlightenment.

> Thus before their eyes
> All things seem to laugh,
> To play,
> And to live.
> —Swedenborg, *Heaven and Hell* (16, #489:3)

When full of this spirit, the world you look out upon is also full of life. So all things seem to laugh, to play and to live.

You may wonder how this poem came to me. It was not labored over, word by word. It came in the space of a few minutes, upon arising, before I even had breakfast. I woke up with many ideas running through my head, so I knew my "Editor," which is what I call the writer in me, had something to say, and I just set it down.

13

Pristine Awareness in Your Center

And you should cultivate joyfulness in thinking
Ah, there is no need for me to install
All these beings in happiness;
Each of them having found his happiness,
Might they from now onwards, until they are
    pervaded
    by limpid clearness and consummate perspicacity,
Never be separated from this pleasure and happiness.
The indication is the birth of joy without envy.
Thereafter comes a joyfulness (as) in pure
    concentration.
Body, speech, and mind are spontaneously calm and
    happy.
The result is steadfastness and joyfulness through this
    inner wealth. . . .

When love is present and acting on hatred, there
    comes in its place
A pristine cognition that is like a mirror,
    and the founding stratum of meaningful engage-
    ment is present.
This founding stratum of meaningful engagement
    is adorned with the major and minor marks
    of Buddhahood.
        —Longchenpa, *Kindly Bent to Ease Us* (55)

My teacher in Buddhism did not refer me to Longchenpa since he is considered so advanced. But in him I clearly recognized a friend across six centuries of time. He is describing pristine awareness which is an utterly simple state anyone can realize in minutes. Before we analyze what he has said, follow me into pristine awareness. The scene is this. I am alone in the house sitting at the kitchen table. It is a darkish rainy morning. In the peaceful quiet I simply gaze out the window and take in the scene.

> It is a dark rainy morning.
> Sitting at the kitchen table
> I look out on my garden and the trees beyond.
> I fall into the mood of it all.
> Cool wet green.
> It is all stillness.
> The trees, of such ancient lineage, stand up and
>   hold out their arms, washed by the rain.
> In the soaked ground thousands of root tendrils are
>   enlivened by the moisture.
> I stand among my brethren washed and refreshed
>   as they are in this ancient sacred ritual of rain.

Pristine awareness is simply opening yourself to experience, to allow the rest of existence to reveal itself. "I fall into the mood of it all." I become aware of cool wet greenery in the midst of stillness. Many images come to me of ancient times, of people taking in the wonder of nature long ago. It becomes an ancient primordial scene. As a person I am aware that the trees are of a more ancient lineage than me. Some time ago I was delighted to learn that plants have the same basic genetic code as humans. The trees seem like me—holding out their arms, being washed by rain. I envisioned what was happening below the ground to the fine tendrils of roots taking in moisture. The identity between the trees and myself has been gradually forming. Suddenly it is as though I am like them, holding out my arms like limbs, being washed like them. I see that this is an ancient sacred ritual practiced by us tree/plant/people. Why sacred? Because life is being imparted. Why ancient ritual? Well, because it has been repeated since ancient times. We tree/plant/people are aware of this. As simple as that.

Pristine awareness occurs when you just let yourself be, and enjoy what comes. You look at a level of experience below that of worldly business. It is very rich and pleasant. Previously I used the image of a pool or pond. You are sitting beside the pool and gazing into it. You wait a few moments for it/you to settle. Then it/you mirrors the universe. Above all I want to convey how extremely easy and simple it is. What are you to do? Nothing, but wait and gaze.

Now let us look at Longchenpa's gazing. He is a Buddhist monk writing six centuries ago. But basically he is doing the same thing as I did. His account looks very different until you get into it.

> And you should cultivate joyfulness in thinking.

Here he is speaking as a monk or teacher. This is Buddhist doctrine—"You should cultivate"—yet it is doctrine cast in such a pleasant form "joyfulness in thinking." But suddenly he remembers an advanced understanding—that ultimately there is no lostness in the supreme awareness of the One. Having come into this awareness the tone shifts from "you should cultivate" to:

> Ah, there is no need for me to install
> All these beings in happiness;
> Each of them having found his happiness,

This is a shift here out of time into the eternal. He is speaking from nirvana—which everyone already has even if they don't recognize it. Then suddenly a shift back into time:

> Might they from now onwards, until they are
>   pervaded by limped clearness and consummate
>   perspicacity,
> Never be separated from this pleasure and happiness.

He is now a Boddhisattva—one who delays the full pleasure until others can have it too. "Until they are pervaded by limpid clearness." He is a monk/Buddha working to give this same pristine awareness to all others. Then he shifts back into the state itself and tries to describe it.

> The indication is the birth of joy without envy.
> Thereafter comes a joyfulness (as) in pure concentration.

The joy of pristine awareness is like this. It is a joy of a pure and natural concentration as you are enraptured. There is no effort in this concentration; it just occurs. This is the same as when I enjoyed looking out the window. Time is of no consequence. One enjoys just staying.

> Body, speech, and mind are spontaneously calm and
>   happy.
> The result is steadfastness and joyfulness through this
>   inner wealth. . . .

Everything is calm. And it is as though one has found an inner wealth. The result is steadfast joy. Longchenpa went on for pages in this joyful vein. But I wanted to also deal with three other lines. Longchenpa is a monk. When he feels any hatred, out of any kind of interpersonal difficulty, he returns to pristine awareness which undoes hatred. He takes hatred with him into pristine awareness and there it is transformed.

> When love is present and acting on hatred,
>   there comes in its place
> A pristine cognition that is like a mirror,
>   and the founding stratum of meaningful engagement
>   is present.

He uses a Buddhist practice of bringing in hatred and looking at it in this state of pristine awareness. Then love acts on hatred and undoes it. You can imagine that in a few sessions like this he becomes a gentle and loving person. Hatred is consumed by love. But he also comes to the nature of pristine awareness itself, which is like a mirror that you can pick up and turn all ways to see all things. The mirror merely reflects, as pristine awareness reflects the eternal. At the same time "the founding stratum of meaningful engagement is present." Pristine awareness is the foundation of mind and experience. In pristine awareness you feel meaningful engagement, so meaningful you enjoy staying. I recall a tale of one monk who proposed to fix a meal for others and fell into this state. His companions waited respectfully day and night for three days before he returned. He had not noticed the passage of time.

> The founding stratum of meaningful engagement
> is adorned with the major and minor marks
> of Buddhahood.

The marks of Buddhahood are signs of enlightenment. In this state you can easily glimpse all time past or future. You can see the design of the whole of creation. It is the source of revelation. It has the marks of the Ultimate all over it.

I have presented pristine awareness, or mirror mind, in a very simple form in my experience and as presented by a Buddhist monk centuries ago. Do not be concerned if at first your own pristine awareness doesn't have any obvious Buddha marks on it. Visit the state regularly and you will eventually find marks aplenty. If there is some art, poetry, or religious writing that pleases you, try enjoying it in this state. Later you can ask major questions in this state and get answers. But first find it and learn to enjoy it regularly. Later you can experiment with other possibilities in it. Longchenpa had been in this state countless times and could easily enter it whenever he wanted.

Let me create an analogy of our situation. Suppose our mind is like a busy apartment house. There are many families. We note babies' cries, children's laughter, busy adults coming and going, and the aged. The apartment house is our mind. Why so many people here? Because in some ways we are like babies, children, adults, and the aged. We are busy in so many different concerns and roles. The builders of the apartment house simply bulldozed the land, made it flat, and built on it. Unknown to all the people here, there is a wonderful stream flowing underneath. Under our mind is this stream, which has the wonderful property that when you step into it you suddenly see everything in its perfect nature. You see from eternity, from the universal. If the people in the apartment house could go down through the basement, into the underground caverns, and visit this stream, it would heal them by enabling them to slip out of limited vision. I speak of this pristine stream not because Buddhism says it is so, but because I have been visiting it a long while.

Pristine means "prior, belonging to the earliest period or state, original, free from drabness, soil or decay because it is fresh and clean." We have in us pristine awareness. It is a natural given to all. It simply needs to be found, and like all mysteries, treated respectfully. In the stream analogy above, if someone tried to bottle the water and sell it, they would find the bottle empty when brought into the light. It can't be treated as a commodity. It is beyond manipulation, because it is of the divine nature. That is why Longchenpa says it has all the major and minor marks of Buddhahood. Its very nature is beyond our manipulation, but it is quite capable of transforming us, and this we can bring into the light of day.

Let me give a minor example of a visit to pristine awareness. After writing the previous chapter I felt drained of ideas. Before retiring I asked to be shown what is next. I had already resolved that if there were no clear indications, I would simply spend a day getting caught up on my correspondence. I woke up a couple of times in the night and checked the bulletin board of my mind. No answer yet. Just before awakening I got, "Pristine awareness." I knew what was meant, but I thought I had so little material on it I would make it the close of the last chapter. I got, "No, a new chapter," and I saw an image. In the lower part of the picture are the heads of several people. In the upper part hands are reaching down and rearranging their thoughts. I recognized this as a picture of pristine awareness which very much rearranges thoughts. I was surprised at several people's hands and several heads. I remember one of the pair of hands was black. I see this as meaning the Universal (represented here as the hands of several races) rearranges everyone's thoughts. And, of course, at that time my thoughts were being rearranged on what I would do next. *You cannot meet pristine awareness until you are open to being influenced and rearranged.* Afterwards, you are free to consider what has been given to you. But your openness is critical to the appearance of pristine awareness.

I know that this guidance is available, that it can answer questions, and that it is a natural given in my experience. I was not surprised that it was given just as I was awakening, when I was least able to manipulate the situation. I suppose some will think the message I received was an auditory hallucination. It wasn't. It was noetic: a wholly-formed thought that appears in your mind with no forethought, planning, or effort. It is just suddenly *there and understood.* Afterward you can reflect on it. No doubt everyone reading this has had this experience already. With long experience I know these are given to me by influx. I do not take credit for them. I misinterpreted its aim and it corrected me—indicating the topic was not to be an addendum to the last chapter but a new one. The image was a surprise to me. If I had made an image it would be one pair of hands working on one head (mine); I was surprised that it presented many. In a sense what I am writing is many (all the mystics I refer to) working on many heads (my readers). This whole book is being written with this kind of guidance. Pristine awareness conceived this project. Even when I am tired, and quite ready to quit, it comes up with more ideas. When I am doubtful and thinking this is impossible, it remains enthusiastic.

Let me make clear what happens if one takes credit or attempts to manipulate this process. Say I have thought about a new gadget for days. The ideas just seem wrong. Suddenly I awaken with an image showing me how to make it work. I patent it, sell it, and get rich. If I take all credit for this process, as though I am a very clever person, it dries up; thereafter I have quite mediocre ideas. Why does pristine awareness withdraw? Its real aim is not invention and material wealth, but to lead into universal understanding. If I take credit, I am going in the direction of ego inflation which is spiritually harmful. So it withdraws to avoid this development. An inspired idea is just its calling card. Inspire means to breath in. Breath and spirit are closely related. The word "inspired" in its roots means to be filled with spirit.

Pristine awareness occurs at the boundary of the Divine and the human, and gifts are given at this boundary. If I take credit for them, I am using gifts from the Divine to aid my separation from the Divine and ultimately my spiritual downfall. Its aim is full enlightenment, so for my sake it will withdraw if not acknowledged as the More-Than-Self. Freely acknowledging what is More-Than-Self is simply being friendly and open with mystery. Think of this mystery as a lonely person who is very able to inspire, but for your sake you must acknowledge it as more than you. As the Sufis indicate, it resembles a love affair. Two join and can relate, yet they remain two. In pristine awareness you are temporarily joined.

One aspect of the Divine is that, by its nature, it chooses to reform people through their own volition. This makes most of its interactions with people gentleness itself. You are left in freedom to accept with thanks, to take all credit, or even to curse the Source. It will not use major visions to enforce your belief, because that would violate your freedom. It is Freedom Itself that created and respects your freedom.

In a real sense we live in a kind of dreadful freedom. I say dreadful because the combination of our abysmal ignorance and our freedom means we can do very badly. People have asked me what I would prefer to be. Everyone is surprised when I have answered, "A rock." They thought I would like to be a lion or an eagle. Human freedom opens all sorts of possibilities both of good and of disaster. Because we are so unsure of our bearings, we might step on a land mine at any minute. As a rock I am solidly and irrevocably in my own nature. Only great heat or pressure can transform me, and as a rock I don't care. From rock, to plant, to animals, to humans I see an increasing chance of losing oneself. Pristine awareness is more like rock. One will never find pristine awareness wondering about its nature or how it should behave. That is strictly a human characteristic. Perhaps a healthy plant, that just lives out its nature, could represent pristine awareness. But plants also have some sort of awareness and ability to respond to light, gravity, disease or injury. Pristine awareness is more like a rock, the rock on which we stand and on which our house is built, the bedrock of our nature.

Getting answers from pristine awareness is a small use to give it. Its greatest use is that it is fully capable of reforming our nature and out of that our perception and our experience. You no longer need *to do anything* either outwardly or inwardly. In pristine awareness you enter the awareness that underlies all existence, experiencing an elevation of spirit that can reach ecstacy. In this experience you are shown and reformed at the same time. Entering upon infinite possibilities, you are inclined to dally, and stay there, because it is so good, and there is an infinity to go through. Far from being an arduous ascetic practice, it is a sheer delight.

I have been quite disenchanted by occult literature that implies that by some complex magical procedure it is possible to create great wealth and even to control the world. Many books imply that someone long ago discovered the secret and only the author knows it, but isn't telling, setting up an impossible contest that only a hero can win. From the viewpoint of pristine awareness this is so upside down and backwards! The way is actually quite simple. Give up and seek the grace of God. When you have ultimate happiness you don't need wealth, and least of all power over others. Every religious tradition gives a way to God as candidly and as openly as possible. It is openly shown to those who approach it with a good heart. So rather than being hidden and mysterious, many have openly talked about the way to God and have led others to it. The sacred is only hidden from the profane. This is a quite natural and God-given protection, which is thoroughly woven into the nature of existence itself. Even priests and ministers may not touch the sacred until they are worthy. How does this happen? They will simply be unable to see, experience, and know it. In this way the sacred is fabulously and most subtly protected. But the way is open to all who approach it with a good heart.

A major implication in all religions is that one approaches God through becoming like God. Religious festivals are a deliberate identification with God. The Roman Catholic goes through the stations of the cross, identifying with Christ's life as though the petitioner is becoming like Christ. The holy is opened insofar as you are holy. You literally cannot perceive and experience what is not of your nature. If you really want to approach God, assume a wisdom that penetrates all sham and sees into your innermost heart. This approach to the sacred requires that you peer into your own nature to see what is the best you have to offer. In this process you approach God, and God approaches you. In the eventual mystical union your effort and God's are one. We cannot create goodness, but we can learn to enter it and to live in it. The sacred is this goodness, and we approach goodness by attempting to act on the goodness we know.

The profane take an opposite tack. "There must be some trick, some way to manipulate my way into the sacred. I will pretend to be holy." Can you picture Wisdom falling for this? While the simple person of good heart has entered and explored the wonders of the whole temple, the profane find themselves trapped in a room of blank walls, looking for the secret device that will release them. The Roman soldiers who sacked the temple at Jerusalem got only a few trinkets and an incredible poverty of spirit—and an awesome load of bad karma. It looks as though the soldiers succeeded, but they actually failed terribly. Sacred objects may need physical protection, but the spiritual in itself is quite beyond violation. The sacred opens easily to those who approach it sacredly, but it is not even in the distant view of the profane. It doesn't exist for them. I was immensely pleased to find this ample safeguard woven into the very nature of the sacred. It is those who have not turned to God contritely who consider God's ways dark, occult, and mysterious. To a mystic they are as clear and plain as can be.

It is an extraordinarily simple idea that if I want to receive a state of being I must be like that state. The gentle receive from

Gentleness! In Zen there are many funny stories about manipulation and effort. In one, the student is in a hurry for satori (enlightenment). He says he will do thus and so, and the master says then it will take five years. The student promises much more effort and the master says then it will take ten years! Effort lengthens the process, and makes it harder.

I was very impressed by one incident in a Zen story. A student asked, "Where is the Buddha nature?" The master answered simply, "The tree in the courtyard." This tree is right in the center of the courtyard, and it has carefully-raked sand circling it. What does this answer mean? Picture the tree in the courtyard as a spiritual image. The answer to the question, "Where is the Buddha nature" is "Nearby, in sight." It is the life that grows up out of the ground, near you, that you are overlooking as you ask your question. It is an honored tree, in the center of the courtyard, sand raked in circles. This is a very precise answer. For the student asking, it was nearby. But for the master the tree of life is right here—answering the student. Pristine Awareness is nearby, in sight—but with effort five years away, and with supreme effort eons away. It is the inverse of effort. It simply is.

The following blank verse came to me when I was in a state of sagging spirit, here represented as a ruin, and I entered pristine awareness through it.

> When all effort has ceased
> When you take delight in the single note
> of a bird
> To lift your spirits.
> When you have collapsed inwardly
> upon yourself.
> There—in the little pile
> The rubble of past involvements
> The core of you that remains is pristine
> Eternal
> Always was and always will be
> Beginning and end
> The original self
> The essential core.
> Do not cry out against God
> That you are in ruin.

How else could you see
The clear stream that flows
Out of nowhere to everywhere?
We should celebrate this ruination
That reduces all to the original One.

This heaped up little ruin
That I am—
So entirely insignificant.
Resting in
All that is.

How to find it ever again?
Let all fall in ruin
All pride
All entanglements.
In this ruin
Find the simple life
That remains
Ever.
And rest in this awareness.
The center is wide open
Spacious
One can wander around
And look at all events
From a new perspective.

Awful concerns
Are like terrible demons
Painted on boards
Colorful pictures
That never move.
Look at those blue teeth
And sharp claws
Painted on wood.

In spacious stillness
One can freely wander
And look at it all
And gain perspective.

No hurry
Take your time
To look at it all

This is pristine awareness
What lies in total ruin?
You die to self
And all entanglements
To become free
To see it all
Things in time
From the steady eye
Of eternity.

Probably you have been in a similar state many times. Perhaps you were just tired and decided to sit and look at the world around you. You weren't doing anything but resting. But your mind opened up, and everything began to be more harmonious and pleasant. This state has a very spacious feeling, as though one could wander, and look, and learn forever. From the peaceful center of this state you could look at your concerns, the demons with sharp teeth and claws; they looked not so bad, painted on wood. Like the Tibetan paintings of awful demons, they are perhaps painted too well, so that their beauty betrays the horror they are meant to portray. The next time you get all tangled in a terrible situation, see a demon painted on wood.

Perhaps in a little while you get up from this rest and think, "I must have needed this," not realizing that you were closer than the tree in the courtyard. The state opens when you just let yourself be. Rather than "I must just have needed rest," the mystic says, "Aha, this is worth cultivating." I am quite convinced that these gentle precursors of mystical experience are quite common. They need merely to be recognized and cultivated. There seems to be very little difference between saying, "I must have needed rest," and "This is worthwhile, I must return again and explore further." But it is the difference between no Buddha tree in the courtyard and one at hand. If I say I was merely tired, I limit it to the physical. If I say this holds promise, I will cultivate it, and start on a whole path of discovery. I have explored this state for years, and as far as I can see, the discovery in it is endless. It contains the Buddha marks, the signs that God is present. One obvious sign is that one enters pure Truth and Wisdom. This is one of endless marks, but you need to find them yourself, and of course you can describe this as Christ awareness or whatever your preference.

Pristine Awareness is an innate, given capacity in everyone. It is not forbidden to try any kind of exercise or manipulation you want, but remember that pristine awareness is the opposite of effort. It is effortless. By what effort can you reach effortlessness? Any effort to create it blocks it. It is well just to state your deepest concerns, and then wait in silence for pristine awareness to appear and guide you. It can answer questions, and it is very gentle. It will suggest, but you are always free to consider and reflect on its suggestions. One of its great uses is simply to reorder your perception, your thought, and your life itself. All that it does drifts toward enlightenment and the direct experience of God as though that was always its goal. Along the way you will make endless discoveries about yourself, nature, and existence. It is not possible to go this way without becoming wiser. Its effect is never to make one feel better than others; rather one drifts toward feeling kin to all others, and kin to all there is. It takes repeated visits to this state to become accustomed to it. Rather than being impossibly difficult, as many have said, it is quite easy. A beginning student may take thirty minutes, an average student five minutes; to the experienced it is there in a moment.

A friend of mine who knew my interests sent me Malidoma Some's *Of Water and Spirit* (56). Malidoma is a contemporary central African Dagara black who was kidnapped by Jesuits at age four and raised to be a priest. He escaped in late adolescence and returned to his people. There he finds he is far behind all other males in his development within this culture. At age twenty he goes off naked into the jungle to undergo initiation by the male elders of the tribe. The initiation is primarily to become opened up to visionary experience, so that he can be guided by spirits and ancestors for the rest of his life. His western Jesuit training had impaired him and made him slow compared to thirteen-year-olds in his tribe. I was struck by the initial instructions to the whole group of naked initiates, because I could say the same thing about pristine awareness. Imagine that you are naked, sitting around a fire in the jungle, about to undergo initiation by your elders. Here is Malidoma Some's account of one elder's instruction:

Somehow what he said did not sound strange to me or—I found out later—to anyone. It was as if he were putting into words something we all knew, something we had never questioned and could never verbalize.

What he said was this: The place where he was standing was the center. Each one of us possessed a center that he had grown away from after birth. To be born was to lose contact with our center, and to grow from childhood to adulthood was to walk away from it. "The center is both within and without. It is everywhere. But we must realize it exists, find it, and be with it, for without the center we cannot tell who we are, where we come from, and where we are going."

He explained that the purpose of Baor (the initiation process) was to find our center. This school specialized in repairing the wear and tear incurred in the course of thirteen rainy seasons of life. I was twenty. Had I been home all that time, I would have gone through this process seven years ago. I wondered if I was catching up too late but then thought, better late than never.

"No one's center is like someone else's. Find your own center, not the center of your neighbor; not the center of your father or mother or family or ancestor but that center which is yours and yours alone."

—Malidoma Some, *Of Water and the Spirit* (56)

Even though I come from a vastly different culture, I agree completely that each of us has a natural center. In the course of life we get busy with things and lose track of our centers. Age thirteen is a good time to repair this damage. But we, being far behind these "primitives," may doubt the center exists, and may never find it. I also agree that each one's center is different. The way of the Dagara is to be guided by spirits and ancestors. This is a level between the personal and the Universal. On a personal level each will be led through a somewhat different drama. But follow the path long enough and you come out on the plain of the universal. The purpose of the initiation was to aid each to find their center, where they would meet this guidance. The Dagara are also aware of the Universal further down the path. I would have several questions of Malidoma. For one, is there a separate initiation for women? It would seem unbalanced to me to only put men through this experience. I would also wonder how this capacity to visit their center for guidance fits into the culture. That his extensive Jesuit training impaired him for direct religious experience is no surprise to me. When he came back from the Jesuits the tribal elders debated if he would be a hopeless case, and he actually did not do as well as most thirteen-year-olds. One of his spiritual tasks in the initiation was to sit and gaze at a tree until he had a vision. The procedure sounds remarkably like my own gazing at an icon—staying with a constant stimulus until the center opens and reveals itself. In his case he met a green goddess who had all his love. Malidoma represents an almost unique example of a "primitive" who is so well-educated he can really tell us like it is. I would like to go through the Dagara initiation myself—if my delicate white feet and bottom could stand the jungle!

There are so many paradoxes in this example I hardly know where to begin. I have heard so much about how terrible paganism is. If this is an example, I think the critics should look a lot closer before they condemn. These spirits and ancestors, since they project out of the people, are simply the higher aspects of themselves, appearing in a form appropriate to the culture. They expect God to come in this form, and God is quite able to adapt to cultural differences! Similarly we are not surprised that God speaks to each of us in our native language. We are so detached from this way of thinking that our central experience is more likely to appear quite different, but the process is the same. The native expecting spirits and ancestors meets God in that form, while Christians may find guardian angels or some other form. I would be a little concerned if a Westerner was meeting spirits and ancestors, but for these people this is an appropriate way.

Basically I look at the fruits of the process before judging whether it is of any good or not. For these people the initiation appears to help them in many ways, and makes them a useful member of the group. The fruit is good. If only we had such fruit in our backward culture! But if a Westerner meets spirits and ancestors in visions, I would immediately check its fruit. If a vision makes him feel superior to others, then it is a different and dangerous process. Heaven is a kingdom of uses; of what joins people together. Hell is a kingdom of splits and divisions created by isolated and impoverished egos.

Pristine awareness is really just relaxed perception. In Zen, pristine awareness is called "the original face." Face here means nature. Swedenborg said that the angels in heaven know your nature from your face. It is paradoxical when the Zen master asks the student to show their original face. Your original face or nature just is. Any effort will only disguise it.

In most of life we get an idea and act on it as a reality. My laundry needs washing; I should go do it. Our mind projects us into the world where we become entangled in events. There are methods that attack this process itself. One simple one is Ramana Maharshi's asking, "Who am I?" (57) The question is not asked lightly, but is repeated silently, becoming a major questing for the source of identity itself. This questioning gets you back into the mysterious source of yourself, beneath and beyond small ego. All easy answers like "I am so and so" are just word signs that don't really answer. Ultimately you find that you can't answer, discovering that you are a process already present, and underway, and quite unknown. Attacking the source of mind or experience works for some, leading back to pristine awareness, the natural mind underlying all we consider mind. I prefer the utter simplicity of relaxed perception. Once you know there is mind underlying your ordinary mind, and how to find it, you have made a good start. Then you need to return to it daily until it tames and teaches you. It is very like discovering you have your own marvelous natural spring.

Yet many people will say "This is not possible." "Such springs don't exist." "They were only known centuries ago." "Only a great one from a distant place and time found it!" Clever reason so easily fools itself. If only they would bend down and try a cupful of the refreshing water. Over and over I have heard it said that revelation stopped with so-and-so, long ago. Indeed. Tell the Dagara. They will laugh and say, "That is the white man's sickness."

> The most desirable of all
> Is never elsewhere
> But simply here
> Waiting to be seen
> With the eye that is
> One's whole being.
>
> Oh, when this eye opens
> Everything is found

In place
Right
All right
Oh, indeed very good.

Within is refuge
Is gathering together
Recollecting—
Setting first things
In first place.

I go home to silence
To have my priorities
Put in order.
First priority
Is to go home
And then it is shown me.

How are they to know
It is within?
When everything appears outside
In such multiplicity—
Busy, busy, everywhere.

Oh, such a dancing disguise
For utter simplicity.
But look now—
To see utter simplicity
In the dancing disguise—
No longer led astray.

14

Some Questions Answered

The autumn floods had come. Thousands of wild tor-
rents poured furiously into the Yellow River. It surged and
flooded its banks until, looking across, you could not tell an
ox from a horse on the other side. Then the River God
laughed, delighted to think that all the beauty in the world
had fallen into his keeping. So downstream he swung, until
he came to the Ocean. Then he looked out over the waves,
toward the empty horizon in the east and his face fell.
Gazing out at the far horizon he came to his senses and mur-
mured to the Ocean God: "Well, the proverb is right. He who
has got himself a hundred ideas thinks he knows more than
anybody else. Such a one am I. Only now do I see what they
mean by EXPANSE!"
—Thomas Merton, *The Way of Chuang Tzu* (58)

Up to this point we have been on a straight course to elaborate
various aspects of the experience of our common God. Undoubted-
ly readers of various traditions and backgrounds will have some
questions. I would like to try to address at least some of these. In
effect we are standing back from the experience to see how this
relates to other areas of religion and psychology. The first and foremost is that religions end up with different representations of the
Divine. In fact this is their most obvious difference. So let us look at
the apparent multitude of our differences.

Diverse Representations of the Divine

I have been dealing with God as the Ultimate One. In Christianity this is the level of the Father, in Islam Allah, in Hinduism Brahman, and in Buddhism nirvana. This One is quite beyond all forms whether conceptual forms and words, or as shown in art. Yet we seem to need some form to relate to. If it is of God and has any form, including words, it is a representation of the Divine. Religions are easily distinguished by their representations. What represents God in one religion may be merely a curious artifact to other religions.

Swedenborg said that God is the Very Human. To me this says at least two things. By capitalizing Very and Human he is saying God is the Divine aspect of the human. Yet he is also saying that since God is Very Human, in our very innermost human nature we have the means to come back to God. Our way of return is in our very nature, and the way to God is through our humanness. The long tour in history from God in the forces of nature, to God in animals, to human Gods may be a gradual zeroing in on the Common God.

Different creeds are like different cultures. The Eskimo lived on animals and wore animal skins, so it is reasonable to me that their religion deals with the spirits of animals. If I lived in the same circumstances, I would want to respectfully study under Eskimo shamans and deal with animal spirits. All religions look to me like different cultures, which grew up in a particular time and place and solved certain human problems their way. I have speculated that if elephants should conceive of God I would not be surprised if their God was at first represented as the forces of nature, and then perhaps as particularly delicious and nutritious plants, and finally as the Great Elephant. I can't believe for a moment they would represent God as a man, since man is killing them and crowding them off the earth. As a mystic I would see it as entirely appropriate if elephants had an elephant God.

Below the level of a culture's principal representation of God there are always a host of lesser figures which are aspects of God, or god-like persons, or messengers of God. Most of these are some mix of the human and the Divine. The great pantheon of figures in Hinduism and Buddhism are not multiple Gods, but different aspects of God. The Hindu Kali represents the creator/destroyer aspect of the One. The Buddhist Goddess Kuan Yin represents the gracious compassion of the Divine. Below this level we have all the saints and god-like persons. I used to have the common prejudice that creating saints was a kind of idolatry. It wasn't until I really saw into the world of icons that I realized there are persons through whom the Divine shows. Many who stand squarely on the Bible and deny saints should look up "saint" in a good Bible Concordance. "Saint" is a synonym for holy. A saint is simply one in whom the holy shows through. This is not to say all will see that holiness, since one must have the holy within to perceive it without.

Additional agents which are representatives of the Divine are angels, good spirits, and in many cultures one's sacred ancestors. There are also sacred places, sacred objects, sacred words, sacred gestures, sacred books, and sacred symbols. If you looked at all of the representations of the Divine in the Bible alone, it would make a multitude. What it comes down to is that pretty much everything has been or could be a representation of the Divine. Paden put it quite well:

> Gods correlate with critical points of a world where humans are most open to the power of "the other." If a world is crucially subject to what comes from the sky, from animal or plant life, from clan or political order, or from ritual purity, we may expect to find gods located in these junctures and conceived in these categories. In societies based firmly on family relationships and social hierarchy, such as traditional China, we are not surprised to find ancestors, elders, and emperors receiving the same reverence as gods. If a community or individual is weary of a despotic, alien world, we are not surprised to find gods appearing as messiahs, redeemers, and inner guides, delivering us to another, better place altogether.
> —William Paden, *Religious Worlds* (36, p. 126)

Gods are often presented as a great revelation out of the distant past, handed down directly from heaven. The cynic, who has no Gods to honor, will say that obviously all these representations of God are man-made and serve human functions. I agree completely. I find it refreshing to think of Gods as very directly related to human needs. To me this does not destroy their power, but rather makes them more understandable and accessible.

Let us look at the process by which something becomes sacred. I can illustrate it by my experience with the ten-cent postcard icon of St. Innocent of Irkutsk, described earlier (4). Instead of the experience becoming boring and limited, it blossomed endlessly in expanding discoveries. At times, while gazing at this static icon, St. Innocents's face went through infinite rapid changes. I found I could express concerns and receive guidance. The experience was much too rich to describe. There developed a kind of dynamic interaction between us. It was obvious to me I was projecting what was in me into the icon, where I could then see it and read it back. But even though it is a very human process of projecting and discovering, the process itself had higher dimensions. I discovered a wisdom that I could not claim credit for. It may have been in me, but I can only touch it in the empty stillness of meditation. This is the process by which something becomes sacred.

Tradition may suggest a way (in this case a combination of Eastern meditation and a Western icon). But one must enter into a relationship and an interaction with the sacred. It becomes sacred when it is found to embody the higher within you. This is the key to the whole world of God representations. You must live with a representation and interact with it for it to acquire meaning. When you can find in it the life that transcends you, it then becomes sacred. Some lose touch with what is in them, so it appears as though the object itself is fully sacred. But the wiser person remains in touch with the source of the sacred in himself. After I became acquainted with this process I could meditate on my icon without it being present. Later any scene could become my icon. The experience generalized to life itself.

People's sacred images and objects represent a rich experience in which they can find the sacred in themselves as represented in the external world. Representations of the Divine are a very humanly-needed aid to interacting with what is higher than ourselves. Instead of feeling that others' sacred things are weird, odd, or pagan, we should be a bit envious that they can find so much in what looks like very little to us. I honor the whole process by which people find something to honor. I may not know the names of their Gods, or what they represent, but I honor the process by which any people contact the sacred anywhere.

Throughout I have tried to avoid sexism in relation to God. At the outset I said God was neither male nor female, and both. The paradox of being neither and both is really to say that neither of these categories works alone. Many representations of God have been male. We should be suspicious when males proclaim that God is male. I can fully appreciate that some will need a goddess. I was charmed by John Blofeld's *Bodhisattva of Compassion* (59). He went on a long search until he found a feminine divine in Kuan Yin. In some ways she corresponds to the Virgin Mary. After I read Blofeld I realized I had a fine white porcelain figure of Kuan Yin unhonored somewhere in the house. She is now atop my rolltop desk, and I work under her compassionate gaze. With all males on my altar I felt a longing for something feminine. My Kuan Yin is decidedly woman. Her gown flows, she stands on a flower and holds flowers in one hand, while the right hand is in the mudra of bestowing blessings. There seems to be little of gender in a need for a female God. Both men and women can feel the need of her. A female representation is appropriate when the god within feels more feminine than masculine.

I honor the whole process by which peoples from all times and places have found such creatively different ways of describing the sacred. I was quite pleased to see a book about primitive Hindu shrines, with photographs of what people had made out of a bit of paint, tinfoil, and whatever (40). Anything can become sacred if someone is willing to find their sacred in it. The mystic has taken but a little further step. In the mystical experience it is found that the Divine shows forth in every aspect of creation. As Swedenborg says, the whole of existence is a theater of representations of the Divine.

Sometimes the Divine is represented simultaneously in its formless aspect and as manifesting in existence. An example from Taoism is, "Twenty-four spokes hath the wheel, but in its empty center is its usefulness." One should say the first part, "Twenty-four spokes hath the wheel" as though stating an amazing and marvelous thing! Imagine twenty-four spokes! This represents the whole of manifest existence. "But in its empty center is its usefulness" refers to the empty center that permits the wheel to go on an axle to do work. The empty center is the One. It is empty; it has no form. It looks like nothing. But it is the means by which everything is done, and the center around which all turns. Of course the twenty-four spokes are also useful. Seen rightly, they point to the empty center. In Buddhism the wheel represents the whole round of events and all turnings and changes. And of course the empty center knows not of change. What is it that changes and remains ever the same? You.

Outwardly you roll like a wheel through changes. But in the empty center nothing has ever changed. Can you not sense the you that has always been the same you? This one is ageless and destined to live forever. It is your still and changeless center in the midst of all the busy turning of existence.

If others' representations do not move us, they appear unsacred to us, and we may act foolishly. Rather we should conclude that we lack the experience that others have. Having learned to experience the sacredness of representations which were at first alien to me, I am now aware of the process by which anything can become sacred. It simply requires understanding and interacting with others' representation until the sacred in you is found to be echoed in the representations. Like learning to appreciate art, this process is an opening and expanding to the more. I read of Zen masters (61) and of the Roman Catholic Jesuit, Jean Pierre de Coussade (62), and discovered that both had come to find that the process of realizing the sacred had generalized until the whole environment had become sacred. They had entered into mystical experience. De Coussade had lived the view that the Divine was dealing with him in all the circumstances of his existence. Some new and unexpected demand on his time wasn't seen as an interruption; the wisdom of the Divine was simply showing in an unexpected way.

You can work with any representation of the Divine until you discover more and more of the sacred within finding expression outwardly. I had not expected my own experience of the icon to generalize, but it did. I had merely asked, "Can I meditate on my icon without it being physically present?" I could. Then I came to see all of existence as my icon. The formal boundaries between religions often lie in what they regard as sacred. When an individual comes to regard everything as sacred, they have reached the plain of the universal.

We can also turn around the experience of the sacred to find its human potentials. Tell me all you consider sacred and I will have an adequate representation of your inner life. Those who consider nothing sacred are in a darkness of understanding themselves. They are often imprisoned as too dangerous for normal human company. For some, sacredness is limited to a few specific things, and this is a reflection of their internal limitations. For some, the sacred is limited to love relations and this becomes their major representation of the Divine. The same is true of those for whom art is sacred. Even more important is how you relate to what you consider sacred. How do you act with your sacred? Is your experience of your sacred theoretical, a matter of talk, or do your actions reflect your real relationship to your sacred?

When I am getting acquainted with someone, I like to see their home. In a glance I can see a reflection of the quality of their inner life in how they shape their space. What we honor and how we honor it is very much a representation of the inner life. The way to the sacred outside is the way to the sacred within. We honor ourselves when we honor creation. Divine representations are at the intersection of the Divine and the human, and partake richly of both. The way to the Divine is also a way of personal discovery. Again we find persons are a microcosmic image of all there is. The puzzle of so many diverse representations of God is at once the creativity of God and of persons. This puzzle is solved when we understand the creative process by which the sacred is found.

Misunderstandings Between Religions

Misunderstandings easily arise between religions, even among well-intentioned people, because religions are not simple objects. *I would not feel I understood a religion until I had really lived within it for some time.* Religions are *of life* and need to *be lived* to be understood. We generally learn a few external details of a religion and try to judge the whole from what we suppose from these details. I will deal with a single misunderstanding between Christianity and Buddhism as an example.

I have seen some religious experts rather taken aback when they hear there is no God in Buddhism. God is so much the supreme element in most religions that a religion without a God hardly seems to qualify as a religion at all. Buddhism is not a theistic religion, and to many religious people this seems like a terrible and irreconcilable difference. But let us examine it.

In most of the world, and particularly in the West, we apprehend things as objects with names. The world is full of things to which we assign names so we can refer to them. So when it comes to the Ultimate we also give it a name, God. When we do this, we are thinking of God as simply another object. But is God anything like an object? It is characteristic of objects that they are only in one place at one time. We have never known, nor will we ever know an object that is omnipresent. Have we ever known an omniscient or omnipotent object? Never. In fact, with a little examination we can safely declare that although we think of God as an object, God is in all critical ways totally unlike any object we have ever known.

Now look at it from a Buddhist perspective. It would be fair to say that the most central subject of Buddhism is Nirvana, the state in which the ultimate is experienced. This state is the aim of every Buddhist, and the whole of Buddhism is devoted to fostering this state. Although we can name this state, the name is merely a pointer toward a possibility that may well be beyond description. Its fullness must be experienced, and we cannot rightly stand outside this experience and manipulate it as a mental construct. The experience of nirvana is full of what in the West we would call God. It is characteristic of Buddhism to have examined mental states so much that they are wary of the vain game of naming states and then manipulating names. The first line of the Taoist *Tao te Ching* "The book of the way" is "The Tao that can be named is not the Tao." If we can name and manipulate it, it is among our mental toys; it is not It in itself.

Christians are quite comfortable with names, even though they will recognize that God is totally unlike any other object named. The Buddhists have spent centuries examining mental games and to my mind quite rightly refer to the Ultimate in terms of Nirvana, the undefined ultimate state available to all, the goal of all Buddhist practice. This choice in part reflects a wish to avoid seeming to make the Ultimate an object, distant from me as a subject. In the actual experience of Nirvana there remains no me there to even look on God. The omnipresent is all there is. The subject/object categories dissolve on the way. This is the meaning of "Only the Son can see God;" only the very Spirit of God sees God. As a mystic I have always been uncomfortable in bantering words about, so I am more comfortable in the Buddhist approach. I would also be in accord with those traditions that forbid naming the ultimate. So what looks like a serious religious difference dissolves upon examination. Other religious differences also dissolve in a similar way if we take the time to really experience what is involved, instead of attempting to apprehend each other by a few names or logical constructs.

Let me close with a quote from a westerner who understood Tibetan Buddhism quite well. Here he defends Tibetan prayer wheels and particularly their flags with prayers on them. Spin the wheel and prayer issues forth.

One aspect of popular Tibetan Buddhism which has drawn disparaging remarks from travelers is the use of prayer-flags and prayer-mills which cause mantras to flutter in the breeze and dharanis to whirl in the streams. These travelers pour scorn on what they take for examples of mechanical religious practice carried to extremes. Even if that were so, one might be tempted to reply that flags inscribed with mantras of compassion are a pleasanter and more improving sight than the concrete structures shaped like torpedoes and rocket-bombs that adorn many cities in the West. As it happens, Tibetans do not suppose that wind or water power will assist them to reach Nirvana, leaving them free to spend their time in earthy enjoyment, for they are acquainted with the Buddhist teaching that liberation is the fruit of a man's effort. The prayer-flags and prayer-mills, set up by people with mantras constantly on their lips and in their hearts, testify to a sort of spiritual exuberance, to a longing for the whole universe to be full of sounds and symbols inspired by the Dharma with even the wind and the water contributing to the auspicious mantric dance. Where everything exists in the mind, what is the difference between words that are spoken and words that flutter in the breeze?
—John Blofeld, *The Tantric Mysticism of Tibet* (21, p. 196f)

We should be very careful of attempting to apprehend a person's whole life by a few mental constructs that we can so easily judge. After Blofeld's defense of prayer flags I would wish to see many more fluttering in the breeze with high and noble sentiments being sent forth. This is the same John Blofeld who helped me to enjoy the goddess Kuan Yin who now looks down on me as I write.

Religious Intolerance
If you asked the average person what is the worst aspect of religion, a great many would point to its remarkable tendency to intolerance. This extends all the way from, "I have found the one right way; all others are lost," to feeling totally justified in killing members of any other religion. The degree of intolerance varies considerably between religions, with Christianity and Islam at the top of the intolerance list and Buddhism barely making the list at all. Of

course many instances in which religions appear to be in conflict are actually due to cultural and economic differences, with religion just a convenient way to identify the adversaries.

The religiously intolerant in general deal with religion in an extroverted fashion. An introvert processes experience through himself before he can react to external events. It is as though he says to himself, "Let me see how I feel about that." But the extrovert doesn't process through himself because for him it clearly is "out there;" he can see and react to the external directly. The intolerant find religion in an extroverted way. "It is of the Book, the doctrine; it is the law," and they are very inclined to seek and find religious people like themselves. Let us say an extroverted person has found the right people, and the right doctrine, and even comes to experience life more deeply through this. It is but a short step to come to the conclusion that *this is the right way for all mankind.* Often there are suggestions in their doctrine and the prejudice of church leaders that reaffirm this conclusion. Then there may follow some concern about what happens to all not of this church. Do they go to hell? Perhaps we should do missionary work to go out and save them. If one's whole life revolves around an in-group that reinforces certain experiences, and avoids all other experiences, it is quite easy to become intolerant. All others not in one's particular church are then lost and probably condemned. Some religions have spells of righteous wars in which it is noble to kill the infidel. Their doctrine may even grant them a place in heaven for this.

There is a type of religious experience one finds in mystics which may superficially look like prejudice. Many mystics only know one religious frame of reference. Because of this, even after they experience the Universal, they conceive of all higher experiences only in terms of their own religion, because this is the only frame of reference they know. Swedenborg is a good example, though I could cite many others. It is immensely clear that Swedenborg is over and over again referring to the Universal, but he does so only in Christian terms. When he says all will be saved who act in the good they know, he is of course referring to people of all cultures and different persuasions. This is reinforced by the fact that the Divine is quite capable of addressing us not only in our own language but in terms of our culture, religion, and even personal experiences. Ramakrishna (19) is a fine example of a mystic who deliberately tried the way of several major religions and found the

Way in each of them. Every mystic meets the Divine in the framework of his own culture. God is very accommodating.

My own experience of the Divine has been primarily as the
Universal which transcends all cultural viewpoints, and I came into
this experience before I knew religions and religious viewpoints
even existed. So the intolerance between religions is particularly
poignant to me. It looks like a terrible misunderstanding in the one
area that should draw us together. I am now accustomed to trans-
lating between religious frames of reference, and I can easily work
with mystics who describe their experience in a new and different
one. Since I have experienced the universal they are all pointing to,
their different frames of reference are no obstacle to me.
Intolerance exists by an opposite way. I have never known a religious intolerant who had any interest in comparative religion or the
discovery of how other religions function.

> The denial of other views is typically a consequence of
> the need to protect or affirm one's own. We reject other
> views when the truth of our own does not appear to be
> acknowledged in them. If one blind man believes the ele-
> phant is like a tree and another that it is like a wall, then the
> reason they argue is not because they understand the alter-
> native accounts and reject them, but rather in order to
> defend their own respective beliefs. The blind men are not
> even aware of each other's different experiences. None of
> them have the slightest idea about how their counterparts
> are relating to the elephant or why they say what they do.
> —William Paden, *Religious Worlds* (36, p. 126)

The intolerant usually avoid any contact that might threaten
their viewpoint. Some religions even forbid exploring other religions. Intolerance acquires and safeguards its own limited point of
view. The intolerant are also usually devoid of any personal inner
search, taking religion as a purely external matter. Meditation and
the internal personal search involved is the cornerstone of
Buddhism, and this alone may account for the Buddhists' remarkable tolerance. Intolerance is the opposite of the mystical experience in that it is ego magnified. "I have the one right way for all
mankind," overlooks the wealth of human differences, different cir-

cumstances, and cultures. It magnifies the ego, and is a form of vanity. From this position it is easier to assert that one's way is the only right way. The mystical experience treads the opposite path in which the ways of all are found and honored.

It is no wonder that religions, being embedded in very different cultures and all the differences they imply, have difficulty understanding each other. If only God were not so fruitful! While I can enjoy these fruitful differences I still can lament that different religions can say the same thing in so many tongues, not recognizing they speak with one voice. Over and over I find people hoping their "one true religion" will sweep over the earth and replace all others. This would be a cultural disaster of incredible proportions. It is like praying that all plants be replaced by the "one true plant." The other plants, and all the animals that live from them, would die off and disappear. God likes diversity. If we are to be like God we need to enjoy it too.

I believe that one day we will routinely treat intolerance like a very human disorder. The treatment will be to demonstrate the living qualities of other views. Tolerance begins when I can experience and enjoy others' ways as also meaningful. When we see the One Life in all, intolerance will be gone.

Misunderstandings of the Mystical

There are so many misunderstandings of the mystical I hardly know where to begin. A central one is that the direct experience of God is only for a few select people—great ones from the past, or a very holy person. This is completely wrong. The experience is available to all people, young and old, saint and sinner. It has been known by infants and children. A problem children often have is that their culture may provide no means of understanding and integrating the experience into their life. I came out of one major vision at age seven feeling that I must have done something bad! At times ministers themselves are unprepared for parishioners with direct experience, and end up casting doubt on their mental stability! Can one be a sinner and have this experience? Yes, I have known criminals in solitary confinement to have been given great visions. Their lives may not have prepared them for so much goodness, so often they cannot make good use of it. I have also known frankly psychotic persons to have mystical experiences. Again they were often not in a position to use it well. There is no class of persons to whom it may not be given. We will never know how many executed criminals walked right into full enlightenment. The near-death experience would suggest that many did, if not all.

Out of this arises the real question, "What is a good use of the experience?" Treasure the experience and honor whatever leads back to it. Hold on to the good in it, and make it the center and focus of your life. Honoring it would include a detailed reflection on what happened, what it means, how it ties in to religious doctrine, etc. Attempt to follow any leads in it as to how you should live. In my own experience I recall the very moment when, as a boy, I came into the experience for the umpteenth time and resolved to seek it rather than to wait to stumble upon it again. This led to making notes, which led to my writing occupation. It also persuaded me to read all the other mystics I could find, opening me out from a lonely seeker to joining countless others.

If a particular setting is conducive, set aside time to come back to it regularly, at least a few minutes a day. In this setting study the role of your attitude. Find what deepens the experience. Find out how you can pose questions and get answers. Be patient if the answers are subtle—right before you, but broader than your understanding. The inner process may use some external events to illustrate the answer to your question. When seeking an answer I've had a few words of a text so stand out I could not pass them by. I had to stop and reflect on what was being shown. A good deal of becoming a mystic rests upon being curious enough to *play* with the process until its dimensions become clearer and more habitual. I deliberately use the word play. When you play with something you are open to intuition and feelings, trying this and that until it is clearer. To me it is very like an infant discovering that banging a spoon on a pot makes an amazing sound. Bang, bang. It is most amazing.

Given that a person is very open to all experience, how does the transcendent appear? It can appear either right out of the circumstances of the world or right in your inner midst as a thought, feeling or impulse to do something good. If it arises in the world, it arises in you at the same time, or else you would be unable to recognize it in the world. Although a given person may be partially blind to the internal or the external aspect, the real experience of the sacred is internal and external simultaneously. Being deeply internal, it colors all external perceptions.

Anything which increases egotism, any separation between you and the world, will block the experience. For some, very cerebral thought blocks it. Anything which emphasizes you and your powers versus the world is harmful. It is in this sense that mystics say you must die to your ego. There is some mystery about getting ego out of the way. In my greatest experiences it was fully as though I was ushered through death. Then the black nothingness opened up into All There Is. I had died to any sense of my own existence and Existence opened up. In later experiences this death no longer seemed necessary. I no longer regard myself as anything; things simply open up.

One can meet God externally in representations, or within, but eventually the inner and outer are one and the same. With influx the Divine is ever-present and comes right in the midst of your inner life *not as something separate but as a broadening and deepening of your inner life.* So I am totally convinced that mystics, and even the ordinary religious can have enriched experiences which many others do not even know exist. Compared to these experiences, even death is a small and trivial matter. The transcendent occurs in the innermost of persons, right in their life, and this transforms outer experience. The individual's world enlarges until it encompasses all there is. Outwardly one is still a very ordinary and limited human. The mystic walks in two worlds, this ordinary one and the spiritual one. How many people have experienced moments when they felt they were carried on high and their vision of life greatly enriched— and did not realize that this is the essence of the experience of God? Is there one who has not? If there is one let this poor creature stand forth and we will examine his total experience to see if such a thing can be true. The experience is for all. The mystic simply remembers and treasures what others forget, and makes it a central focus of his or her life. The experience is as intimate as your inner life; it is not other than your life itself! The experience of God is an enlargement of the meaning of life right in the midst of your living.

The literature has a great many examples of philosophers and mystics who tried to define stages of the experience. I am wary of stages; it has led some to compare their experience to some great mystic and to find themselves wanting. Mysticism is not a game or sport with great winners and the rest losers. Comparison is inappropriate in this realm. At one time we were all ignorant and struggling beginners. The task of the mystic is to aid all. It is too early to try to describe the mystical experience of all humans in a single format. For the sake of other seekers I would de-emphasize stages and any invidious comparisons between people. If you are working at your relationship to God in any way, you are on your way, and that is enough in itself. In this realm the simplest beginning is quite as precious as the most saintly development. Another doubtful aspect of stages is that they set an external criterion, while the essence of mysticism is in the intimate, personal and *largely unknown details of one's relationship to God.* This relationship is the reality. Stages is an intellectual theory.

There is one account of stages with which I do feel in full accord: the Zen ox-herding pictures (63)*. These pictures don't come out of speculation but rather out of the experience of many mystics. They depict ten stages of mystical insight in a series of paintings of a person and an ox. The person is the spiritual seeker; the ox is the Divine in a wild, unknown, untamed form. Some may find it surprising that the Lord is represented here as an ox. Well, at first it is as though you are in the woods (1), and now and then you find the

1. Seeking the ox

*From THE THREE PILLARS OF ZEN, by Philip Kapleau. Copyright © 1965, 1989 by Philip Kapleau. Copyright © 1980 by The Zen Center, Inc. Used by permission of Doubleday, a division of Bantam Doubleday Dell Publishing Group, Inc.

2. Finding the tracks

3. First glimpse of the ox

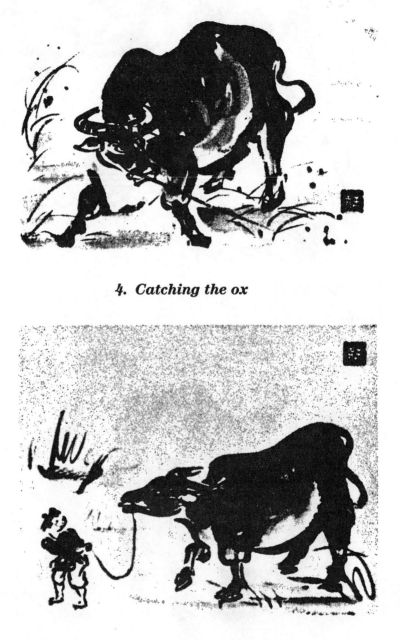

4. Catching the ox

5. Taming the ox

6. Riding the ox home

footprints of some heavy beast (2). You would like to see it, so you track it. Finally you catch a glimpse of it (3). Many are at this stage, having caught only a glimpse of the beast! Finally you catch him but he's a tough one (4). He once stepped on me and I can testify he is heavy. Finally the ox starts to work with you (5). Finally you two are in accord and you can ride the ox home (6).

This whole book is about the first six stages, in which one reaches friendship with the Divine; one can contact the Divine and learn from it. But there is still some dualism, that of the rider versus the ox, though now there is enough friendship and understanding that there is no longer opposition.

I have felt little need to describe the last four stages because the person who has reached stage six is well on their way, and will be shown the last four stages in time. In the seventh picture the ox is forgotten. The monk came to realize he could reflect on the very Life in himself. Ox and self are now the same thing. There is no other. The life one sees and feels within is the One life. The cut-off self never existed. There always was only Life. The repeated experience of the eternal, of coming back to the Divine, gradually weak-

7. *Ox forgotten, self alone*

8. *Both ox and self forgotten*

9. *Returning to the source*

10. *Entering the marketplace with helping hands*

ens the ego sense of "I am a separate entity." Finding the One in so many people and contexts overcomes the sense of separateness. Finally we experience separateness and ego as illusion (Maya). Just as we repeatedly stepped from time to the eternal and back, we can also step from separateness to no separation and back again. Let us look at the last three stages, but realize that only direct experience makes these stages real. In the eighth picture we see just a circle drawn on the page. Even the seeker has vanished. This is the ultimate illumination. There is only this unity. In the ninth picture the world and all its beauty returns, but this is the world transfigured, permeated with the One. There is nothing to seek. It is obvious the One is everywhere. In the tenth picture the adept returns to the marketplace with helping hands, doing what he/she can. What was given is multiplied by being shared. The Zen ox-herding series represents the experience of many, and they are in a nearly universal language. You may have some sense of where you are in this series.

Dualities and The Dark Side of the Divine

There are two basic approaches to reality. In one we simply accept all things as they are and then observe and accept their dynamics. This leads to a non-dual conception of reality. In the other way *we* look for major categorical dualities and use these to explain reality. I stress *we* because it is mankind that creates these dualities. Examples of major dualities are male and female, light and dark, good and evil. Having created and elaborated a duality, we come to depend on it for explanation, and come to assume it is a real part of existence, rather than our invention. Light and dark is a good example. The stark contrast of light and dark is clear in itself, but then what do we do with all the shadings in between which partake of both? Dualistic thinking is convenient, but it creates its own problems, such as how to respond to the shadings in between. Male and female seems to be a very clear and simple duality, but there are people who do not clearly fit into these neat categories. The issue of non-dual versus dual is critical in understanding the universal experience of God, because at the level of the One *all dualities are transcended.* The highest mystical experience is always non-dual. Bearing this in mind, let us step back to the more mundane level of mankind where there appear to be dualities.

Let us take another duality like life and death and look at it. If we seriously reflect on the way things actually are, we see that life and death are part of the same process. If all plants did not die, leaf by leaf or as a whole, the earth would have become one dense mass of plants eons ago. It would be a plant disaster. All nutrients would have been taken out of the soil, and no new plant would have room to live. Dying is a vital part of living. The same is true of every form of life. The design we see about us is a harmonious balance of life and death. Such a balance permits new life while older life returns to its origin.

Similar things happen within us. Today I am enthusiastic about an idea, and set it down. But at the end of the day I am tired and drag myself off to bed. Life in us blooms and dies in a harmonious round. Inwardly we are like plants, with some aspects just starting, others mature, and thankfully some dying.

At the highest level all dualities are transcended. But one that is usually embedded in religion itself is good and evil. Religions usually describe God as all-good. What then to do with evil? If you ask most people what evil they have encountered they will describe events contrary to their wishes. When the mystic Swedenborg describes evils he is basically describing what is a poor way to go, since it leads away from God. This concept of evil or sin is personally useful. It is like a road sign that says, "This is a fruitless way to go." But some people use evil as a way of putting down others. Such a person prefers the limited company of their own kind; all others are potentially evil and dangerous. The more you cut yourself off from others the more you become inwardly limited in human experience. I've seen a few who, after long thought, come to the conclusion they are the only person who really understands religion. They become an odd church of one, unable to get along with anyone, not even God.

I am amazed at how badly the issue of good and evil has usually been handled over the centuries. The answer is given by Swedenborg and other mystics, and is best illustrated by an exercise. You be God for a while. You want to create as free a world as possible for yourself, now going forth as all creatures. Can you really do this by smoothing out every bump in the road? No. That would then be like a possessive parent who doesn't permit their children to play freely, for fear of their being hurt. If you want the ultimate in freedom they must be allowed to explore the full range of existence, the good and the bad. This is done out of the supreme value put on freedom. The price is that some will be hurt. Yet even here be a real God and consider. A child plays with matches and gets burned. The temporary pain, and the choice to be careful in the future, is a part of the depth and qualities of being human.

In the midst of this argument the opponent will eventually say, "Yes, but what if the child dies?" This is usually thought of as if it is all over, a terrible injustice forever. Arjuna presented this same argument to Krishna in the *Bhagavad Gita,* a sacred work to the Hindus. In the midst of a battle, Arjuna of the warrior caste has the duty to go forth in battle to potentially kill his own brothers in the opposing forces, and he didn't want to do it. Krishna, the Divine in human form, began his answer with, "In the first place, no one ever dies!" One must look beyond the temporary little events of this world. On this ground the Christian saints walked calmly to their death, prizing eternal life over this life itself. We can choose evil because our freedom has a supreme value. Evil happens to us so that we might use even that to seek what is higher. And besides, this life is really but a moment, while eternity is a different matter. Even as God I would suppose allowing such a degree of freedom to creation was a really hard decision. Knowing there is no death and how all things balance out helped to make it easier.

When we become very passionate about a duality, with ourselves on the "right side," it is a nice illustration of how we conceive reality to suit ourselves. A marked duality such as God versus the devil weakens the One into two gods fighting. I still remember the moment when I read the following from Isaiah, for in it God clearly takes credit for creating weal and woe, the dark side of existence.

> I am the Lord, and there is
> no other;
> besides me there is no God.
> I arm you, though you do not
> know me,
> so that they may know, from the
> rising of the sun
> and from the west, that there is
> no one besides me;
> I am the Lord, and there is
> no other.
> I form light and create darkness,
> I make weal and create woe;
> I the Lord do all these things.
>
> —Isaiah (25, 45: 5-7)

So there is one God which creates good and also weal and woe, or all human difficulties. We do not need two gods contending. But why the weal and woe? It is part of our learning. How are we to learn if we are not free to make mistakes, and through this to learn of wrong ways? Our freedom is divinely-ordained, and out of this comes the possibility of doing good or ill. Fundamental freedom is a part of fundamental learning. The apparent problem of good and evil is designed to be solved.

Though we easily create dualities in existence, when we really examine them, they are seen to be parts of a functioning whole. Our own ignorance and wondering is part of a possible higher attainment. Our ignorance and doubts are very necessary. They lead us to wonder, inquire and learn. Our mistakes are like high points where we can learn. And if we did not learn in time, what would eternity be like? In this way we credit the One with it all. We have one God. Equipped with this understanding we can now explore God's dark side.

Suppose we decide to do something really wrong. I have always liked chocolate malts. I will buy five and stuff myself. Later I will suffer. The suffering is like a road sign that says, "Dangerous; do not go further." I need money. I will go to a town where I am not known and rob a bank. On the way I suffer all sorts of "what ifs." I will be frightened during the robbery. Even though I appear to get away safely with the money, my conscience plagues me. I suspect that every policeman I see is looking for me, etc. There are built-in safeguards against doing wrong. And if you are religious, and realize that you are under the All-Seeing Eye, it becomes nearly impossible.

But suppose a person is not religious and overcomes all conscience. Where are the safeguards? Suppose a person is alcoholic and they have access to an abundance of alcohol. Some weeks later we meet the same person having drowned all conscience in alcohol. He is now in an alcoholic psychosis. Not only does he feel terrible, but voices are coming out of the vents or out of thin air, saying things like, "I think we should kill this stupid bastard," and he hears someone cocking the hammer of a gun. Our friend is a nervous wreck. His demise and his worthlessness is the constant talk of these demons. He can't sleep, being disturbed by another demon who is all for strangling him. Apparently conscience did not dissolve in alcohol, because it has returned in a very rude, assaultive form.

In some ways the punishment fits the crime in the alcoholic, but how about the poor schizophrenic who also meets the demonic? After a long and careful examination of chronic schizophrenics I have concluded that they did not willfully violate what was in them; they violated it by a mistaken conception of their own nature (64). The schizophrenic seems to split between what they are consistently trying to do in consciousness, and inward forces bent on undermining their every effort. The alien inner forces are the unrecognized other side of the self that also wants to live. The more this core of oneself is rejected, the more persistent and malevolent it becomes. Its malevolence is created by their own negative reaction. The more they reject the inner, the more negative it seems, proving it should be rejected, a real "catch-22." It is very like trying to flee one's own shadow, which thereby seems darker and more persistent and dangerous. So many fail to recover because the solution is not apparent. The solution lies in someone helping mediate between the distressed client and their other side. As they accept the shadow as a natural part of them, it ceases to distress them. As they cease to run from it, it ceases to chase them.

After knowing hundreds of schizophrenics, I conclude that it is perilous to overlook any part of your real nature. In chronic schizophrenia this split-up and struggle gradually can erode away all the normal powers of a person to perceive, judge, and understand. The person is progressively injured and lost in the battle. Old chronic schizophrenics often tell a wild tale of a person who was taken over, killed, and buried. This is an accurate mythological account of what has happened to them. The way back becomes progressively more difficult as more of them becomes lost in this process.

In this way the palpable demonic does exist. It is an actual part of reality itself. It is often represented in Eastern religions by demons with as horrible an aspect as the artist can create. When seen in their proper function they are like Guardians of the Way. Depart from the way a little bit and you feel uncomfortable; conscience starts talking. Go further, and you become sick. Go as far as you can and you will meet Guardian Demons, whose assaultive rudeness matches your stupidity in straying so far. These Guardians are God's compassion in a big, bright road sign saying, "Go no further, stupid; this is the wrong way." I have met many a demon in work with the mentally ill. The main difference between schizophrenic demons and those the saints encounter is that the schizophrenic is ill-equipped for such a cosmic struggle, while the saint enters the battle deliberately, and better-equipped. Mature saints who have transcended this heroic ascetic struggle often live in great modesty and simplicity thereafter.

Once you understand demons as Guardians of the Way, then even these are an intimate and unexpected sign of God's goodness, worthy of honor and respect. When honored and respected, these demons no longer attack us. The essence of what I would say to demons of schizophrenics is, "Don't so overplay your hand. Those who meet you also need some direction and guidance, for they are very lost." Many patients' demons feared I would kill them. Now that I understand them, I would not want to kill any. But to the rudest of them I would say, "Be gentle; remember how lost we are and what guidance we need."

In many temples there are guardian demons or fierce animals at the gate. They protect what is most sacred. I would address all such honorable guardians seen and unseen directly, "I respect your role to frighten, but also be considerate of all the poor lost mentally ill who stumble unwittingly into your strange realm. Balance fright with help."

I will end with a rare little incident involving the demonic that happened to me. I was at work in a mental hospital, dining with other staff. For some reason I was being inwardly tormented by nameless and multiple forces. I was about to take a bite of mashed potatoes when I decided that the way out was to directly recognize these demons as from God. I inwardly said, "Please Lord, cut out this nonsense." Suddenly there was the Lord of heaven about to take a forkful of mashed potatoes. I did not battle with demons, which are rather like the shadow of a divine being. I went to the very Source of the demons. In an instant they vanished and the Author of All was there, affirming the Divine is their source. It all happened so fast the people I was with noticed nothing.

Buddha himself went through a long spiritual struggle. He credited his finding the middle way of Buddhism to the comment of a passing boatman, who remarked that a string too tight will break, and one too loose will not make music. The middle way between extremes makes music.

Other Questions

I can picture so many questions being asked. We are, after all, dealing with the very ultimates of our existence and of the nature of the universe. There is actually a very fine and fitting answer to all possible questions. Questions arise out of your own needs. All your needs can be met by your own experience of the One. "Seek first the

Kingdom of Heaven and all things else will be added to you." This is not just a saying. It is actually the best answer. The way to God answers all questions. You will always have questions until you recognize the way you are already on—the way you will always be on. No words, no matter how clever, can ever take the place of direct experience.

> In the stillness by the empty window
> I sit in formal meditation wearing my monk's
>   surplice,
> Navel and nose in alignment,
> Ears parallel with shoulders.
> Moonlight floods the room;
> The rain stops, but the eaves drip and drip.
> Perfect this moment—
> In the vast emptiness, my understanding deepens.
>   —Ryokan, *Three Zen Masters* (65)

15

The Overall Picture

The Sea Bird

Once upon a time
A great sea bird was blown far inland.
Exhausted, he found himself among people.
They caged him.
He was used to great rolling waves.
He could soar all day long on the wind
Skimming waves
Occasionally diving for fish.

But this was so strange a place.
No water, no waves, no wind.
People cackled strangely over him.
The butcher thought of the meals he would make.
The hat merchant eyed his feathers.
Others' kindness led to his safety in a cage.
But in this alien place
He became quiet
For he was dying.
Thinking him tame, he was let out
For a few hours each day.
When no one was looking
He opened his magnificent wings

And this reminded him
He was a sea bird.

Then one day, when free in the sun
He decided it was either fly or die.
He opened his wings
And with unaccustomed effort took off.
Which way to the sea?
He thought of rolling waves
And simply turned the right way.
His strength returned while in flight.
The sight of distant water
Caused him to climb high.
He glided down from a great height
And dove and caught the first glistening fish.
He then lounged in the swells.
Everywhere bright light
And glistening water
And the power of the ocean.

Enlightenment is remembering you are
A sea bird.
You have wings
And instinctively know the direction.
It is not as though you fly
To what you have never known.
Rather it is of your very nature.

In many ways poetry, art, or music are more appropriate media for mystical experience. Dense, rational argument certainly isn't suitable. Of all the world's many mystical traditions it is Zen that has made the fullest use of artistic expression.

As a sea bird myself it is quite as though I have been blown into a strange place. This is a quite suitable start for mystical experience—simply to look at the world as a strange, and even a humorously peculiar place. Yesterday I got a catalog from a military book club. For very few dollars I can get books that rehash great killings. Oh delight! I also received a catalog of mystical items that promise to confer great power. I can buy miraculous stones that come from the exact center of North America. They supposedly alleviate pain by closing holes in the human energy field. Only $22 for a male and female pair of stones. Pages and pages full of sacred, mystical, transforming items! In the newspaper I learn that Sweden is selling synthetic wolf urine to Kuwait. When sprinkled alongside the road, it keeps camels from crossing and being hit by cars. How strange a world this is. Perhaps this life is not to be taken seriously!

Often people look at a sea bird in terms of their self-interest. How many meals I would make, or how my feathers could decorate their hat. They would lock me up out of loving kindness. Sickening and dying arises simply out of allowing yourself to be wholly subject to circumstances that don't suit you. You forget you can fly, and feel trapped. One of the great values of meditation is that you can practice little flights into freedom. Church services and prayer may also do this for you. All people need to remember and practice letting go and letting things be—taking the pressure off themselves. It is like finding one's own personal sanctuary.

When you set out to fly, there is a problem of which way to turn. Visualize the highest you know of, and you will have turned the right way. It is very like returning to some primordial state that something in you remembers quite well. You find you can rise to a great height, and the higher you go, the more you can see and understand. The glistening fish that is caught is a bit of understanding given you because you need it to sustain you. Soaring over the waves and lounging on them is the mystic simply appreciating things as they are. The central idea here is the contrast between losing sight of your inborn nature in an alien world, versus simply soaring on your visceral, inborn instinctive nature. To understand wings, one must fly. How many birds have you seen in academic discussions of flight? To a real bird, flight is too well-known to be discussed. The weightier the words of academic birds the less they fly!

We have an opportunity now to try to bring together all the strands into a single fabric of understanding. By the mystical experience we are referring simply and awesomely to the direct experience of our common God. Cultural and historic accidents have led to an immense assortment of names and even namelessnesses of God. But however it is said, or not said, we understand it is the same One, common to us all. Instead of being put off by our differences, let us celebrate them, because each represents a whole rich discovery. In this realm we have an abundance of riches, not a poverty of them.

Those who have had the direct experience of God have a very

wide area of essential agreement. The apparent differences between them merely reflect differences in language, culture, and religious frames of reference. It is common that a mystic of one tradition can recognize a similarity in the mystic of another tradition. I am still a little amazed and delighted that I can walk with mystics of any century and tradition. This will disappoint some religious people, who would like to feel that they guard the only way. Fortunately God is generous enough to provide ways for all people. I have tried to emphasize this by quoting and referring to various traditions, but of course I have been unable to refer to all the world's major mystics. And of all the world's mystics, it must be only a small number who have left a written record that is still available. Evelyn Underhill's classic work (66) describes only a portion of Western mystics, while the bulk of mystics are Eastern. Most are now known only to God. It is very significant to me that those who have had the experience are in a wide agreement, suggesting that the total nature of existence can be understood. This corresponds in natural science to the fact that there are physical laws which appear to apply throughout the universe. This enables little humanity to get a glimpse of it all.

Those who have had the direct experience do differ in the depth, range, and frequency of their experience of God. But in spite of this human difference, they agree that there is a One (of countless names). This One is the All, being ultimately all there really is. This One is without beginning or end, since it transcends time which is one of its lesser creations. The One is self-subsistent, sufficient in itself, formless (transcending all forms) and is all love and wisdom. Ultimately all superlatives apply to It. I also agree with the apophatic theologians such as Dionysius (67) that it is best described as "not this and not that." This illustrates quite well that the categories by which we pretend to grasp the One are themselves insufficient. I also agree with and understand those who prefer not to name It at all, as an attempt to emphasize that It is beyond naming. In some respects our bantering names about is presumptuous. It is a pretense at grasping the omnipotent, omniscient, omnipresent, and formless. But to aid limited human understanding we point toward all this with the word "God."

The world's mystics are agreed that the One has created out of itself (not out of nothing) all that exists. It is out of itself, since some of its very nature permeates creation. All that exists on every level can be metaphorically described as a theater showing forth potentials of the One. Time and space themselves are part of the show, and are lesser potentials. The whole physical universe is a lower representation of the All. If you want some understanding of immensity, study the presently-understood size of the physical universe.

In the midst of this immense theater of representations, each of us is a mini-universe or microcosmic representative image of the whole. We are made in the image of God. Our bodies are made of atoms blown out of supernovas eons ago. But we are also inwardly, in our mind, full participants in all the higher spiritual aspects of the universe, living in both a material and a spiritual world. We cannot be fully understood as only material, nor can we be fully understood as only spiritual/mental. It is part of the paradox and mystery of our existence that we exist in these different worlds. Even the spiritual is not one world but is a hierarchy of worlds as described by Swedenborg.

There are some awesome mysteries involved in why the One creates itself into this vast theater of representations. Some mystics have seen and reported this creation and they agree it was done with the greatest of ease and in a light-hearted and even playful spirit. If it were not done, neither we nor anything else would exist. The forms of existence are a direct expression of the Formless. We see the Formless as though it has form, all forms. The One transcends the time that is woven into the very nature of forms. Creation is not a one-time, big event, but is actually continuing in every moment.

Seen rightly, change speaks eloquently of the changeless. We ourselves participate in changes moment-by-moment throughout our whole life. Where is the changeless in us? We are the same person from beginning to end. It is as though there is a Watcher in us that sees, but is not caught up in the change. From the viewpoint of the Watcher it is a passing show. Sometimes it is delightful, other times dull, and at other times frightening or painful. We are Sameness discovering Itself in change. We couldn't know ourselves as well without this change. The show seems very necessary if we are to grow in wisdom and eventually to meet the Wisdom itself which designed the show. The show is, of course, "Maya," illusion in Hinduism and Buddhism. Maya seems very substantial from the viewpoint of time, but is illusory from eternity.

The sea bird, in its natural element, transcends time; but in a cage, it is caught in time. We badly need to shift back and forth both ways. In time is stress and learning. Out of time is peace and wisdom. When we have enough of stress we need the eternal. But out of the eternal comes a wake-up call that brings us back into time. Both are useful. Like light and dark, time and the eternal are aspects of one reality, each with their uses. We wander, get lost, have troubles in time, that we might be wise in the eternal. This drama was represented in Hindu mythology by the One God who would meditate forever and never do a thing. So he was sent a most seductive lady to seduce him into creating. We and the rest of existence are the result of this seduction, without which there would be nothing but the infinite. When we are stressed in time, we long for and need to take a vacation in the eternal. In the eternal we can watch events in time and see the One as obvious in all things. The tragedy is to think we are trapped in time. You are also of the eternal and are free to go back and forth.

Contained in all this is the drama of the ego which it is said must die to see God. What makes such a formulation puzzling is that it is unclear what ego is. The root of self-identity is a mystery in itself. The more you think of yourself as separate and superior to others, or even superior to things, the more you have an ego. Ego is most plain when you feel in conflict with others. It is then ego versus all else. If you habitually notice and consider others, you have less ego. In effect ego is in opposition to all that is. When you appreciate all there is, there is no ego; so the death of the ego is a delight, permitting the enjoyment of all there is.

The mystical experience is not the discovery of something alien. It opens right in your midst. Meaning and perception expand, and this expansion can go on and on until there is only the One, and there is no "me" left to look. Enlightenment is an enlargement of identity beyond the human, beyond all things, into the All. On the return to human identity it is as though the All chooses clothes to put on. I chose my not-very-impressive figure just as it is.

In this process did ego really die? It is possible to go through the experience of death and enter darkness before the illumination opens up to all there is. With greater familiarity, the experience of dying is apparently unnecessary. I no longer really consider myself to *be anything*, so the enlargement of whatever I am into all there is takes place easily. What it comes down to is this: since the very root of our life is Life itself, our life can open to its full nature any time. If you really think you are and have an ego, maybe then there is something that needs to experience death, perhaps many times, depending on how stubborn you are. The easy egoless way is very like enjoying any form of art, or anything higher. In enjoying a symphony you aren't concerned with yourself. There is just the wonder and pleasure of the music. By giving it your full attention the music lives in you. It is quite the same with the Divine. Remember the incident of the monk who asked to be shown the Buddha. The master answered, "The tree in the courtyard," meaning "For you, close by." There is still a dualism of monk-versus-Buddha. He is expecting the other than himself. But that isn't the way it is. The Divine is the very root of life, everyone's life, all life. But it acts like a dumb monk and goes hunting for Itself. This misconception that goes hunting is ego. With no ego it is plain, simple, and apparent. The One is here since it is ever-present and all there is.

The ultimate result of the mystical experience is represented in the ox-herding pictures as returning to the marketplace with helping hands. The great mystic doesn't glow in the dark or do amazing wonders. He is not proud; she is the simple one, doing what he/she can. See how many there are. Enlightenment is an exuberant expression of Life which furthers life itself. Swedenborg described this in his beautiful doctrine of heaven as a kingdom of uses. Heaven is a society where each finds their love of the life and fully lives out their uses, working each in their own way to aid the society, where the joy of one is the joy of all. But at our level the mature mystic attempts to do what he/she can. What do you do after enlightenment? Why, of course, you chop wood and carry water! My highest use is in attempting to share this with you.

The Way

The concept of the way is fairly traditional in the mystical literature. Taoism describes the way into the fullness of life with no God label involved. In other traditions it means the way into the experience of God itself. Ultimately these two are related ideas. The way into the fullness of life is also the way to God.

There are a number of difficulties in understanding the way. We may as well face them and get them out of the way. We are in an age of techniques. Do thus and so and in seven or seventy days you will meet God. The hubris in this is obvious. Only God gives the experience of God. This is a realm that is far more spiritual than it is technical, so I prefer the concept of a way rather than a technique.

One of the problems is our hurry, and God's patience. Many

reckon mankind is God's greatest project! Well, what do you think of a One that would take over fifteen billion years to get around to His "main project"? Perhaps hydrogen gas was Her real favorite, since it predates us by quite a bit, and is found everywhere astronomers have looked.

The main emphasis of the world's mystical literature is on ways to finding God. Very often an adept finds God by a way and describes that way as an appropriate one for all mankind. Individual differences in relation to ways is hardly known. So much depends on the nature and quality of one's effort that I am convinced that the dumbest procedure on earth, sincerely applied by a contrite seeker, could work well. How much dumber can you get than my simply gazing at an icon daily? I am sure I could succeed by gazing at a spot on the wall, or even by gazing at my own hands. Could I do as well as a whirling dervish, an Islamic way? I don't really know, not having tried it, but in general the quiet and simple way suits me better than something flamboyant. Individual differences do play a role.

In effect this whole book has been about ways. I have chosen to attempt to get at the human aspects that lie below techniques or cultural frames of reference. Ways are often couched in the frame of reference of a particular culture or religion, so one needs to learn that frame to fully grasp their way. Knowing that I am a microcosm, I can search in my little world. I no longer need to travel to an exotic place and get esoteric instruction.

But in spite of these difficulties, we can look at the issue of ways more specifically. But first let me ask a very serious question. Does the way have to have a God label on it? Many would say immediately, "Yes, of course." What good is it if it doesn't? Picture someone who has found their way to an amazing fullness of life experience without specifically knowing God. They are unusually productive, do much, aid many, are paragons of all the virtues. Yet they seem to know nothing of God and attend no church. Do you not suppose that they die honored by others, and go from a fullness in this life to a fullness in the next? Swedenborg spoke of persons as a church in the least form. If you visit their church, there are no candles and altar. Instead there are busy people making up food packages for the poor, or engaged in some similar activity. There is a whole subsection in this church for the care of animals, and one that goes out to beautify the natural environment. But in this church there is no central altar. Maybe it is in a corner, heaped up with cans for the poor. Being of use to others is the altar. In a mystical sense it is indeed a quite adequate church. There are so many who speak of God, yet whose lives are dubious, that it is refreshing to see the opposite—a church in the least form that simply is goodness. It would be a fine place in which to study ultimate theology! Most would concede that this person was of the way, whether he knew it or not, because of so much good done for others. One could find quotes in all the religious traditions that emphasize this. The most recent one I heard was from a Jew. He said there were three Jewish ways, all adequate. One is to attend the synagogue, another is to study the Torah, and the third is to be concerned for others. My friend was of this third way. He was forever working at understanding human foibles and aiding others.

There is a story about a devout Buddhist who pledged himself to publish a sacred sutra, a discourse of the Buddha, that had not been seen in centuries. He managed to save the money to print it, but the province had a dreadful flood. Many suffered. He sent his money to aid them. He saved money again. It took some years, but then there was an earthquake. He debated with himself, but ended up using the money to aid the earthquake victims. He saved money again, and in his later years managed to publish the sutra. It was said that the first two editions were superior to the third.

We easily accept good works as a proper way. But here is another case. A person attends no church and never speaks of God. Instead there is a life of beauty. She creates beauty and enjoys the artistic works of others. Whereas others live a life of drabness, this person is forever finding and creating beauty and bringing it to the attention of others. To me, this is a way equal to others. Although perhaps not formulated, she has a God called beauty. When she dies she will enter ultimate beauty, what she looked for her whole life. God does not demand a God label on everything. Anyone who in any way works to improve the quality of life, is on the path and on the way. Honor goodness in all its forms. Be open to new ways to the good. All things of good are very much a part of the way.

The simplest way is to cultivate your smallest possible experience of God. If you are really on the way, you see how to do this. Do nothing; simply appreciate this moment as it is. If you could do that I would feel secure that you knew the way. Here I sit noticing I am alive. What is in this aliveness? Inwardly all of my life, all my possibilities, at hand. Looking out I enjoy things as they are around me. What a lively balance: me, unknown to myself, amidst the wonder of creation as it is. The raw experience of life is like that; it is given here. It lives here, and yet in no way can I grasp what is fully here. It is. My appreciation that it all just is, is precisely my honoring what is beyond grasping. Life is Living Water, gushing forth. We can drink of it and enjoy it but never fully know all its ways.

That is a smallest example of the way. It would probably even be wordless, simply enjoyed. Now what technique can lead to this? None. Do nothing. And in doing nothing, simply notice and learn from what is there. Attend the school of Letting Be. It is a very subtle school. Once you have become competent in the smallest and simplest way of all, then you can experiment with technique. But you are never to forget your simplest way. Because there will be times of worry and stress when even the simplest way will seem mysterious and lost to you. The simplest way requires balance and harmony. Much of the practice of meditation is learning how to find your way through stress and concerns to the place of balance and harmony. To those who have balance and harmony, centering on what is here is simple. And it is a very little way from the simple letting be to samadhi, coming into the fullness of your own center.

Techniques are only ways to lead you back to the simplicity of letting be. In several ways techniques are all nonsense. Each finds their own way and then tends to tout their own private discovery as the way for all the rest of mankind (without even bothering to test if it works for anyone else). After a long and varied journey, many adepts come back to give us the standard doctrine of their faith as the one right way. I have read many such accounts of saints. All the uniqueness of their own wandering and discovering is omitted and they end up repeating standard church doctrine. They went through all the vicissitudes of the personal journey and discovered that their particular faith contained the universal way, so that is what they described. As one who is driven by a need to understand all the ways, I very much miss the personal details of the journey itself. Someday I may be able to see the whole panorama of all the vast territory of ways and techniques, which is the main content of most mystical literature. I can only describe some salient points:

1. The experience of God can only be given by God. There is no clever technique for forcing God's hand. Like grace, it is given out of love.

2. The simplest way of letting be is at the root of all techniques. I suspect that many vigorous seekers simply need to wear them-

selves out on ascetic practices or in techniques, and it is perhaps when they give up to letting be that they are rescued.

3. Though we are all human, there are such great differences between us that different ways suit different people. The dream of one way for all is a dream, not a practical reality.

4. The issue of finding God is so spiritual and human that a bad and monumentally stupid approach will work very well in the hands of a sincere seeker, and the finest technique will fail in the hands of the insincere. God responds to what *we are* rather than to the cleverest doing. So if God holds out on you, look to the very nature of your relationship.

The Way of the Book

In this way, the seeker takes a book as itself revealing God, reading and reflecting on what the book says as though God is present and aiding them. Any book that the person feels is sacred will do. Swedenborg read the Bible in this way, Buddhists have used Buddhist texts and the Koran is appropriate for Moslems. Some religions have used books of prayer in this way. A few have used their liturgy. This process is far more subtle and experiential than most outsiders would suspect. Adepts of this way find that certain words and passages leap out at them and become meaningful in great depth. Swedenborg wrote a work now called *The Messiah About to Come* (68) which is a collection of Bible passages. Swedenborg scholars paid it no real heed because it appears to be merely a collection of Bible quotes. These are the passages that leaped out at him, full with meaning, and all had to do with the Messiah coming into his life. In the last lines God penned the words through his hand. Generally this sort of reading is very sensitive and intuitive, rather than intellectual. The person discovers what God is currently leading them toward. One may well work with one slim volume the rest of their life. A Russian pilgrim used the only book he owned, a volume of the *Philocalia* (69). This method requires only an initial faith that God is present and will reveal wisdom through the volume at hand. I know of no instances in which the volume was other than religious. Such a process doesn't make them a scholar, even though they come into considerable knowledge of their book. Rather they use it to enter into a direct relationship with God. Since many different books have been used, it would be foolish to say God can only be revealed through one volume. Above all, it is a very personal seeking and finding.

The Way of Prayer/Reflection/Meditation

I put these together because they are internally related. Prayer that is verbal can easily become nonverbal, in which case it is like reflection, which easily becomes meditation. Verbal prayer and petitions to God are only a starting point. Real dialogue is speaking *and listening.* Listening easily becomes reflection on whatever presents itself. In reflection one is noticing what is given internally, or some lesson from the world might be given. I was once reflecting while sweeping the floor. I noticed the balls of lint would escape the broom if I was too hasty. The lint was teaching me about my own impatience. I have also made deep philosophical discoveries while splitting wood or weeding the garden. Reflection is simply remaining open to discovery.

The realm of meditation has a vast literature. In many ways reflection or meditation is the most basic of the spiritual methods. Yet there are whole religions that pay it no heed. Meditation as a spiritual method is simply opening one's self to whatever comes. It can begin with a prayer, or a concern one seeks guidance on, but thereafter it is a state of attentive openness. It is common in meditation to discover that one's own mind and being is not at all what you thought it was like; it has a will and a life of its own. One then enters and discovers the real Life that is present within you. There are a few religious practices that seek concentration and control. Concentration produces its own problems; those who don't know this should try tiring themselves out with concentration. Meditation and self-reflection is like drifting in, and enjoying, and discovering in the present. In early stages ideas and impressions may float by like flotsam in a stream. But later an internal wisdom comes to guide the process. Total illumination as to the nature of God is possible this way. In meditation you can find your own peace and harmony. It is a fundamental approach in religion that all should explore, because it is training and experience in openness, and this openness leads to the discovery of the root nature of existence.

The Way of a Mantra

A mantra is a sentence or phrase said inwardly and repeatedly. One major example of this in the West is the repetition of the one-line Jesus Prayer, "Lord Jesus Christ, Son of God, have mercy on me a sinner." (70) In the East various sacred phrases are used such as, "Om mani padme hum" (the jewel in the lotus) (71). One can have the mantra assigned to them by a holy person while some people discover their own sacred phrase. The method is to repeat it silently within, as much as possible. For some Christians it was an answer to the injunction to pray constantly. There is a whole world of experiences within this method. The prayer can become quite automatic, as though something in you is saying it. A mantra can be used inwardly to ward off unwanted thoughts and return attention to spiritual matters. Each word and syllable may acquire profound meaning. It teaches mindfulness (72), an inward concentration on the sacred which then opens and reveals itself. Because of this centering on the sacred, one becomes alert to all aspects of the sacred in one's life.

The Way of Church Services

I am hesitant to list church services as a way, and this hesitance is curious in itself because such services are the main way prescribed by church authorities, both East and West. I hesitate to list attending them because they do little for so many, and it may well be a way for only a few. Taken in the right spirit they certainly remind one of the sacred and may prepare you to find it by another way. I suspect that liturgy becomes a full way insofar as it is taken personally, as addressed to you specifically. The method would then work just as though you consulted your holy book. What was meaningful to you would leap out at you and become quite memorable. Certainly the services need to be seen as for you personally, not just about God in general. In this personal realization you receive from the services what you most especially need. If nothing else, church services are a supplement to other ways. How they could become a full way in themselves would be a most useful bit of information to religious leaders of all kinds.

The Way of Identification With God

This way underlies most other ways. The Christian Eucharist ceremony has its greatest meaning in such an identification. There is an identification with God in many church services. Looking at Christ crucified, the worshipper would have the full realization that they themselves are on the cross in this life. The deeply religious person tries to live as their God does, an attempt to be like God. There are a lot of mystical states in which the identity floats between human and Divine, and this is part of the necessary learning. Some

Buddhists have exercises in which they visualize themselves creating the universe. For the person who consistently stands outside God's view, I often ask them to seriously try to visualize things from God's way. Some are afraid of this approach for fear of the blasphemy of thinking one's self God. Such presumption is so easy to treat; if they think they are God, ask them to move a mountain.

The way of identification is quite unlike presumption. It is best to start with identifying with others, animals, and even rocks and clouds. A little loosening of identity is therapeutic. Then the identification with God is not so challenging. You'll not find cruelty in those who identify with other people and animals. What is crime but a failure to identify with the victim? We always feel we could improve the design of existence. But the humble way of identification can reveal Divine Providence already quite adequately at work. Identification with the Divine is at the heart, the real life, of religious ritual. And as the priest, rabbi, or shaman acts in the ritual, you too should be there doing the same. The whole quality of existence depends on you.

The Way of Use of Ordinary Experiences

In this approach one assumes that God is good and that *all* circumstances given to one are from God, and somehow are for one's good. It is perhaps a way for the mature mystic—one who already knows much of God and realizes God acts in even the smallest of life's circumstances. Whatever happens to you, you reflect how God's good is present in it. For instance, illness is merely a nuisance and an obstacle if so viewed. But viewed as a message from God, the emotional aspects of the illness are readily discovered, which may cure by itself. Illness also does much to teach patience. Orthodox saints made no distinction between what is given within or what came "by chance" from without. They looked at both for God's goodness and were quite able to find it. The French Catholic de Caussade (62) desscribes this way quite well.

In Buddhism it is part of the way that what you get to eat depends on the generosity of others, for you are to beg for your food. In some respects this way really puts one's relationship to God to the test. This is an ancient way, discovered over and over in all cultures. Instead of turning away from the world, it sees the world as God incarnate for the personal guidance of each, and making maximum use of it—which is in itself a form of respect for existence.

The General Way

I would not be surprised if you sensed a certain underlying similarity to all these ways as I have described them. There are countless other ways not elaborated here; I have just touched on the most prominent. The same process occurs in all of them:

1. The person is seeking God.
2. They choose or stumble upon some avenue or way.
3. Because they are seeking, they find God actually entering their life and instructing them.
4. All these ways involve an openness to discovery. Using the repeated mantra may not appear to have this quality, but while they are occupied with their phrase, the sacred can slip in.
5. A friendship with God is established, under any name, and even as beauty or service to others, etc.

All of these can be summarized in the single sentence, "Seek and ye shall find." Techniques or methods are merely external considerations. The quality and persistence of the seeking is absolutely central. Given these, anyone can find a way, anywhere, in any circumstance. We all die sometime, and I agree with the traditions that death itself is part of the way and is a grand opportunity for seeing into the nature of things.

Are some people disadvantaged in this seeking? I am not sure. Certainly there are religions in which mystics are very rare. These are usually very external and doctrinaire religions that disregard meditation or any sort of personal exploration. There are religions that have a long history of badly understanding mystics, prohibiting them from speaking or publishing, and even executing them or sending them into exile. Religions should seek and foster the direct experience of God, but they may have so little experience in this area that they see the mystic as a dangerous troublemaker, a heretic. The higher the church authority, the more the perceived threat. Mystics in these religions appear to be better off not saying anything.

Perhaps the greatest drawback is simply living in a culture that knows nothing of the direct experience of God, and hence makes no provisions for it. What the culture does not look for, its members will less likely find. In contrast there are cultures where mystical experience is acknowledged and quite common. So both religion and culture can be an impediment, but not to the real seeker.

But are others disadvantaged? I suspect the mentally retarded are not. Their simplicity of outlook and faith appears to be a secret advantage. Certainly God takes their situation into consideration. Major mental illness may be a disadvantage. I am not sure even here, because psychotics can be directly introduced into cosmic dimensions which the sane rarely experience. I am also in doubt about those in a life of crime. I have seen too much of an odd connection between ethics and crime to make a hasty judgement. Criminals are often obsessed with ethics; it was injustice and officials' lack of ethics that turned them to desperate crime. If no one they knew was ethical, why should they be? In group therapy with criminals, I soon discovered they had a remarkable sense of the phony and the real. They were more sensitive than I could hope to be in this regard. In the history of saints there are some who turned from a life of crime into a saintly way. Could it be that God is able to reach all?

I suspect that individuals with a powerful logical mind, proud of its powers, have a fairly serious impediment. Such a mind banters words and ideas about as though thoughts are bricks and wood. I have shocked a few such people by saying that the essence of life has nothing to do with logic. There were shocked that I had so little use for the wonder of human logic. The essence of life is much closer to grass, or clouds, or soft music. When the super-logical become sick, Japanese Morita Therapy forbids them to speak for weeks and puts them to work raising their own food. Beware of trying to explain with words to the super-logical. They may be quite impervious to learning because of their ego and separation.

The way into the direct experience of God is actually very simple and available to all. Our rich and varied religious traditions all point toward it. It is a cosmic love affair between the individual and God. But it is a unique kind of affair. On God's side we have all wisdom that seeks the return of this part of itself sent out into ignorance as a person. Yet this One also has an ultimate respect for the freedom of the individual. So it longs but leaves free. Our side of this love affair is fraught with a host of difficulties—ignorance, misinformation and just plain entanglement in the struggle for existence. How is this affair to come to a happy conclusion? The return and union of the lovers is written in the most intimate way into the whole fabric of our microcosm and into existence as a whole. The varied riches of religion, art, and human speculation are all clues to the resolution.

The solution to this love affair is "written on the heart" in the inner and intimate details. Whereas the sacred is totally and awesomely protected from any presumptuous assault, it opens easily to the simplest love and respect. Persistent love and respect overcomes even time itself. Though we are thrust forth into profound ignorance and forgetfulness, the loving way of the return is our innermost nature and identity. This love affair was written to have a happy ending, because the seeking and the finding are the same process. When both lovers seek there is bound to be a finding, especially when one of the lovers designed the way and is all the seeking and all the finding. There is an intimate mystery in this affair. You cannot even seek without the one sought being there in the very search itself. The One, launched into profound ignorance and seeking the way back is the same as the One leading the way home. There is only God, even in the midst of profound ignorance. It is quite fortunate that all the barriers to the simple and easy return to the One are in ourselves, near at hand. The barriers are not elsewhere in some occult or cosmic problem to solve. It is a clever design that we must know ourselves to find God. There is no dodging around that one. The Lord is the Very Human.

I have written this book as a representative of the one great stream of mystics. Like them I have simply tried to clarify the ultimate mystery. Where you find faults here, freely blame the author, whoever he is. Where you find a good you can resonate with, surely credit the Author of All.

These little points are the essence of this whole book:

1. The experience of God is mainly a matter of consistent seeking, even though it only comes from God. Your seeking and God's become one.

2. Enjoy the simplest approach of letting be and coming to appreciate things just as they are.

3. Look for the smallest signs.

4. Once the Source is found, it is your guide ever after.

Amen. So be it.

16
A Hand Puppet

You know what a hand puppet is—
Cloth, someone's hand in it—
It moves, waves arms
Opens its mouth and talks.

See, I am a hand puppet.
I wave and talk—
As though alive
In myself.

My own experience showed me
There is only God
In the whole of creation.
Swedenborg says we are
Recipient vessels—
The One Life flows in
And animates us.
The ancient Vedas said
There is only Brahman.
But how are we to apply
This vast insight?

It is easy
Waving arms and talking
Just don't take ourselves

Too seriously.
See today
I am green Kermit the Frog
Arguing with pink Miss Piggy.
It is all in fun
Not to be taken too seriously
Least of all—ourselves.
Called selflessness.

There is a colossal experience
Available in this.
As cloth ego puppet
I am most honored
That my simple cloth
Is given life
Even a little while.
Any life—
Thus my simple cloth
Experiences all Life.

Even tossed in a corner
It is not so bad—
Quietly waiting to be animated.

But when I am given life
It is so wonderful
Look I can wave my arms
Talk, and seem quite alive in myself.
Knowing All Life
Through me.

How many puppets there are!
Everywhere!
Same Hand
Doing all this
By golly—I moved again
Saying intelligent things—
Isn't it a wonder!
This is the most direct way
Back to the Source

Realize you too—
Are a hand puppet
A recipient vessel—
Not alive in yourself
But animated by all Life.
Takes getting used to—
Not taking yourself too seriously
All in fun.

When you live
In such an insight
There is a sense
Of utter freedom.
For freedom is to live
In your deepest love.
And all you wonder about
Is shown.

This enlightened cloth
Is honored to receive
Such a Hand.

Now take Kermit the Frog.
Only green cloth?
No. He's a witty fellow
Playing a role
Meant to illustrate ourselves
Playing a role.

His/our role is a mixed reality.
Green cloth
And an animating conception.
Our green cloth
Matches our role as frog.
Our role is a relative reality
Very real, relatively—
If you don't get too caught up in it
Your role/life is your very way
To the Source
And to the whole Theater of Existence

To the Real in Itself.
What to identify with?
Green cloth?
Our role?
Or Life itself?
Your choice.
Cloth
Or the role
Last only so long,
But Life Itself—
Oh, that is another matter.

Overhead a raucous crow
Caw, cawing
Having a good time
Full of life—
Making noise
Even in flight.

About the Author

In the past some great religious figures have had some notable events surrounding their birth. Wilson Van Dusen has minor qualifications. He was conceived on Christmas Day and his birth was attended by a rare full eclipse of the sun in San Francisco, California in 1923. His grandmother was a spiritualist minister, and with a slight grandmotherly bias, found the signs auspicious. But he was born into a totally unreligious family.

At the age of one he had an ecstatic experience of God while lying in a crib, an experience he remembers some seventy years later. He had many mystical experiences in his youth. By adolescence he set about to understand how this happens, so that he could return to it at will. At this time he first connected this experience to the only formal religion he encountered, in radio sermons. Formal religions seemed lost in comparison.

He had just completed high school when World War II started. He served in the U.S. Merchant Marine, ending the war as a Second Mate. Nearly every ship he sailed on had explosive cargoes, and in this delicate state they met three enemy subs and thirty-nine bombing raids. After the war he raced through university getting a B.A. and M.A. in three and one half years and a Ph.D. in Clinical Psychology in two more years. His middle years were taken up with raising a family and dealing with every form of madness as a clinical psychologist. In his later years he became a real scholar of the mystic Emanuel Swedenborg. He discovered that his grandmother had willed him her Swedenborg collection when he was seven, and

272

his parents "protected him" by throwing it out. Grandmother won in the end.

It is as though his direct experience of God became a hidden occupation. Most of his friends don't know of his knowledge and expertise in this area. He has studied the mystics of various traditions, and considers himself a living representative of this universal tradition. He finds that the more widely one explores in this area the more apparent is a universal consensus on the nature of things, transcending individual religious traditions. One mystical friend remarked that he seems to have a knowledge tree that grows new understandings. He says that whatever he has really wanted to know in this area the Lord has graciously shown him.

We have here an unusual representative of the experience of God. He regards this experience as essentially simple and quite available to everyone, in or out of any religious tradition. It is the ultimate answer to everything. He helps make this wisdom available to others in this book.

He is also the author of *The Natural Depth in Man, The Presence of Other Worlds*, and *The Country of Spirit.*

References

1. William James, *The Varieties of Religious Experience*, Chapter on mysticism, various editions.
2. Evelyn Underhill, *Practical Mysticism*, Dutton, NY, NY, 1915.
3. Wilson Van Dusen, *The Natural Depth in Man*, Swedenborg Foundation, West Chester, PA, 1990.
4. Wilson Van Dusen, "The Rediscovery of an Ancient Way to Work With an Icon," *Sacred Art Journal*, 3/91, Vol. 12, No. 1, p. 3-10.
5. St. Theresa of Avila, *Interior Castle*, Doubleday and Co., Garden City, NY, 1961, p. 9.
6. Longchenpa, *Kindly Bent To Ease Us*, Dharma Publishing, Berkeley, CA, 1976, Vol. II, p. 73. A Tibetan Buddhist, circa 1300's. To a mystic his writings are radiant.
7. Rabindranath Tagore, *Gitanjali #43*, Macmillan, India, 1981. Tagore is a Hindu mystic who won the Nobel Prize for literature.
8. Panayiotis Nellas, *Deification in Christ*, St. Vladimir's Seminary Press, Crestwood, NY, 1987, p. 148.
9. Rabindranath Tagore, *Collected Poems and Plays*, Macmillan, NY, NY, 1993, p. 341. His best-known and most mystical work is *Gitanjali* which is also in this volume.
10. Emanuel Swedenborg, *Arcana Caelestia*, 12 volumes, Swedenborg Society, London, 1983-on. Swedenborg's works are in numbered paragraphs which I will give with the reference number. They may be obtained from the Swedenborg Foundation, 320 North Church St., West Chester, PA, 19381-0549 or

Swedenborg Society, 20 Bloomsbury Way, London, WC1A 2TH England.

11. Rabindranath Tagore, *Selected Poems*, Penguin, NY, NY, 1993, p. 109.
12. Emanuel Swedenborg, *Divine Providence*, Swedenborg Foundation, NY, NY, 1964.
13. Pir Vilayat Inayat Khan, *Samadhi With Eyes Open*, Sufi Order Publications, New Lebanon, NY, 1978.
14. Rabbi Lawrence Kushner, *Honey From the Rock*, Harper & Row, NY, NY, 1977, p. 11.
15. Emanuel Swedenborg, *The Worship and Love of God*, Massachusetts New-Church Union, Boston, MA, 1956, p. 164.
16. Emanuel Swedenborg, *Heaven and Hell*, Swedenborg Foundation, West Chester, PA, 1984. Dole Translation. Swedenborg spent some decades in the direct experience of heaven and hell and dutifully described his experiences. Each person is potentially a heaven in the least form so this is also a description of our interior nature and of heaven simultaneously.
17. Emanuel Swedenborg, *True Christian Religion*, Swedenborg Society, London, England, 1988.
18. St. Nikodimos of the Holy Mountain and St. Makarios of Corinth, *The Philokalia*, Faber and Faber, London, England, 1979, 3 vols. The *Philokalia* is a collection of fairly ancient religious writings used in the Eastern Orthodox faith.
19. Sri Ramakrishna, *Teachings of Ramakrishna*, Advaita Ashrama, Calcutta, India, 1971, p. 11.
20. George De Charms, *Imagination and Rationality*, Swedenborg Scientific Association, Bryn Athyn, PA, 1981.
21. John Blofeld, *The Tantric Mysticism of Tibet*, Dutton, NY, NY, 1970, p. 170.
22. Emanuel Swedenborg, *Apocalypse Explained*, Swedenborg Foundation, West Chester, PA, 1972.
23. Emanuel Swedenborg, *The Divine Love and the Divine Wisdom*, Swedenborg Society, London, England, 1963.
24. Jelauddin Rumi, *This Longing*, Threshold Books, Putney, VT, 1988, p. 52.
25. *Holy Bible*, American Bible Society, NY, NY, 1995. This is the Contemporary English Version.
26. Swami Nikhilananda, *The Upanishads*, 4 volumes, Harper, NY,

NY, 1949. This quote is from memory. I am unable to give the exact source.

27. Emanuel Swedenborg, *Divine Love and Wisdom*, Swedenborg Foundation, West Chester, PA, 1985, Dole translation.

28. Shaun Mc Niff, *Earth Angels*, Shambala, Boston, MA, 1995.

29. Swami Vivekananda, *Jnana Yoga*, Ramakrishna-Vivekananda Center, NY, NY, 1995.

30. Kenneth Ring, *Life at Death*, Quill, NY, NY, 1982.

31. Brent and Wendy Top, *Beyond Death's Door*, Bookcraft, Salt Lake City, UT, 1993.

32. Jeffrey Moses, *Oneness*, Fawcett Columbine, NY, NY, 1989.

33. Valentine Zander, *St. Seraphim of Sarov*, St. Vladimir's Seminary Press, Crestwood, NY, 1975.

34. Wilson Van Dusen, *Swedenborg's Journal of Dreams*, Swedenborg Foundation, West Chester, NY, 1986.

35. Thinley Norbu, *White Sail*, Shambala, Boston, MA, 1992, p. 137.

36. William E. Paden, *Religious Worlds*, Beacon, Boston, MA, 1994, p. 52, 53, 51.

37. William E. Paden, *Interpreting the Sacred*, Beacon, Boston, MA, 1992.

38. Emanuel Swedenborg, *Heavenly Doctrine*, Swedenborg Society, London, England, 1911.

39. Eknath Easwaran, *The Upanishads*, Nilgiri Press, Tomales, CA, p. 143-144. The Upanishads are among the oldest religious books in the world. They were probably set down from an even older oral tradition. In this selection much of the immense amount of Sanskrit has been removed so that the teachings stand out clearly. If I were asked as a Western mystic what convinces me I am in an ancient tradition I would simply point to the Upanishads.

40. Mother Meera, *Answers*, Meeramma, Ithaca, NY, 1991. Mother Meera conducts electrifying and silent spiritual sessions. I was pleased to discover this is possible. In many ways silence is stronger than words. In silence we are face to face with ourself.

41. Namkhai Norbu, *Dream Yoga and the Practice of Natural Light*, Snow Lion, Ithaca, NY, 1942.

42. Stephen La Berge, *Lucid Dreaming*, Ballantine, NY, NY, 1985.

43. David Rapaport, *Organization and Pathology of Thought*, Columbia University, NY, NY, 1959, Chapter 8.

44. Wilson Van Dusen, "The Phenomenology of a Schizophrenic Existence," *Journal of Individual Psychology*, 1961, 17, p. 80-92.

45. Wilson Van Dusen, "Another Key to Swedenborg's Development," *New Church Life*, July, 1975, Vol. 45, No. 7, p. 316-319.
46. St. Nikodimos of the Holy Mountain and St. Makarios of Corinth, *Writings from the Philokalia on Prayer of the Heart*, Faber and Faber, London, England, 1954.
47. Sandy Ryrie, *Prayer of the Heart*, SGL Press, Oxford, England, 1995.
48. Vladimir Znosko, *Hieroshemamonk Feofil*, Holy Trinity Monastery, Jordanville, NY, 1987.
49. John 10: 1-6
50. Bruce Glenn, *The Arts, An Affectional Ordering of Experience*, Bryn Athyn, PA, 1993.
51. Stephen Pepper, *Aesthetic Quality*, Scribners, NY, NY, 1938
52. Leonid Ouspensky and Vladimir Lossky, *The Meaning of Icons*, St. Vladimir's Seminary, Crestwood, NY, 1983.
53. Plotinus, *The Essential Plotinus*, Mentor, NY, NY, 1964, p. 40-41.
54. Lobsang Lhalunga, *The Life of Milarepa*, Penguin, NY, NY, 1992.
55. Longchempa, *Kindly Bent to Ease Us*, Part 1, p. 118 & 120, Dharma, Berkeley, CA, 1975. Longchempa lived 1308-1364. He was a Tibetan monk and a leading exponent of Vajrayana Buddhism who was hailed as a second Buddha.
56. Malidoma Some, *Of Water and the Spirit, Ritual, Magic and Initiation in the Life of an African Shaman*, Tarcher, NY, NY, 1994, p. 198-199.
57. Lex Hixon, *Coming Home, The Experience of Enlightenment in Sacred Traditions*, Tarcher, NY, NY, 1989, Chapter 3.
58. Thomas Merton, *The Way of Chuang Tzu*, Penguin, NY, 1969, p. 84. Though it doesn't show in this excerpt, Chuang Tzu is one of the most humorous of mystics. He appeared at the beginning of Taoism, approximately the 4th century B. C.
59. John Blofeld, *Bodhisattva of Compassion, The Mystical Tradition of Kuan Yin*, Shambala, Boston, MA, 1988.
60. Priya Mookerjee, *Pathway Icons, The Wayside Art of India*, Thames and Hudson, London, England, 1987.
61. Those who enjoy the literature on the mystical and have not yet seen the Zen literature have a great treat in store. It is typical in Zen to be so familiar with the mystical experience as to be able to read it in all natural beauty.
62. Jean-Pierre de Caussade, *Abandonment to Divine Providence*, Doubleday, NY, NY, 1975.

63. Roshi Philip Kapleau, *The Three Pillars of Zen*, Doubleday, NY, NY, 1989.
64. Wilson Van Dusen, "A Central Dynamism in Chronic Schizophrenia," *Psychoanalysis and the Psychoanalytic Review*, 1959, 46, 85-91.
65. John Stevens, *Three Zen Masters*, Kodansha, Tokyo, Japan, 1993, p. 114.
66. Evelyn Underhill, *Mysticism*, Dutton, NY, NY, 1961.
67. Colm Luibheid, *Pseudo-Dionysius*, Paulist Press, NY, NY, 1987. Whoever Dionysius was, he certainly soared in the highest realms and greatly influenced others. His dates are unknown but probably early in the Christian era.
68. Emanuel Swedenborg, *The Messiah About to Come*, Academy of the New Church, Bryn Athyn, PA, 1949. See also reference 45.
69. R.M. French, *The Way of a Pilgrim*, Harper and Row, San Francisco, CA, 1952.
70. Archimandrite Lev Gillet, *The Jesus Prayer*, St. Vladimir's Seminary Press, Crestwood, NY, 1987. There are many accounts of this way.
71. Lama Govinda, *Foundations of Tibetan Mysticism*, Weiser, York Beach, ME, 1969. See mantra in the index.
72. Thich Nat Hanh, *The Miracle of Mindfulness*, Beacon, Boston, MA, 1987. Though this is on Zen, mindfulness has appeared in many cultures but is most prominent in Buddhism. It is perhaps another way in itself.

Index